M000288957

THE FALL AND RECAPTURE
OF DETROIT IN THE WAR OF 1812

William Hull, governor of Michigan territory, brigadier general. (Courtesy of the Burton Historical Collection, Detroit Public Library.)

THE FALL AND RECAPTURE
OF DETROIT IN THE WAR OF 1812

In Defense of William Hull

ANTHONY J. YANIK

Wayne State University Press   Detroit

© 2011 by Wayne State University Press, Detroit, Michigan 48201.

All rights reserved. No part of this book may be reproduced without formal permission.

Manufactured in the United States of America.

16 15 14 13 12   6 5 4 3 2

Library of Congress Cataloging-in-Publication Data

Yanik, Anthony J.

The fall and recapture of Detroit in the War of 1812 : in defense of William Hull / Anthony J. Yanik.

p. cm. — (Great Lakes books series)

Includes bibliographical references and index.

ISBN 978-0-8143-3598-7 (cloth : alk. paper)

1. Detroit (Mich.)—History—Surrender to the British, 1812. 2. Hull, William, 1753–1825.

3. Michigan—History—War of 1812--Campaigns. 4. United States—History—War of 1812—

Campaigns. I. Title.

E356.D4Y26 2011

977.4'03—dc22

2011001497

Designed and typeset by Maya Rhodes

Composed in Fairfield LH and Engravers LH

CONTENTS

PREFACE

Because I am a native Detroiter and a historian, it was inevitable that at some point I would become interested in one of the more dramatic episodes of the city's past—the surrender of Detroit by Brigadier General William Hull during the War of 1812.

As I delved into the subject, I was struck by the invariably negative characterizations of Hull, made not only by his peers but by many historians over the past two centuries. In one account after another, he has been pictured as a "senile American commander, a trembling old man," a "blithering idiot," a general who "appears on the edge of a nervous collapse," a man who, as the bombardment of Detroit was taking place, sat for hours "in a daze, spittle mixed with the tobacco juice that dribbled down his chin, over his beard and neck cloth, and onto his vest."[1] The more I read, the more I began to question whether these characterizations of Hull and his conduct, though they've persisted over the years, were historically accurate. I discovered that most historians were merely repeating accounts that could be traced back to three sources: *The Robert Lucas Journal,* in which Lucas gives his eyewitness account of the events surrounding the surrender; the inflammatory letter that Lewis Cass wrote to the secretary of war describing those same events (Lewis's account also borrowed from Lucas) that was published in newspapers across the country at the time; and the court-martial testimony of the Ohio volunteers and regulars involved in the campaign, testimony *not* given under oath. All three sources revealed a deep animus toward the general, and I felt that I owed it to Hull to examine whether he truly was the coward his peers repeatedly portrayed him as. This investigation led me to the question of whether Hull's surrender of Detroit was justified.

In my search for materials that would lead me to the truth of the matter, I am deeply indebted to the librarians at the Sterling Heights Public Library who never failed to unearth for me obscure, out-of-date publications as well as scholarly articles that have appeared in journals dealing with the 1812 period. The Michigan eLibrary system, through which they were able to access much of the material, is a historian's delight. I am also indebted to Dr. Charles Hyde, professor of history at Wayne State University, who monitored the progress of the manuscript, and to the three unknown persons selected by Wayne State University Press to review my original manuscript. Their corrections, suggestions, and recommendations resulted in a final draft far superior to the original. Finally, special recognition must be given to Mark Bowden, coordinator for Special Collections at the Detroit Main Public Library, and the library's collection of early Detroit artifacts and photographs. Thanks, one and all!

I should also add that the proper name of the British/American post on Mackinac Island is "Fort Mackinac," and I employ that usage in this book despite documents dating back to the 1812 era that refer to it as "Fort Michilimackinac." The original Fort Michilimackinac was built by the French on the northern tip of the lower Michigan peninsula in 1713 and passed into the hands of the British in 1761. It was replaced by a new fort in 1780, built on Mackinac Island, which was given the name "Fort Mackinac," as it still is known today.

INTRODUCTION

Brigadier General William Hull waited patiently as the members of the court assembled. It was 10:00 Saturday morning, March 26, 1814. On trial since the previous January, Hull was accused of treason, cowardice, neglect of duty, and unofficerlike conduct stemming from his surrender of Detroit to the British during the opening campaign of the War of 1812.

Hull firmly believed that his surrender was a decision based upon humanitarian principles: that by surrendering he had avoided unnecessary bloodshed, especially that of the men, women, and children who inhabited Detroit. He hoped that the court would accept his defense on these grounds.

The court did not.

As the verdict was announced, Hull realized that his plea had failed. He was acquitted of the charge of treason, not surprisingly, considering the weak ground on which it was based. Nevertheless: "The court in consequence of their determination respecting the second and third charges [cowardice and neglect of duty], and the specifications under those charges, exhibited under the said Brigadier General William Hull—and after due consideration, do sentence him to be shot to death, two thirds of the court concurring in the sentence."[1]

How could such a sentence have been passed on a brigadier general and Revolutionary War hero—the only sentence of death ever rendered against a commanding general in the annals of U.S. military history? That the verdict was based primarily upon the hearsay testimony of militia officers and men involved in the Detroit campaign, none of whom had any military training and who, as indicated in their testimony, were on a mission to malign the reputation of their commanding officer, would seem entirely unjust. One suspects that the members of the court acted in response to the deep embarrassment that Hull's surrender brought to the administration of President Madison, then still struggling to justify the war itself.

Hull was in his third term as the governor of Michigan territory when war was declared. He allowed the administration to persuade him to accept command of the newly created North Western Army, a decision he would regret his entire life. The president, Congress, and the nation itself were ill prepared to fight this war, which was primarily over the maritime problems that the United States had faced for several years: the boarding of U.S. ships, both those privately owned and U.S. Navy vessels, by the British Royal Navy; the British impressment of American sailors suspected of English heritage; and the requirement that U.S. masters purchase a license for continental trade. To declare war over maritime matters, though, would seem to be the height of folly. The nation's miniscule navy was no match for England's powerful fleet, then engaged in shutting down the flow of supplies to Napoleon. Congress realized the position it was in, but had determined that although England controlled the seas, the United States controlled the land, the land of North America. And the key to that land control was to take possession of Canada, whose trade England vitally needed in its war effort against Napoleon. Members of Congress had been gulled into believing, from the arguments of Henry Clay and the War Hawks, that Canada was weak and ripe for the taking. Westerners also were receptive to this argument, assuming that the conquest of Canada would eliminate another festering problem, Indian attacks on the frontier settlements that were prompted by British agents.[2]

However promising a land war against Canada initially appeared, the military soon discovered that it was an enterprise built upon a weak foundation—the use of raw militia. When war was declared on June 18, the regular army numbered only 5,260 men. This guaranteed that militia volunteers, hastily recruited, untrained in war, would do the bulk of the fighting in the war's early stages. Their training would be conducted by officers who were themselves untrained and whose conduct too often was unsatisfactory and at times disgraceful.[3] The Ohio militia, for example, would prove to be Hull's undoing during the Detroit campaign.

Originally the War Department intended to make a simultaneous three-pronged attack on Canada: at Detroit, the Niagara River, and Lake Champlain. However, it was at Detroit that the opening campaign of the war took place, beginning in early June, months before the other two campaigns were under way: October in Niagara and November at Lake Champlain. It was unfortunate that Hull, as commanding general of the North Western Army, began his campaign months before the other two went into action, thus depriving him of the diversions he could well have used.

The Detroit campaign is the subject of this book, particularly its most significant action: Hull's surrender of Detroit to the British on August 16, 1812. The surrender, completely unexpected, shocked the administration and the nation. Condemnation of Hull was immediate, widespread, and angry, the anger fanned by vitriolic statements made predominately by the Ohio volunteer officers of Hull's command, especially Lewis Cass. A court-martial of William Hull was inevitable. What was unexpected was the delay of 18 months before it took place, and that the verdict of guilty was followed by a sentence of death. A close examination of the testimony of the witnesses at the court-martial, an analysis of Hull's defense, and a review of the actual events themselves raise many questions about the credibility of that verdict, as this book investigates.

CHRONOLOGY OF HULL'S
DETROIT CAMPAIGN

APRIL 8

U.S. Senate approves appointment of William Hull as brigadier general of the North Western Army.

MAY 23

Hull arrives at Dayton, Ohio.

MAY 25

Governor Meigs of Ohio transfers command of three Ohio volunteer regiments to Hull.

JUNE 1

Troops depart from Dayton; arrive at Urbana, Ohio, on June 7.

JUNE 10

Lieutenant Colonel Miller and Fourth Regiment join rest of North Western Army.

JUNE 11

McArthur's regiment begins cutting road ahead and on June 16 builds crude blockhouses on south bank of Scioto River, calling them Fort McArthur.

JUNE 15

Troops leave Urbana; arrive at Fort McArthur on June 19.

JUNE 21

Findlay's regiment begins cutting road 30 miles ahead to Blanchard's Ford; constructs blockhouse and picket fence arrangement it names Fort Findlay.

JUNE 25

Rest of troops arrive at Fort Findlay.

British general Brock learns of declaration of war and sends alert to all posts.

JUNE 26

Hull receives dispatch from War Department with no mention of war declaration.

Cass's regiment leaves to cut road through to Rapids on Maumee River.

JUNE 28

British Fort Malden alerted of war declaration.

JUNE 30

Hull's troops cross Maumee River into Michigan Territory.

JULY 1

Hull hires vessel *Cuyahoga* to carry sick soldiers and heavy baggage by water to Detroit. Troops set off toward Frenchtown (Monroe).

JULY 2

Dispatch reaches Hull with news that war has been declared. Efforts to catch *Cuyahoga* before it sails fails, and vessel is captured by British.

JULY 3

Troops reach Swan Creek, nine miles north of Frenchtown.

JULY 4

Camp made at Huron River, 21 miles from Detroit.

JULY 5

Troops arrive at Spring Wells, three miles from Detroit.

JULY 7

Hull conducts council with southern Michigan Indians.

JULY 8

Army enters Detroit; camps behind the fort.

JULY 9

Hull orders army to prepare to cross Detroit River to Canada next day.

JULY 10

Rowdy militia ruins plans for surprise crossing, which then is cancelled.

JULY 11

McArthur's regiment marches south to dupe British into believing crossing will be made below Detroit.

JULY 12

Army begins actual crossing near Belle Isle at dawn. By end of day Sandwich is secured and proclamation promising safety to Canadians handed out.

JULY 14

McArthur and 115 men set off on foraging expedition to Thames River, 35 miles away.

JULY 16

Cass takes 280 men on scouting trip to Canard River, 12 miles south of Sandwich on road to Fort Malden. Captures bridge and so informs Hull, asking permission to hold it.

JULY 17

Cass returns to Sandwich when Hull leaves the decision whether to hold bridge up to him and his officers.

Findlay returns on scout in evening to discover the British *Queen Charlotte* now guarding the bridge with its guns.

McArthur returns from successful foraging expedition to Thames River.

Fort Mackinac in Upper Peninsula surrenders.

JULY 18

McArthur takes 150-man patrol to Canard River and is fired upon by gunboat.

JULY 19

Cass joins McArthur at Canard with his regiment and exchanges shots with British. Both detachments camp in area for the night.

JULY 20

Cass and McArthur renew exchange of fire with British, finally drawing back to Sandwich.

July 21

Hull and Lieutenant Colonel Miller cross river to Detroit to check progress of building carriages for heavy guns planned for attack on Malden. McArthur left in command at Sandwich.

July 24

McArthur orders Major Denny to take 117 men and set up ambush against Indians crossing Canard River bridge.

July 25

Ambush fails. Denny's troops attacked instead and flee back to Sandwich.

British colonel Procter arrives to take command of Fort Malden.

July 29

Two Chippewa Indians traveling south inform Hull that Fort Mackinac has surrendered.

August 2

After a council that lasts four days, Colonel Procter convinces the Indians on the American side of the river to defect to the British and cross over to Canada.

Lieutenant Hanks arrives at Detroit under parole, confirming his surrender of Fort Mackinac.

August 3

Captain Brush with 69-man guard arrives at Rapids with supply train for Hull. Requests an escort from Detroit to travel the rest of the way because of the heavy presence of Indians on the trail.

After holding council of war, Hull's officers vote to wait before attacking Malden until carriages for heavy guns are ready.

August 4

Hull orders Major Van Horne with 150 men to proceed to Frenchtown and bring the Brush supply train in to Detroit.

Procter calls for Canadian volunteers to assemble and join him in setting an ambush for American troops headed for Frenchtown.

August 5

Van Horne's detachment surprised at Monguagon and sent reeling back to Detroit with loss of 17 men.

AUGUST 6

Hull convenes council of war, then determines that the army will march on Fort Malden on August 8.

AUGUST 7

Hull receives an express from Niagara stating that a large body of enemy troops is moving in his direction and that he cannot expect help from Niagara. The news causes Hull to cancel the Malden attack and order the troops back across the river from Sandwich to Detroit.

British troops and Indians cross river at Brownstown in anticipation of another attempt by Hull to rescue the supply train at Frenchtown.

AUGUST 8

Miller leaves Detroit with 600 men for Frenchtown.

AUGUST 9

Miller severely attacked near Monguagon but routs the British and Indians.

On Niagara front, British adjutant general Baynes and U.S. general Dearborn agree to temporary armistice that does not include the Detroit front but frees British to send men and supplies to Malden.

AUGUST 10

Miller's troops spend day in camp waiting for McArthur to arrive with supplies and take wounded back to Detroit.

AUGUST 11

Miller's troops still in camp at Monguagon, having requested more supplies.

AUGUST 12

Hull orders Miller back to Detroit, fearing his troops have remained at Monguagon too long and are susceptible to British counterattack.

Cass sends round-robin anti-Hull conspiracy letter to Ohio.

AUGUST 13

General Brock reaches Fort Malden near midnight with 300 more men.

AUGUST 14

Brock sends most of his army to Sandwich.

Hull receives message from Brush to rendezvous with supply train at Huron River (Ypsilanti).

Hull orders McArthur and Cass with 400 men to meet Brush, then discovers them still on-site late in afternoon, finally getting them on the trail at dusk.

AUGUST 15

At 1:00 p.m. Brock demands surrender of Detroit. Hull refuses.

Hull sends courier after McArthur and Cass, ordering them to return to Detroit immediately.

Brock constructs gun battery across river from Detroit and commences firing at 4:00. p.m. Hull's guns reply in kind.

At sundown, Hull orders Captain Snelling to take 40–50 men to Spring Wells, across from Sandwich, and report before morning on enemy activity in area.

At dark Indians cross over to River Rouge in preparation for morning attack on Detroit.

AUGUST 16

In predawn hours Snelling's detachment returns to Detroit with nothing to report.

At dawn British cannons open fire on Detroit, signaling British troops to cross river at Spring Wells, rendezvous with Indians, and converge on Detroit.

By 8:00–10:00 p.m. British are in vicinity of Detroit.

At 10:00 a.m., having had no response from McArthur or Cass (who, unknown to Hull, are camped at River Rouge), Hull flies white flag on wall of Fort Detroit and halts heavy gunfire. Brock sends escort to question meaning of flag. Hull replies with request to discuss terms of surrender. Escort returns and meets with American officers to draw up terms. These are completed and agreed to by 11:00 a.m., with official surrender taking place at noon.

Late afternoon, McArthur and Cass surrender their detachment to Captain Elliott of Essex Militia.

[1]

DETROIT AT THE OUTBREAK
OF THE WAR OF 1812

Detroit in 1812 was a small town of 800 people living on the very edge of the frontier. It was over 200 miles from the nearest large American community, Urbana, Ohio, separated by wilderness and Indian tribes that vacillated between friendship and hostility. During peacetime, Detroit's distance from large American towns posed no real problem, although Indian lands surrounded the town to its north, west, and south. It could rely for help on friends in Upper Canada, a more settled and populous region extending east from the Detroit River to Montreal.

When the War of 1812 began, Detroit had been in existence for over 100 years, having been established as a French colony by Antoine de la Mothe Cadillac on July 24, 1701. Detroit enjoyed a strategic location: furs shipped south by water from the upper lakes inevitably had to pass Detroit before descending into the lower lakes on the journey to Montreal. The settlement experienced a major problem over the years, however, with its food supply. Although farming was practiced along the river on either side of the town, settlers never were able to raise enough of a crop to make Detroit self-sustaining. The town also was faced with the specter of Indian attack at any time. Thus during its early years it existed as a combination fort and town, homes and military quarters alike enclosed within a stout stockade that gradually expanded as more homes were built.[1]

The British government took ownership of Detroit in 1763 after its victory in the French and Indian Wars. Almost immediately, the fort/town endured a four-month siege led by the Ottawa Indian chief Pontiac. Pontiac's defeat brought an end to the widespread Indian uprising he had fomented, which had resulted in the capture of all British forts west of Niagara except Detroit. A major rebuilding of Detroit then followed: a section of the interior area, called the Citadel, was enclosed to house the fort's troops and military stores.[2]

Detroit became a center of attention during the Revolutionary War when in 1778 George Rogers Clark captured British forts at Kaskasia, Vincennes, and Cahokia in present-day Indiana. Henry Hamilton, the British governor of Detroit, led an expedition south to reclaim those forts but was captured in a surprise attack at Vincennes. Clark then threatened to march on Detroit. Alarmed by the news, Captain Richard Lernoult, who had been placed in charge of Fort Detroit after Hamilton had left, came to the conclusion that it could never withstand a siege from a determined enemy like Clark, especially if Clark succeeded in mounting cannon on a high rise of ground directly north of the stockade. To prevent this, Lernoult ordered a regular fort to be constructed on the rise, with the town itself taking up the space between the fort and the river. Christened Fort Lernoult, it was a substantial structure surrounded by an earthen rampart 11 feet high, 26 feet wide at its base, and 12 feet wide across its top. A ditch 12 feet wide and five feet deep formed an outer ring around the base of the rampart and contained a single row of upright cedar poles 12 feet high. Along the outer edge of the ditch a second, low rampart called a "glacis" was constructed, in which were imbedded rows of sharpened tree branches facing outward. The inside of the fort contained the officers' quarters, barracks, storehouses, and a bombproof magazine. The main entrance faced south toward the river and could be accessed only by drawbridge. The stockade walls that formed the town perimeter extended up to the rampart of the fort.[3] As the tide of the Revolutionary War in the Northwest changed, Clark's attack never materialized, but the new fort did provide excellent protection against Indian attacks.

The Treaty of Paris terminating the Revolutionary War in September 1783 came as a distinct disappointment to the British in Canada. Michigan became part of the Northwest Territory of the United States, effectively closing off a great part of the favorite hunting grounds of British fur trappers and traders. Moreover, the loss of Detroit, which controlled the water transport of furs down the Great Lakes to Lower Canada, was especially bitter. The British fur traders convinced the government to ignore the treaty and retain possession of either Detroit or Mackinac Island. Indian tribes in the region who favored trading with the British rather than Americans actively supported this violation.

Fort Lernoult (later Fort Detroit) and the town of Detroit at the time of the Jay Treaty, when the British relinquished command to American forces, 1796. (Courtesy of Adam Lovell, Detroit Historical Society.)

Heeding both parties, the British contrived to hold Detroit and other Northwest posts until the signing of the Jay Treaty on November 19, 1794. It required that all British forts on U.S. territory be turned over to American authorities no later then June 1, 1796. The American flag finally replaced the British flag over Fort Detroit on July 11, 1796, when Colonel Richard England formally surrendered it to American captain Moses Porter, and then transferred his troops across to the south side of the Detroit River.[4]

During the next nine years Michigan was first divided between the Northwest Territory and the newly created Indiana Territory, then was entirely within Indiana Territory, finally coming into its own on January 11, 1805, when Congress created the Territory of Michigan with Detroit as its capital.[5]

This change in Michigan's status did little to increase Detroit's population. In 1810, for example, 770 people lived in the town, but their numbers had grown to only 900 by 1817.[6] New settlers expanding outward from Ohio tended to avoid Michigan, since 200 miles of wild country separated the two, in the center of which was the Black Swamp, a 30-mile-wide swath of impenetrable morass south of present-day Toledo through which no decent road had been constructed.

Michigan now being a territory, it was required by law to be administered by a governor, secretary, and three federal judges. The man President Jefferson selected as governor was William Hull, who accepted the post on April 11, 1805. As governor, Hull automatically became the superintendent of Indian Affairs for the Detroit area as well. His post paid him a salary of $2,000 per year. Jefferson's appointment of Hull, an easterner, to administer a frontier region may have been a political move since Hull had been a loyal Jeffersonian Democrat who had held several offices in his native Massachusetts, despite it being a strong Federalist state. Or the appointment might simply have reflected the reality that at this point in the country's political history, the West still had fewer talented and qualified people than the East, limiting Jefferson's choices.

Michigan would take Hull far from the more urbane setting of the eastern seaboard to a rough frontier society made up of French-speaking settlers intermixed with a sprinkling of Americans who were primarily westerners of an independent spirit. Nevertheless, his qualifications for governor were impeccable, though perhaps better suited to a more civilized society. Born in 1753 in Derby, Connecticut, Hull graduated from Yale at the age of 19 and was admitted to the bar at 22. When the Revolutionary War began, he volunteered as a militia captain for his area and

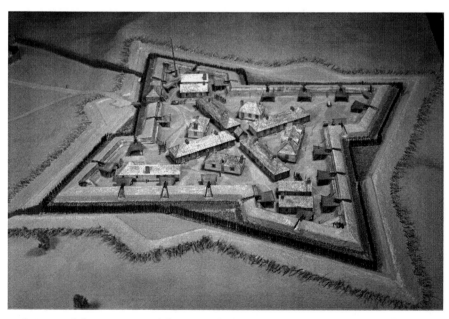

Fort Lernoult (later Fort Detroit). (Courtesy of Adam Lovell, Detroit Historical Society.)

fought in 13battles, in several of which he led bayonet charges and was cited for bravery. By the end of the war he had progressed from the rank of major to that of a full colonel in the regular army, and had the distinction of retaining that rank in the only infantry regiment kept on active duty after the war ended. He resigned from the army in 1786, moving to Newton, Massachusetts, his wife's hometown, where for the next 19 years he served as justice of the peace in common pleas court. He continued to hold the rank of major general in the Massachusetts militia, giving it many years of faithful service. In 1802 he became a member of the state senate, a position he occupied until selected as governor of Michigan.

After his appointment, in May he traveled to Albany, New York, where Vice President George Clinton administered to him the oath of office.[7] From Albany he set out with his wife, son, and two daughters for Detroit, a trip that would take almost two months and remove them hundreds of miles from the civilization to which they were accustomed.[8] Traveling overland to Lake Ontario, they then boarded a boat that took them to Niagara, then traveled by portage to Buffalo, where they were forced to wait until a ship put into port that had business on the west side of Lake Erie. Detroit, being primarily a wilderness town, did not attract frequent commercial travel.[9]

While they were en route, Detroit became the scene of an unprecedented disaster. On the morning of June 11, 1805, a fire broke out inside the stable behind John Harvey's bakery. It has never been conclusively established how the fire began. In one version of the incident, an employee of Harvey had stopped in front of the open stable door to tap out the ashes from his pipe, only to see a gust of wind whisk them through the door into a pile of straw. Before he could react, the interior of the stable was a mass of flames, which the wind carried off in every direction. Someone sounded the alarm. Men quickly assembled, bringing up the town's small hand-pumping fire engine, which had to be constantly refilled with water from the river via a bucket brigade. Soon the townspeople began tearing down the houses and other buildings near the bakery in an effort to contain the blaze, but the fire prevailed. By nightfall all 300 houses in the town were in ashes. The only structures left standing were a warehouse and a few brick chimneys. The fort itself had been spared, being separated from the town homes and buildings by gardens and a large stretch of common grounds. Families were left homeless and destitute. Farmers from the surrounding area offered refuge, as did Canadian settlers across the river.[10]

View of the town of Detroit and the Detroit River, looking south from the fort. (Courtesy of Adam Lovell, Detroit Historical Society.)

Less than one month later, on July 1, 1805, Governor Hull and his family disembarked from their ship at Detroit. The scene that greeted them had to have been disheartening. The capital of the State of Michigan was in ashes. The governor himself had no place to house his family until a nearby farmer offered the Hulls temporary lodging in a small farmhouse one mile up the river.

Hull acted quickly to set up a government. On his first day in office he administered the oath of office to two of the federal judges appointed by Jefferson: Augustus Woodward (a close friend of Jefferson), and Frederick Bates. A third selection, Samuel Huntington, a justice of the Ohio Supreme Court, had declined the nomination, which meant that Michigan would have to make do with only two federal judges for some time. Hull also administered the oath to the new secretary of the territory, Stanley Griswold, previously a Connecticut minister and also a strong Jefferson backer. Both Woodward and Griswold would prove to be highly contentious men who often went out of their way to oppose the governor. Woodward in particular at times acted as if he, not Hull, were in charge of the government.[11]

But that lay in the future. Both judges and the governor had an immediate, important task to resolve together—the rebuilding of Detroit before winter set in. All favored replacing the previous crazy-quilt town plan with an official plat of streets and lots. The new design, revealed to the homeless citizens on July 19, received a mixed reception, especially when the townspeople were informed that the plan would have to be reviewed by Washington before any building could proceed. Woodward and Hull journeyed together to Washington in December 1805 for approval. Thus Congress passed a law in which lots were to be awarded to those who had owned property before the fire, but since the new plat called for these to be larger than the ones they replaced, a fee would have to be paid before taking ownership. Bickering between the settlers and the land board (consisting of Woodward, Hull, and Bates) over the size and locations of the lots grew so rancorous that no new houses were authorized until 1807.[12]

One of Hull's ongoing problems concerned the inhabitants of Michigan Territory: they were primarily of French extraction, understanding little English, they had been loosely governed by the British, and most were poor, illiterate, and not politically active. Neither were they too happy to discover that their placid life was to be ruled by a governor, a secretary, and two federal judges who were empowered to adopt laws they believed were best suited for the territory. It all seemed too complex for a small pioneer settlement.

Hull unwittingly aggravated the citizenry as well by the way in which he established the first territorial militia, which he was required to do by law. The men of the town had no problem with volunteering to serve in the militia, but when Hull prescribed a dress code to which they were to adhere when on duty (a dandified uniform for the officers and special dress for the others), they refused to obey. When the material Hull had ordered for their uniforms arrived from the East, it transpired that most of the militia members could not afford to pay for the cloth. It did not help matters that Hull arrested those who could not or would not buy the material.[13]

Yet the importance of forming a militia could not be denied, especially after Hull had been alerted of the possibility of an Indian uprising. On May 20, 1807, he received a letter from a Captain Dunham stationed at Fort Mackinac warning him that belts of wampum were being circulated among the tribes. Dunham believed that the Indians were poised to make a "desperate and decisive blow" sometime in the near future.[14] The following month Dunham sent Hull another letter, reporting that the Indians had become angry with the Americans for depriving them of their lands, and that if all of them united they would be strong enough to "crowd off every white man that now dares to set foot on their ground."[15]

At around the same time, Hull received reports from Washington of a British warship's infamous attack on the American frigate the *Chesapeake* on June 22, an incident that came very close to precipitating a war with England. The American public, especially along the eastern seaboard, was so outraged by the *Chesapeake* incident that the British government in Canada, fearing an invasion in retaliation, debated whether it should attempt to bring the Indians on the western frontier to its side.[16]

The previous January Hull had been commissioned by President Madison to conduct treaty talks with the Indians in the Michigan area. Madison desired the purchase of two tracts of land, one extending from the Miami River at the mouth of the Auglaize River to a point directly north on a line extending across to Saginaw Bay. Although Michigan had been declared a territory by the government, the only land actually purchased from the Indians was a strip six miles deep along the Detroit River from Lake St. Clair to the Raisin River, and a small portion of Mackinac Island.[17] Hull held the council on November 7 at a gathering of the chieftains of the Ottawa, Chippewa, Wyandot, and Potawatomi tribes. The outcome was a rather surprising treaty (since it went against the wishes of Tecumseh) in which the tribes ceded the southeastern quarter of the Lower Peninsula to the United States in exchange for $10,000 in money and goods plus an annual payment of $2,400. Called the Treaty of Brownstown or the Treaty of Detroit, it represented the first significant purchase of Indian lands by the United States within Michigan Territory.[18]

Hull also made an extra effort to protect Detroit from any potential Indian problems in the future. The stockade pickets that had originally enclosed the town were destroyed in the 1805 fire and had never been replaced. Hull had the militia reconstruct it with pickets 18 feet high, which extended to the pickets surrounding Fort Detroit. Nevertheless, while the town and fort were admirably suited to defend against Indian attack, they were in a poor position to face an enemy on the other side of the Detroit River since the fort's guns would be required to fire over the roofs of the town's houses and buildings, thus limiting their effectiveness.

As the war fears engendered by the *Chesapeake* episode gradually subsided and an Indian threat seemed more remote after the 1807 treaty, Detroit drifted into what proved to be a false sense of security. By the spring of 1810 its citizens had gone so far as to remove portions of the timbers that made up the stockade walls, using them for building materials or even firewood. Hull was not in a good position to halt them from doing so since the stockade walls were built not on public property but on their private lands. Hull had all of the remaining stockade timbers taken down and placed in storage to prevent their gradual loss in the event that they might be needed for a future emergency. Except for the Citadel, which existed outside the fort but was connected to it by a stockade remnant, the town was completely open to attack. If Indian trouble should erupt, the entire population would have no choice but to crowd into the fort.[19]

As the year 1810 passed into 1811, little occurred to disturb the complacency of Detroit. Hull had been confirmed for a third term as governor on January 9. News periodically surfaced regarding Indian problems in Indiana Territory, but that area seemed quite distant, considering the wilderness separating it from Detroit. However, news did reach Hull that a Shawnee warrior named Tecumseh was circulating among the Indian tribes to the south promoting his plan for a grand Indian confederation.

Reports from Washington had kept Hull aware of another potential threat—the ongoing maritime struggles with England which, should they escalate, could lead to war. If nothing else, such news must have made him more acutely aware of Detroit's position should war become a reality. Detroit depended on food supplies obtained from the Ohio area to supplement its own farming output. The easiest and safest form of transport for these supplies for much of the journey was by boat rather than by pack train through the wilderness, which was more vulnerable to bad weather and Indian sorties. The water route, unfortunately, took the supply boats past the British Fort Malden, which was in a position to control all ship traffic by virtue of its location. Although the mouth of the Detroit River was four miles wide, large boats were forced to navigate by way of a narrow, deep channel that passed between Bois Blanc Island and the Canadian shore, directly under the guns of Fort Malden.

As long as there was peace between the United States and Upper Canada, this did not present a problem.[20] But with war talk continuing to surface, the supply situation did worry Hull. On April 3, 1809, he first expressed his concerns over this matter with the War Department. "I would suggest for consideration the expediency of building some armed vessels on Lake Erie, for the purpose of preserving communication; consider that you have three military posts, to the north and west of these waters and not other communication with them."[21]

Again on June 15 he wrote:

> From the present state of our foreign relations, particularly with Eng-
> land, I am induced to believe there is little prospect of a continuance
> of peace. . . . A wilderness of near 200 miles separates this settlement
> from any of the states. Besides, the Indiana Territory and states of
> Ohio and Kentucky are thinly populated, have extensive frontiers,
> and their forces will be necessary for their own defense. With respect
> to the Indians, their situation and habits are such, that little depen-
> dence can be placed on them. At present they appear friendly, and
> was I to calculate on the profession of their chiefs, I should be satis-
> fied that they would not become hostile. Their first passion, however,
> is war. The policy of the British government is to consider them their
> allies, and in the event of war, to invite them to join their standard.
> . . . Under these circumstances, if there is a prospect of war with Eng-
> land, what measures are most expedient? In my mind there can be no
> doubt. *Prepare a naval force on Lake Erie superiour to the British, and
> sufficient to preserve your communication.*[22]

No such action was taken by the administration despite Hull's warnings.
It was as if Detroit's problems were not a matter of concern to the government.

In the summer of 1811, Hull requested permission of Washington
to return to Massachusetts for an extended vacation. He left for the East
on September 29, having turned over the reins of government to Reuben
Attwater, now the secretary of Michigan Territory, and took passage from
Detroit to Buffalo aboard the British sloop of war the *Queen Charlotte*.[23]

A week after he left, events suddenly erupted that shattered the
peace that he had left behind. On November 6 William Henry Harrison,
governor of Indiana, and his army of 960 men came under surprise attack
by the followers of Tenskwatawa, otherwise known as the Prophet, while
camped outside the latter's village near Tippecanoe, present-day Lafay-
ette, Indiana.

Harrison had been wary of Tenskwatawa's intentions for some time.
A charismatic Shawnee who had abandoned his debauched life in April
1805 after having a vision, the Prophet believed that he had been selected
by the Master of Life to lead the Indians away from their bad habits and
bring them to a life of peace with all mankind. He preached that those
who heeded his words were to eat only the game that they killed in the

forest, discard their metal tools for those made of wood or stone, and hunt with bows and arrows. Guns were permitted only in self-defense. He specifically cautioned his followers to avoid all contact with Americans, as they were the children of the Great Serpent who, according to the Shawnee cosmology, opposed the Master of Life. As the spokesman for the Master of Life, the Prophet warned that anyone who did not obey his injunction would become an enemy of the Master of Life.[24]

Together with his brother, Tecumseh, the Prophet established a village at Greenville, Ohio, after failing to take over the leadership of the Shawnee. Their followers increased dramatically after the summer of 1806. Earlier that year, several astronomers had traveled through the Indian country setting up observation posts from which they could view an eclipse of the sun that was forecast to take place on June 16. The Prophet, learning of their prediction, planned to use the eclipse as a means of further establishing his prophetic credentials. He announced to his followers that he would darken the sun on the June 16 date. His apparent success in having done so so startled his followers that his influence among them and other Indian tribes spread rapidly.[25]

By 1807 the numbers in his village had become so great that Tenskwatawa was at pains to assure Harrison that his religion offered no threat to the Americans so as to forestall any military action the governor might have contemplated. However, white settlers in Ohio had become alarmed by the growing numbers of Indians passing through their lands on the way to Greenville, which depleted the area's game, on which settlers and Indians alike depended for food. On the advice of his followers and at the invitation of Potawatomi chief Main Poc, during April 1808 the Prophet moved his village to a new site at the junction of the Wabash and Tippecanoe rivers, where game was much more plentiful, as was timber for fuel. They named the village Prophetstown.[26]

Although Tenskwatawa continued to preach peace to his followers, not all of them adhered to his message, and raids continued to take place along the frontier. Harrison had hoped to defuse the problem through the September 1809 Treaty of Fort Wayne in which friendly tribes sold over 3 million acres of land to the United States in Indiana and Illinois. Tenskwatawa strongly opposed the treaty and swore that he would kill those chiefs who had signed it. Also opposed was Tecumseh, who up to this point had made no effort to usurp his brother's leadership. After the Fort Wayne treaty, however, he assumed a greater role among the tribes, believing that his brother's movement should be not only religious but political as well. Between 1810 and 1811 he traveled extensively among the various tribes espousing the need for unity if and when frontier trouble should erupt.[27]

Still not trusting the Prophet's peaceful intentions, Secretary of War William Eustis sent Harrison a dispatch, which the latter received on October 12. In it he ordered Harrison to raise an army and confront the Prophet and his followers, encouraging them to disperse in peaceful fashion. If they refused, he was to attack, take Tenskwatawa prisoner, and raze Prophetstown.[28]

Harrison and his army reached the outskirts of Prophetstown on November 6, having been shadowed throughout their march by Indian scouts, and made camp about a mile from the settlement. The Prophet sent a delegation offering to negotiate in council the next day. Harrison agreed, although several of his officers argued for an immediate attack. That evening a black cook in the Indian camp, who was either a captive or a deserter from Harrison's army, convinced Tenskwatawa that Harrison intended to use the council as an excuse to attack instead. Now galvanized into action, the Indians prepared to strike first, that night. Although outnumbered by a ratio of two to one, they were emboldened by the Prophet's promises that they would be immune from enemy bullets and that even in the dark of night, the inside of the American camp would, for them alone, be as light as day.[29]

In the early morning hours the Indians suddenly struck at Harrison's camp, uttering terrifying yells. The advantage of the ensuing battle swayed back and forth between the combatants, but as daylight approached the Indians realized that the Americans could see just as well as they, and as they were running low on ammunition, they finally broke off the action, gradually filtering back to Prophetstown. Harrison's troops remained fixed in their camp, the following day expecting another attack, which never came. They then cautiously made their way to Prophetstown. Finding it abandoned except for an elderly, infirm woman, they burned it to the ground along with 5,000 pounds of food supplies.[30]

Tecumseh returned from his journey to the southern tribes in January. Although his brother's defeat made him realize that his and Tenskwatawa's attempts to form an Indian confederation had been badly damaged, it was not a total disaster. While it was widely believed that Harrison's victory had put an end to such aspirations, Tenskwatawa had reestablished Prophetstown near its original site by the end of January 1812, with a following of 550 from different Indian tribes. By June the number had grown to 800.[31] For his part, Tecumseh actively sought the support of the British to carry on his mission and journeyed to Fort Malden in June with a number of Shawnee to help lead his Indian allies against the Americans in the forthcoming war, which could be fruitful in furthering his and the Prophet's aspirations.[32]

News of the battle at Tippecanoe reached Detroit by mail on December 7. It was disturbing from the standpoint that it might excite the Indian tribes in the Detroit area to seek revenge for the defeat. A Committee of Public Safety was formed, which addressed a memorial to Washington pointing out that the entire Michigan Territory had only two points of defense should trouble begin: Fort Detroit, with a garrison of only 94 men, and Fort Mackinac with 74.[33] Acting governor Attwater also wrote Hull in Massachusetts to inform him "that there were strong appearances of hostility among the Indians, and that the territory was in danger."[34]

On the Canadian side of the river, however, the British were looking to head off any such uprising. Their Indian agents were ordered to maintain friendly relations with the Indians and continue to furnish them with supplies, but discourage them from taking any overt actions against the Americans. If attacked, they were to retreat.[35]

Disturbing to Hull were comments coming from Congress strongly advocating war with England, which would mean taking the war to Canada. This, he knew, Detroit was in no position to do. On March 6, 1812, he wrote to Secretary of War William Eustis his estimate that the number of Canadian militia members the British could raise and bring against Detroit would outnumber the Michigan militia by a factor of 10 to 1, not including the British-friendly Indians. He added that even if the Michigan militia were augmented by more troops, the additional numbers could not easily be supported, inasmuch as the United States did not have command of the inland lakes, and supplies would have to be freighted by packhorses. "The answer probably may be," he told Eustis, that "it is more expedient to leave the Michigan Territory to its fate, and direct the force to Montreal. This will prevent all communications by the St. Lawrence with Upper Canada, and it must of course surrender."[36]

Unfortunately, near the end of his letter, Hull added a comment that he later would regret: "A force adequate to the defense of that vulnerable point [Detroit], would prevent war with the savages, and probably induce the enemy to abandon the province of Upper Canada without opposition. The naval force on the Lakes would in that event fall into our possession—and we should obtain command of the water without the expence of building such a force."[37] This statement defies explanation: it is completely counter to Hull's long-standing views on the need for control of the lakes to prevent an interdiction of his supply route. In the months to come, he would repeatedly request a presence of U.S. naval power on the lakes, especially Lake Erie. He was not alone in this view. The previous January, John Armstrong, who later would replace Eustis as secretary of war, had suggested that Detroit anchor the country's western defense. "Why not Detroit, where you have a strong fortress and a detachment of artillerists? Recollect, however, that this position, far from being good, would be positively bad unless your naval means have an ascendancy on Lake Erie."[38]

In March 1812 President Madison took the precaution of authorizing Governor Return Meigs of Ohio to recruit volunteers to reinforce the defense of Detroit should war ultimately be declared. On April 6 Meigs asked for 1,200 Ohio men to volunteer for this duty and gather in Dayton at the end of the month. Governor Hull was chosen by the president to take command of this force, but he declined, preferring to continue as governor of Michigan Territory. The War Department next turned to Colonel Jacob Kingsbury, the commander of Fort Detroit. Unfortunately, Kingsbury suffered a severe attack of gout just as his orders were being cut. He, too, therefore declined.[39]

Kingsbury's illness proved to be providential for him. When asked by Hull during the latter's court-martial proceedings, "Did you estimate that force [the Ohio militia and additional regular troops] sufficient for offensive operations against Upper Canada, in case of war with Great Britain?" Kingsbury answered, "I did not."[40] Unfortunately, the question never was posed to him by the War Department prior to the Detroit campaign.

With Kingsbury no longer available, the command of Governor Meig's volunteer force (to which regular troops later would be added) again was tendered to Hull, this time with the provision that he could continue as governor of Michigan. Hull again refused. Eustis approached Hull a third time, offering him the rank of brigadier general. Hull reluctantly accepted despite his strong misgivings that an army consisting primarily of untrained militia volunteers could be effective in battle, especially against the caliber of the men attached to Fort Malden. Nevertheless, he prepared to take command of his new army at Dayton and march it to Detroit.

Why Hull, now a man of 59 who had been out of the regular army for the past 26 years, finally agreed to Eustis's request is open to question. Although he was still and healthy and physically fit, by no means the senile old man his critics portrayed him as, he had never held an independent command, even during his Revolutionary War service. It was his misfortune that the U.S. army at this time was woefully short of experienced, mature military leaders and had to make do with those men who were available.

PREAMBLE TO AN UNNECESSARY WAR

The War of 1812 is one that never should have been fought. For France and England, involved in their great struggle in continental Europe, it was merely a sideshow. It came about simply because these two great nations, in their stubbornness, each attempted to shut down the other's trade with neutral countries. In doing so they ignored the maritime rights of the United States. Great Britain especially was unwilling to believe that the young country would have the temerity to challenge its policies. That being said, had Britain not gone to war again with France, there would have been no reason for a war to erupt between England and the United States.

The seeds of the conflict between the United States and England were sown on May 18, 1803, when England once again declared war on France. Within the next two years, Napoleon defeated Russia, Austria, and Prussia, and put England to the test. The renewal of the war meant a rapid expansion in England's navy, its first line of defense. Having discharged 40,000 sailors after the Peace of Amiens in 1802, England now found itself woefully short of naval manpower. To quickly regroup, the country instituted a policy whereby its ship captains were to stop neutral ships on the high seas and search them for seamen the captain deemed ex-British citizens. These were impressed immediately into the British navy. Sometimes an American ship lost so many sailors through such impressment that it barely had enough hands to sail back to port.[1]

France depended on foreign trade to feed its armies. Britain vowed to stop that trade. Immediately after the war was renewed, France opened its West Indian ports to all neutral vessels. England countered with the

Orders in Council of June 24, 1803, which stipulated that any product acquired from a French possession that a neutral country desired to trade with England had to be carried in British ships. While this may have been a minor impediment to such trade, it did not unduly hamper it.[2]

It was the issue of impressment that made the United States sit up and take notice. Once the French fleet had been soundly defeated by Britain's Lord Horatio Nelson in the battle of Trafalgar on October 2, 1805, and the English were now in control of the high seas, thus preventing any invasion of the British Isles by France, the United States expected the issue of impressment to disappear. It did not. England made no effort to relax its impressment policies, which did not set well with President Jefferson. He became further aggravated when England instituted its "Essex" policy under which any neutral ship that had traded at a French-controlled port, gone on to a neutral port, then stopped again at a French port was open to capture, its neutral status notwithstanding.[3] Then, on May 16, 1806, a new Orders in Council was issued, establishing a British blockade of the European coast from the Elbe River to Brest. Neutral countries like the United States never could trade unmolested by the British in ports outside this continental zone. Two months later Britain announced the American Intercourse Bill, which permitted U.S. and other neutral ships to trade commodities with the British West Indies.[4] While Jefferson welcomed such conciliatory moves, they did not address the still-festering problem of impressment, which remained unresolved despite extended diplomatic exchanges between the United States and England.

Napoleon now attempted to interpose his own type of economic trade warfare. On November 21, 1806, he issued the Berlin Decree, closing off European ports to the ships of any country regardless of their nationality if they also traded with England; if ships attempted to enter port regardless, their goods were confiscated. England could not allow this to take place without challenge and issued a new Orders in Council. This decreed that any ship attempting to trade with the continent would be considered an enemy. It would be stopped by the Royal Navy, searched, and required to purchase a trading license before it could proceed. The United States argued that this was a violation of neutrality rights under international law, but England chose to ignore this logic in its effort to starve out Napoleon.[5]

This exchange of sanctions between England and France had a critical effect on the United States, which had built up a brisk trade with Europe. Before long U.S. ships were being routinely stopped and searched by British warships. And as before, any American sailor identified as having previously been an English citizen was impressed into the British navy. Most galling to Washington was that the English halted not only commercial ships but U.S. Navy ships as well. Under such circumstances, it became only a matter of time until a spark would ignite a reaction that could lead to war.

Such a spark was struck on June 22, 1807. A few months earlier, sailors of the Royal Navy, whose ships routinely stopped for supplies in Norfolk, Virginia, when on patrol, had engaged in a shouting match on the streets of the town with one Jenkin Ratford. Ratford was a deserter from a British ship who had fled to America and enlisted as a seaman on the frigate the USS *Chesapeake*. The British naval officers did not take kindly to his taunts and voiced their complaints to their higher authority, Vice Admiral Sir George Berkeley, the British naval commander on the American station. Berkeley reacted by ordering his ships to halt and search the *Chesapeake* should it set sail. Ratford was to be removed along with any other deserters they encountered. When the *Chesapeake,* under the command of Commodore James Barron, next left Norfolk harbor, the HMS *Leopard* brought it to a halt just outside U.S. territorial waters, otherwise known as the three-mile limit. Captain Salisbury Humphreys of the *Leopard* ordered the *Chesapeake* to stand by for boarding. Barron refused. The two captains kept yelling at one another across the water separating the two ships until an exasperated Humphreys fired a shot across the *Chesapeake*'s bow. When Barron still refused to submit, Humphreys discharged several of his 50 guns into the *Chesapeake,* killing three American sailors and wounding 18. Barron, who had not been prepared to fight a battle during peacetime, had no choice but to strike the *Chesapeake*'s colors. Humphreys sent across a boarding party. It lined up the American crew and removed four men it claimed were deserters, including the unfortunate Ratford, who later was hanged.[6]

The reaction to the *Leopard*'s attack was immediate and widespread. The American press issued scathing editorials against the British Crown. Norfolk refused to supply those British ships still at its docks, and the local militia was placed on active duty to quell any trouble that might arise. Rioting erupted along the coast from Norfolk, eventually spreading to New York City, where the English consul's house was placed under police protection. A British ship in the New York harbor was boarded and its guns, rigging, and sails destroyed. Public meetings were held along the seaboard demanding war. Canada became so leery of the uproar its government called out the militia in case trouble spilled across the border.[7]

More important, the uproar in the States caused the British to take a second look at their Indian policy, fearing that any attack on Canada probably would first occur in the Northwest. This meant securing the assistance of the Indian tribes in Ohio, Indiana, and Michigan. For the past three years, however, they had been discouraging the attempts of Tecumseh to form an Indian confederation to defend Indian lands, and they had been wary of the Prophet, fearing he might trigger an Indian war into which they would be drawn.[8] During December 1807 Sir James Craig, the governor-general of Canada, forwarded new instructions to his Indian agents. They were to avoid any actions that might be construed by the United States as enticing the Indians to frontier warfare, but at the same time meet with them privately and assure them that the British would come to their aid if necessary.[9]

Almost two weeks after the attack on the *Chesapeake,* President Jefferson responded with a proclamation ordering all British ships to leave American ports. He also dispatched the schooner *Revenge* with a message to James Monroe, the American minister to England, instructing him to demand that the British refrain from searching U.S. ships, return the four men who had been impressed from the *Chesapeake,* and remove Sir George Berkeley from office for provoking the *Chesapeake* incident. The British government, which considered the action quite trivial, was surprised by Jefferson's strident response. To calm relations with the United States, it completely disowned the attack, agreed to compensate the relatives of the men who had been killed or wounded, and recalled Berkeley to England. It also added that it had never been its intent to order that American warships be stopped and searched.[10]

Seemingly unaware of the uproar caused by the *Chesapeake* incident, on October 16, 1807, King George III ordered the Royal Navy to conduct rigorous impressment procedures on all commercial ships that flew the flags of neutral countries. Although his order impacted all American shipowners, they continued to hire English deserters simply because these men had become an integral part of their workforce. According to a survey conducted by Albert Gallatin, secretary of the treasury under Madison, as many as 3,000 British deserters were employed in U.S. maritime trade; therefore shipowners chose to tolerate the stoppage of their vessels rather than do without the sailors.[11]

Napoleon reentered the international shipping controversy on December 17, 1807, when he issued the Milan Decree. It stated that any neutral ship that docked at a French-controlled port after it had sailed to England or had been searched by an English warship would be seized along with its cargo. It was Napoleon's warning to neutral countries that if they traded with England they would be excluded from trade with the European continent. (Over the next five years France confiscated about 468 American merchant ships.)[12]

The Milan Decree and England's Orders in Council had sorely tried President Jefferson's patience. The wisdom of his response, however, is questionable. At his recommendation Congress, on December 22, 1807, passed the Embargo Act prohibiting international trade to and from American ports. The act was meant to cripple England's brisk trade with the United States and thereby place a greater pressure on England to cancel its Orders in Council.[13] It shifted the U.S. quarrel with Britain from one primarily about impressment to one of issues involving ships and cargo.

The Embargo Act produced an effect opposite to the one Jefferson had intended. Given the many miles of American coastline, it was too difficult to enforce. Smuggling was rampant, especially by land across the border with Canada. By the end of 1808 U.S. export trade had dropped to only 20 percent of what it had been in 1807, although there was one redeeming benefit: the lack of imported machine tools from Britain forced the development of domestic manufacturing, especially in the middle states.[14] Conversely, British exports for 1808 were scarcely affected. British trade was redirected to new market opportunities in South America, offsetting what had been lost. When Jefferson realized what was taking place, he proposed to the British that he would cancel the Embargo Act if England would drop its Orders in Council, which the latter refused, there being no advantage in doing so.[15]

During December 1808 the British minister to the United States, David Erskine, warned George Canning, the English foreign minister, that there was a danger of war being declared by the Americans if the Orders in Council were not repealed. He suggested that with a new president taking office in the coming year, it would be a providential time for the two countries to reach an agreement over trade policies. Canning responded to Erskine's suggestion with new instructions. England would cancel the Orders if the United States agreed to trade with England but not with any French possessions, and if America accepted the fact that any of its ships that attempted to trade with France or its allies were open to capture without recourse. If such terms were acceptable, England would rescind the Orders in Council by the spring of 1809. Erskine conferred with Robert Smith, the U.S. secretary of state. Realizing that the United States would never agree to Canning's terms as stated so bluntly, Erskine ignored them, working with Smith to draw up a new set of alternatives, which hopefully would satisfy Canning. They now had to wait for the latter's response, which they did not expect to see for at least three months, ocean travel being as it was.[16]

With pressure building to rescind the Embargo Act, which had hurt the United States more than England, Congress in February 1809 rushed a bill through chambers repealing the act, which Jefferson signed three days before leaving office. By a vote of 81 to 40, Congress immediately replaced the old act with the Non-intercourse Act. This allowed American ships to resume trade with all countries except England and France and their possessions. Trade with England and France was conditional upon their abandoning their search and seizure policies, and their ships would not be allowed to dock in American ports.[17]

James Madison, who had taken office as president on March 4, had high hopes that news would arrive from England signaling that the terms negotiated between Erskine and Smith were acceptable and that the Orders in Council would be canceled, allowing the two countries to restore trade. On July 21 Canning's answer finally arrived. He categorically rejected the terms to which Erskine and Smith had agreed. The Orders in Council would continue to be in effect unless and until the United States met all of England's terms. The news came as a bitter blow. Congress was beginning to believe that only war could bring America the respect it felt due as a sovereign nation.

A year passed, with neither England nor France making any effort to respond to the opening given to them over trade with the United States by the Non-intercourse Act. France further aggravated the situation when on March 23, 1810, Napoleon issued his Rambouillet Decree ordering that every American ship entering a French port be immediately confiscated.[18]

Having failed to elicit any good response on trade policies from either England or France, Congress threw up its arms and passed Macon's Bill No. 2 on May 1, 1810. It permitted American ships to resume trade with England and France but only if those countries would repeal their trade restrictions. A refusal would mean that the United States would close all further trade with them. After learning the provisions of Macon's Bill No. 2, France had second thoughts about its trade policy with the United States. The French believed they might be able to use the bill to their advantage by creating a situation in which U.S. trade with England would be shut down but that with France would be permitted. Word of France's intentions came in August 1810 when John Armstrong, the U.S. minister to France, was informed that that country's Berlin and Milan decrees would be revoked after November 1, allowing the United States to resume trade with France.[19] Madison accepted this report at face value, and without confirming its validity informed England that all trade with it would cease in three months unless it canceled the Orders in Council.[20]

This news greatly disturbed British manufacturers, suffering as England had slipped into a deep depression, and they urgently petitioned the government to drop its Orders in Council inasmuch as the value of exports to the United States had fallen by 90 percent during the past year. Trade with western Europe had been all but closed to the British as well, its only markets being Russia and Portugal. Warehouses were crammed with goods for which there were no buyers. Factories were shutting down. Workers were rioting. Still the government refused to concede.[21] An exasperated William Pinkney, the U.S. minister to England, disgusted with England's intransigence over its trade policies, departed for the United States on February 13, 1811. His departure meant that the United States had no official representative in London to argue its policies. In Washington, the general impression grew that England was forcing the United States to choose between a peace on England's terms or war.[22]

Members of Congress had few doubts over what the choice should be. Driven by the "War Hawks," young new members led by Henry Clay, they were eager to fight for freedom of trade. If it came to war, so be it. They ignored the fact that the United States had a miniscule navy and could scarcely hope to damage England on the high seas. If England was to be hurt, it would have to be by land, which meant invading and capturing Canada. Taking Canada, however, might not be simple: the United States would be faced with a large Canadian militia as well as with the Indian tribes on the frontier whose friendship the British had been fostering for decades. Though Britain's friendship with the tribes was not calculated to lead to war unless its hand was forced, in fact, its Indian policy had been modified again since 1807, to the point where Major General Isaac Brock in 1811 specifically warned the tribes that the British would no longer supply them with food and ammunition should they create a war on the frontier—the tribes still constituted a threat, at least in the perception of the settlers on the frontier.[23]

To these settlers, the possibility of war also brought the possibility of ending the Indian threat within their midst, which they were convinced was being promoted by British officials in the Fort Malden area, where the tribes regularly gathered for their supplies. The influential and dangerous Indian leader Tecumseh, still fuming over the defeat of his brother at Tippecanoe and well aware of the possibility of war with England over maritime issues, planned to use such a war, should it occur, as a means of removing Americans from the Indians' northwestern tribal lands. On November 15, 1811, during a council meeting with Matthew Elliott, the British Indian agent, he proposed an alliance between the Indian tribes and the British. Elliott in turn made Tecumseh's suggestion a part of a British Northwest defense strategy in which he suggested to Brock, his superior, that 500 troops be stationed at Fort Malden together with 500 Indians who would be gathered by Tecumseh. If war should be declared, he wrote Brock, they would be able to hold the Americans in the area at bay.[24] Brock used Elliott's proposal to formulate his "Plans for the Defense of Canada." It called for the British to first capture Fort Mackinac in order to convince the Indians in Michigan that they should join the cause, then he would forward the entire 41st Regiment of Foot to Fort Malden under Colonel Henry Procter with orders to go on the offensive against Fort Detroit. This would create a widespread uprising of the Indians, which would freeze American military operations in the area. He also planned to build seven gunboats and add new men to the Provincial Marine squadron.

He forwarded the plan for approval to Lieutenant General Sir George Prevost, who had recently arrived as governor-general of North America. Prevost hesitated to approve it. He doubted whether the 41st Regiment would be able to hold off the Americans for any length of time even if initially victorious. Moreover, he considered it more important, should war be declared, to defend Quebec rather than go on the offense in Upper Canada supported by only one British regiment of regulars. At present he could count only 1,658 trained, paid troops scattered around a dozen posts across that vast territory. Although they could be supported by up to 11,000 militia, the latter were poorly trained and poorly equipped. Also, most of them had been born in what now was the United States and had emigrated to Canada for various reasons, and therefore their loyalty was suspect.[25]

On the American side, members of Congress were optimistic, if unrealistic. Far from Indian country themselves, they did not view the potential Indian threat with the same importance as those living on the frontier; they considered the problem to be one represented only by the territories of Michigan, Indiana, and Illinois, and therefore not a primary issue if it came to war with England. They naively assumed that the annexation of Canada would not only eliminate the Indian problem but would force England to rescind its Orders in Council. In a rather fatuous speech to the Senate, Henry Clay went so far as to say, "The conquest of Canada is in your power. I trust I shall not be deemed presumptuous when I state that I verily believe that the militia in Kentucky are alone competent to place Montreal and Upper Canada at your feet."[26] How wrong these words would prove to be.

Although war talk was rampant in Washington, there still was no guarantee that one would take place. Nevertheless, President Madison, on January 11, 1812, signed a bill that called for the War Department to recruit a regular army of 35,000 men, about six times the number then on the rolls. On February 6, he also approved a bill to raise a militia force of 50,000. While such numbers sound impressive, they existed only on paper for some time. In fact, six weeks later not a single officer except a commander in chief had yet been appointed.[27]

The news that convinced President Madison that war was his only option came on May 27, when the British foreign minister asked to meet with both President Madison and James Monroe. He informed them of the latest word he had received from Lord Wellesley, the British foreign secretary: because he did not believe that the French had actually rescinded their decrees against U.S. shipping, there was no reason for his government to cancel the Orders in Council. They would be continued.[28]

Madison was left with no alternative. On June 1 he forwarded a message to Congress recommending that it meet and vote in favor of war (see appendix 1). Explaining the reasons for his decision, he wrote:

> We behold our seafaring citizens still the daily victims of lawless violence, committed on the great common highway of nations, even within the sight of the country which owes them protection. We behold our vessels, freighted with the products of our soil and industry, or returning with the honest proceeds of them, wrested from their lawful destinations, confiscated by prize courts no longer the organs of public law but the instruments of arbitrary edicts, and their unfortunate crews dispersed and lost, or forced or inveigled in British ports into British fleets, whilst arguments are employed in support of these aggressions which have no foundation but in a principle equally supporting a claim to regulate our external commerce in all cases whatsoever.[29]

The debates in Congress that followed were closed to the public, including newspaper reporters, despite efforts by members of the Federalist Party to keep them open. On June 4, the House, led by the War Hawks, voted in favor of war by a 79 to 49 margin. Ironically, the majority of members casting negative votes represented eastern seaboard states extending from New Jersey northward, states that were heavily involved in overseas commerce and were most affected by Britain's maritime policies. The House measure then was forwarded to the Senate, where it was discussed for the next two weeks. During this entire time the American public was aware that a debate of serious import was taking place in Congress but had no idea that it was about war with England. On June 18 the Senate finally approved the House war bill by a vote of 19 for and 13 against, not exactly an overwhelming majority, which made Madison a bit uncomfortable. The president was said to have been as white as a sheet as he waited to receive the news. Of the total members of Congress, one of three voted against the war, most of these belonging to the Federalist Party. Madison signed the bill on June 19, but it was not until the following day that the nation realized that the country was at war, thanks to an announcement in a Washington newspaper, the *National Intelligencer.* The debates and voting had been conducted so quietly that many across the country had difficulty accepting the truth of the news.[30]

Had Madison delayed signing the bill for another month, the war might never have taken place. Shortly after 5:00 p.m. on May 11, as Prime Minister Spencer Percival entered the lobby of the House of Commons, he was met by James Bellingham, an irate merchant upset with the continuance of the Orders in Council. Bellingham drew a pistol and fired directly at Percival, killing him instantly. After the prime minister's death, cabinet members resigned en masse rather than face the wrath of the public if the Orders in Council were continued.[31]

Relief from the Orders in Council finally came in the form of Robert Banks Jenkinson, the second Earl of Liverpool, who had agreed to form a new government but only on condition that he open the Orders in Council question to debate. When he did, he was amazed to discover that he could not find a single member of the House of Commons willing to vote that they be continued, nor could he discover who had originated them. Allegedly, it had been Sir James Stephen, but when Stephen was asked to testify in their behalf, he refused. Finding no support for continuing the Orders in Council, Liverpool repealed them. He announced his decision on June 23, 1812, only four days after Madison signed Congress's bill for war, a war whose purpose was to force England to cancel those same Orders in Council.[32] But it was too late. There was no turning back.

President Madison wanted war. Congress wanted war. No one gave thought to the fact that the country was totally unready to conduct war. Madison, "who had never heard a shot fired in anger," viewed it as a giant chess game involving maneuvers that would be made by small bodies of troops. Diplomatic moves rather than fighting would take place until England was finally convinced to terminate its Orders in Council.[33] "Madison wanted no British territory, no reparations, no humble surrender. His war aims were limited. All he desired was an admission by British leaders that the United States was not a second-cousin dependent but an honest-to-God sovereign power in the world family of nations."[34]

The thinking of Congress seemed equally naive. Its War Hawk members viewed an invasion of Canada as a cross between a picnic and a shooting party. As one member put it: "I believe that in four weeks from the time a declaration of war is heard on our frontier, the whole of Upper Canada and a part of Lower Canada will be in our power."[35]

However, not all members of Congress agreed. John Randolph came closer than any of his colleagues in Congress to accurately assessing the nation's readiness for war. "Go to war without money, without men, without a navy! Go to war when we have not the courage, while your lips utter war, to levy war taxes! When your whole courage is exhibited in passing resolutions."[36]

Totally glossed over by Congress was the state of the nation's navy, which was miniscule in comparison to England's arsenal of 600 ships. Of these, 120 were huge ships of the line that normally carried as many as 100 guns stacked between three and four decks. Another 116 ships were the smaller but faster frigates, each of which contained 28 to 30 guns on its lower deck level and another six to eight topside. The U.S. Navy, by contrast, was prepared to face this formidable array with 10 frigates (five of which were in dry dock in various stages of repair) and 62 gunboats still in commission as holdovers from the Jefferson administration's efforts to police American shores when the Embargo Act was in effect. Each gunboat was only 60 feet long, carried a single gun fore and aft, and was seaworthy only in calm waters. Naval manpower consisted of 4,000 enlisted seamen and boys backed by about 1,800 Marines. The sheer number of ships that the British could bring into action at any given time probably could keep the entire U.S. Navy from leaving port.[37]

Creating a wartime navy, however, was not on the administration's list of priorities. The Republican Party, which dominated Congress, had been congenitally opposed to a standing navy as long as it had held power. When South Carolina Republican Langdon Cheeves introduced a bill to provide appropriations necessary to construct 12 ships of the line and 20 frigates, it was defeated by a vote of 62 to 59, despite the fact that Congress's most influential member, Henry Clay, in another bit of bravado, argued that such ships would be necessary to protect the United States after Canada had been conquered.[38]

Considering that the country had been at the brink of war for so many months, one would expect that the Madison administration would have sought to improve the War Department's readiness to conduct a war. It did not. The department could easily operate out of a single room. It consisted of only nine men: Secretary of War William Eustis, a chief clerk, and seven minor clerks. Eustis had no experience whatsoever, having served as a military surgeon during the Revolutionary War. He had no military training, but he was an ardent Republican in the Federal stronghold of Massachusetts. Presumably this was sufficient to bring him a post in government.

Congress was no help. Never having been involved in a war before, it was not quite certain what the duties of a War Department should be, and it carried the traditional Republican Party baggage of a fear of a professional standing army. As during the Revolutionary War, Congress simply assumed that Americans would volunteer in great numbers if the need arose.

In defense of Eustis, he did keep in close communication with the commanders of the nation's army garrisons, and he did a creditable job of arranging for their food, housing, and clothing. The task was not very complex. The typical ration for the individual soldier of that era, for example, was bread, beef or pork, and rum or whiskey. Any other food item, such as a vegetable, the soldier had to pay for out of his own pocket. Eustis, however, was ill prepared to deal with the huge demands that a rapidly increasing number of regulars and volunteers were to make on his office. Simply to transport foodstuffs to large bodies of troops in the field would become a major operation in itself and take Eustis completely out of his depth.[39] His most serious handicap was that he had no general staff, no cadre of professional officers who could advise him on civil or military matters.[40] To compensate, he created the office of Quartermaster General to purchase military stores, the office of Commissary General to obtain the necessary arms, clothing, and other supplies that the army might need, and an Ordnance Department to take charge of the machinery of ordnance and ammunition. It helped as well that Congress appropriated $1 million for the War Department's use.[41]

In early June, Eustis informed Congress that the nation's professional army consisted of only 6,744 regular troops scattered among various posts extending from the frontier to the seacoast. Although Congress had called for an increase in the regular army to 25,000 men the previous December, only about 5,000 had enlisted. On April 10 Congress also authorized the president to request as many as 100,000 militia from the states to volunteer for a six-month period of duty.[42] These men were to be selected from outside of the states' normal standing militia. (By the Volunteer Militia Act of 1792 each state was required to maintain a standing volunteer force made up of free males between the ages of 18 and 45.) For the most part the new recruits who enlisted for six months were farmers or artisans, not the poorest, the most unfortunate, or least productive members of society. If the country had been forced to rely on enlistments from this latter group, it could never have been able to raise an army of any significant size.[43]

States were expected to recruit the new militia in numbers appropriate to the quotas assigned to them. They also were to be responsible for their training, arming, and equipment, a requirement that most states did not take too seriously. When volunteers lined up for muster, for example, they most often reported with no weapons. They had no trained officers to lead them either, so they usually elected a commanding officer from their own ranks. Because their officers were their own friends, volunteers felt free to ignore them. As a consequence, they were totally devoid of discipline.[44]

Appointing suitable high-ranking officers for a growing army proved to be a challenge. Already in service were three brigadier generals: James Wilkinson, at age 56, a man of dubious character; Wade Hampton, a wealthy, 60-year-old South Carolina planter who had served as a colonel in the Revolutionary War; and Peter Gansvoort Jr., another ex-colonel of the Revolution. To their ranks were to be added two new major generals and three brigadier generals in accordance with the Army Act of January 4, 1812. Finding qualified candidates to fill these five senior appointments proved to be a problem. West Point had been in existence for only 10 years. Over that time it had graduated 71 officers, but they were still too young for promotion to such high command. The only pool of experienced officers from which the president could draw were veterans of the Revolutionary War, all well past their prime. Hampering the entire process as well was the political factor: Madison was not about to select anyone, despite his qualifications, who either was a Federalist or had been critical of the administration.[45]

For major general Madison finally selected 61-year-old Henry Dearborn, a Revolutionary War colonel who had never before commanded a large body of troops nor planned a battle campaign. For his second major general he chose 62-year-old Thomas Pinckney, a former governor of South Carolina. The three new brigadier generals he created were Morgan Lewis of New York, Thomas Flournoy of Georgia, and William Hull, still governor of Michigan.[46] For lesser command positions he was forced to sift through a long list of commission seekers who had no military experience, his primary criterion for selection being that they not be of the Federalist persuasion. Winfield Scott, then a captain in the regular army, was of the opinion that most of these applicants were ill-educated party hacks "unfit for any military purpose whatsoever."[47]

The military status of Upper and Lower Canada at the war's outbreak was arguably just as shaky as that of the United States. Canadian militia volunteers were primarily farmers and apt to disappear during the fall harvest season regardless of what was taking place. The government estimated that there were about 60,000 militia members in Lower Canada and about 11,000 in Upper Canada. Major General Brock (about whom we will learn more later), commanding the forces of Upper Canada, had a very poor opinion of their military capabilities. He preferred to leave any fighting to British Army regulars whenever possible, even if they were outnumbered. Although there were 5,600 British regular troops stationed throughout Canada, almost as many regulars as there were in the American army, only about 1,200 were in Upper Canada, and even they were scattered piecemeal across the territory in small garrisons.[48]

Brock, however, did have one distinct advantage over the Americans—the presence of the Provincial Marine on the Great Lakes. The 16-gun brig *Queen Charlotte* and the six-gun schooner *General Hunter,* for example, gave him complete control of Lake Erie and the Detroit River. The only American warship on the lakes was the brig *Adams,* carrying 14 guns—except that it was in dry dock at a River Rouge shipyard outside Detroit. Its guns had been removed for storage within Fort Detroit, making the *Adams* completely useless to American forces at the outbreak of war.[49] All other American warships operated on distant Lake Ontario, and therefore were unavailable for a Detroit campaign. Secure in the knowledge that it controlled Lake Erie, the British government in Canada was confident that it could move troops quickly to defend Upper Canada wherever they would be needed. Its navy, being unopposed, would be unhindered when it sought to interdict the transport of supplies by the United States to its own forces via the waterways, as would prove to be the case during the Detroit campaign.

The only American who appeared to be concerned about this state of affairs was William Hull, governor of Michigan. On three different occasions he had reminded the War Department that it must establish a naval presence on the lower lakes if war was to be declared, but each time his recommendations were ignored.

The lack of preparedness that the governments of both the United States and Canada displayed at the outbreak of the war is surprising in retrospect. Both had high expectations of victory, but they were expectations built upon preconceived notions of the other's weaknesses, which is why the opening campaigns of the war were fraught with so many setbacks. The most astonishing of these was the surrender of Detroit within two months of the declaration of war.

[3]

Through the Wilderness
to Detroit, May 23–July 9

On April 8, 1812, Congress approved the appointment of Governor William Hull as a brigadier general in what would become the North Western Army of the United States. The formation of the army already was under way. A call had gone out from the president to Governor Return Jonathan Meigs of Ohio two days previously to recruit 1,200 volunteers from his state for duty in Detroit. Simultaneously, orders had been issued to the Fourth Regiment of regulars stationed at Vincennes to augment the Ohio volunteers with their trained military force. When possible the volunteers were to be recruited from those men not attached to the Ohio state militia.

Meigs designated Dayton, Ohio, as the assembly point for all those who desired to enlist and selected the end of April as the date of rendezvous. Meigs's call was met with enthusiasm across the state. Those from the poorer class, unaware of what they were expected to bring to army camp life, were lacking arms and proper clothing, which created a problem Ohio was not prepared to meet. It would not be until the middle of May that the state acquired a sufficient number of blankets and tents to house the volunteers after they arrived.[1] Despite their discomforts, the new volunteers kept themselves busy. Once the allotted number of volunteers was reached, they were divided into three regiments. The men in each regiment selected their own commanding officer, who received the rank of colonel regardless of what office he may have had in the Ohio volunteers. The First Regiment, for example, chose Duncan McArthur, with James Denny and William Trimble as majors. McArthur, then 40 years of age, was a logical choice. He was a self-made man, quite wealthy through

Ohio land speculation, and had served as a scout with General Harmar's expedition against the Indians when he was 18. Later, as a surveyor, he helped lay out the town of Chillicothe, Ohio. Elected to the Ohio Senate in 1809, he became its speaker shortly thereafter. Although a major general in the Ohio volunteers, he left that rank behind when he chose to enlist as a volunteer in the North Western Army.[2]

The men of the Second Regiment selected James Findlay as their colonel, with Thomas Moore and Thomas Van Horne serving as majors. Findlay, 42, was a career politician. A member of the territorial legislature, he was able to secure such federal appointments as the U.S. receiver of public monies and U.S. marshal (1802). In 1803 he was elected to the Ohio House of Representatives, and was mayor of Cincinnati in 1805 and in 1810. He too was a major general in the Ohio volunteers prior to joining the new force.[3]

The men in the Third Regiment appointed Lewis Cass as their colonel, with Robert Morrison as major. Cass, 33 years of age, was the youngest of three brigade leaders. A successful lawyer and federal marshal, Cass also had been serving as a major general in the Ohio volunteers before joining the new volunteers. Extremely ambitious, he was always looking for opportunities to advance his name and his fortune.[4]

Of the three new colonels, only Duncan McArthur had had any previous military experience, and that was minimal. What military expertise Lewis Cass could claim he acquired through discussions with his father, Jonathan. The elder Cass had fought in the Revolutionary War and remained in the regular army at the war's end as a captain in the Second Infantry. Promoted to major, he then served under General Anthony Wayne in the battle of Fallen Timbers in 1794, after which he resigned as commandant of Fort Hamilton in the Northwest Territory in 1801 to take up homesteading in Ohio's Muskingum County.[5]

Since the North Western Army had been recruited too hastily for Ohio to be able to supply it with proper uniforms, the state resolved the issue in the most practical fashion: volunteers were to wear homespun shirts and pants and low-crowned felt hats. Lewis Cass proved to be an exception. Unlike his peers, he reported for duty wearing a full uniform topped off "by the highest plume of any officer in the army" with his father's military sword banging at his side.[6]

Guns were at a premium. Many volunteers reported without arms, including the riflemen, who usually owned their own arms. Even the regular army troops were not exempt from such problems inasmuch as a number

Lewis Cass in 1813. (Courtesy of the Burton Historical Collection, Detroit Public Library.)

of their government-issued muskets were in need of repair. Gunpowder also was in short supply.[7]

General Hull left Baltimore with his new commission on April 21. With him came his son, Captain Abraham Hull, and his son-in-law, Captain Harris Hickman, both of whom had received commissions as his aides for the coming campaign. Eight days later they reached Pittsburgh, where they were joined by 40 new volunteers, and finally arrived in Cincinnati on May 7. The following day Hull was joined by Governor Return Meigs, but over two weeks would elapse before he formally met with the officers of his new army and watched them pass in review. He was appalled by what he saw.

> Their arms were totally unfit for use, the leather which covered their cartouche boxes was rotten and no better security to the cartridges than brown paper; many of the men were destitute of blankets, and other necessary clothing; no armourers were provided to repair the arms; no means had been adopted to furnish clothing; no public stores to resort to, either for good arms, or suitable clothing; and no powder in any of the magazines, fit for use—and what is more extraordinary, no contract, or any other measure adopted, to supply these troops with the necessary article of provisions during their march through a wilderness of more than 200 miles, until they arrived at Detroit, the place of their destination.[8]

On his own responsibility, Hull ordered gunpowder from Kentucky, collected blankets and clothes from local families, and arranged with armorers in Cincinnati and Dayton to repair the soldiers' arms.[9] Having heard nothing from Augustus Porter, who had been contracted by the government to supply the needs of the army while it was on its march, Hull made his own terms with the Cincinnati firm of John H. Piatt for supplies, thus placing his personal finances at risk.[10]

On the morning of May 25 the army assembled at Camp Meigs, three miles north of Dayton on the bank of the Mad River, to hear of its formal transfer from the State of Ohio to federal service. The traditional flowery speeches were delivered to the troops, with Governor Meigs congratulating them for having been placed under the command of such a distinguished officer as General Hull. Hull in turn reminded them that they would be passing over ground that had been stained with the blood of their fellow citizens from previous Indian battles. Carried away by the moment, Lewis Cass called for the troops to render three cheers for the speakers. The following day he delivered a brief patriotic speech of his own.[11]

After weeks of preparation, the men were eager and ready to begin their march through the wilderness, but many felt ambivalent about their commanding general who, neither a frontiersman nor an Ohio man, was therefore not one of their own kind like the three regimental colonels. Lewis Cass, despite his enthusiasm for the army and its upcoming campaign, especially appeared to have difficulty accepting Hull. Even before Hull had arrived to take command, he had questioned his leadership. "He is not our man. I saw him at Cin[cinnati] and was prepossessed in his favor. But I am now told by men capable of appreciating his talents that he is indecisive and irresolute, leaning for support upon persons around him."[12] (Although a man of no previous military experience, Cass would question Hull's decisions throughout the coming campaign.)

On June 1, the army finally left Dayton, its officers still undecided as to the best route to take to Detroit: the most direct was the most difficult, leading through a wide morass called the Black Swamp, a slightly elevated flat basin of clay covered by black loam. Thirty miles wide and 50 miles deep, the Black Swamp extended between present-day Toledo and Findlay, Ohio. Because it was flat, it had no natural drainage, and depended primarily upon evaporation for lowering its water level. This in turn resulted in a ground surface clogged with impenetrable forests and vegetation, effectively blocking travel between Detroit and the Ohio settlements.[13] Like others before him, Hull decided that it would be best to bypass the Black Swamp. His initial alternative was to march along the Greater Miami River to Loramie's Fort, then travel straight north until he came to the Auglaize River. At this point the army could be transported by boat to the Maumee River leading northwestward into Lake Erie, thus circling around the Black Swamp.[14] The troops had proceeded no further than 24 miles north of Dayton when it became apparent that the water level of the Greater Miami was so low that transport by water would not be feasible. Having no better choice, Hull now opted to march about 25 miles eastward to Urbana, from where he could strike directly north toward Detroit; but taking this route, unfortunately, meant cutting a road through the dreaded Black Swamp. Once the road was cut, however, it would prove of future use, providing a direct avenue for the transport of supplies from Ohio to Detroit.

The army arrived at Urbana on June 7 and was met by Governor Meigs, who had received the news of Hull's change of route. Meigs also had put together a council with the Indian tribes whose lands would be in the army's path as it marched toward Detroit. Twelve chiefs attended, representing the Wyandot, Shawnee, and Mingoe tribes. They signed a treaty authorizing the American army to create a military road through their lands and erect blockhouses at periodic intervals. The treaty also stipulated that Americans would not be allowed to settle on the lands along the route.[15]

Although anxious to begin the march northward, Hull delayed until Lieutenant Colonel James Miller and the Fourth Regiment of the regular army joined him. Miller's regiment had left its original post at Vincennes on May 14, but had to pass through 200 miles of wilderness to reach Urbana, arriving almost a month later on June 10. The three Ohio volunteer regiments gave Miller's men a rousing reception, greeting them one mile out of Urbana and escorting them into town through a triumphal arch. Hull immediately sent Miller an effusive congratulatory note: "The first army of the state of Ohio will feel pride in being associated with a regiment so distinguished for its valor and discipline." Alluding again to discipline, he closed his comments with: "The patriots of Ohio who yield to none in spirit and patriotism, will not be willing to yield to any in discipline and valor."[16] Hull's expectations that the Ohio volunteers' discipline would equal that of the regular troops would prove to be unfounded.

The enthusiasm that greeted Miller and the regular troops soon was dispelled over a problem of command. Lieutenant Colonel Miller discovered that, despite his regular army ranking, he would not be the senior officer beneath Hull. The three volunteer Ohio colonels, none of whom had any military experience, outranked him, which meant he would come under their command should anything happen to Hull. This did not set well with him. He expected at the least that each regimental commander would hold the same rank. He appealed to Hull, who claimed he had no authority to resolve Miller's complaint. The root of Miller's problem lay at both the state and federal level. State volunteer regiments selected their own commanding officers, who automatically were awarded the rank of colonel, as required by the Ohio constitution. The War Department apparently did not realize this, nor did it appreciate the difficult position in which it had placed Lieutenant Colonel Miller. When Hull asked the secretary of war to correct his command situation, Eustis threw the responsibility back into Hull's hands, saying he was confident that Hull could maintain peace between Miller and the Ohio volunteer officers. This was not fair to Hull. The Ohio colonels already had made it quite clear to him that according to Ohio law their rank could not be questioned. Eustis could easily have settled the matter by promoting Miller to a full colonel, but he did not, forcing Hull to tread softly whenever he had the need to give Miller, his most experienced officer, a separate command function.[17]

Because of the long, arduous march that the regulars had made from

Vincennes, Hull felt obliged to give them several days' rest while he ordered McArthur's regiment to begin carving out the road ahead. By June 16 it had progressed roughly 30 miles to the Scioto River, present-day Kenton, where it constructed two blockhouses joined together by a stockade enclosing about a half acre of land. Creating a new road through such a wilderness was difficult work, requiring the use of axes, shovels, spades—any type of implement that would help clear a swath through the trees and swampland. The bulk of the army reached McArthur's blockhouses, christened Fort McArthur, on June 19. Next it was Colonel Findlay's regiment's turn to take the lead, with orders to forge ahead to Blanchard's Fork, the site of current-day Findlay, Ohio, on the Blanchard River, about 25 miles to the north. The rest of the army followed, only to become bogged down by several days of rain that turned the trail into a quagmire over which the loaded wagons could scarcely travel. After only 16 miles of strenuous effort, Hull called a halt and had the men construct another blockhouse, which the troops christened Fort Necessity. In it they stored their unnecessary baggage to lighten the loads in the wagons and make their travel easier.[18]

While the army was at Fort Necessity it was met by Robert Lucas and James Denny, whom Hull had sent to Detroit the previous month with dispatches announcing that the army soon would be on its way. Lucas's role in the army has remained an enigma. Although a captain in the regular army (but without orders) and a brigadier general in the Ohio volunteers, he had enlisted as a private in the volunteer army, preferring to be employed as a scout by Hull during the coming campaign.[19] Lucas reported that while in the Detroit area he had seen Major General Isaac Brock arrive by boat at Fort Malden with 100 British regular troops, and also had noticed a large number of Indians on the move between Detroit and Canada. He had attended several Indian councils on the Detroit side of the river, and while the Chippewa and Ottawa tribes seemed disposed to be friendly, Walk-in-the-Water, chief of the most influential of the Indian tribes in the Detroit vicinity, was not. Lucas thought the Indians were only waiting for a signal from the British to turn hostile to the Americans.[20]

The weather having cleared on June 25, the army completed the remaining 13 miles or so to Blanchard's Fork the same day. Findlay's regiment had already completed Fort Findlay, a wooden stockade anchored by blockhouses at each corner and with a ditch across the gate entrance. In it Hull stored all of the army's unnecessary baggage to facilitate the last legs of the trip to Detroit. On June 26, while still at Findlay, Hull received an express dispatch from Secretary of War Eustis by way of Chillicothe, Ohio. It was dated June 18, the day on which Congress declared war on Great Britain, but no mention of this was made. Eustis wrote, "Your letters May 26 and June 3d have been received, your arrangements for ensuing supplies for the troops are approved. Circumstances have recently occurred which render it necessary you should pursue your march to Detroit with all possible expedition, the highest confidence is reposed in your discretion, zeal and perseverance."[21] The letter's only purpose appeared to be to urge Hull to speed up his march. In responding, Hull informed Eustis that he had taken the time to build blockhouses on the route from Urbana. "To preserve the communications in the event of War, I have placed in them small Garrisons, and left the few sick & Invalids with their Arms, medical aid, and all necessary comforts. I suggest to you whether it would not be expedient to relieve the troops of this Army stationed in the Blockhouses by the Volunteers of the Ohio."[22]

Colonel Cass's regiment now took the responsibility for cutting the remaining stretch of road to the Rapids. The rest of the army followed closely behind. By the 29th it had reached the Maumee River opposite the Fallen Timbers battleground where General Anthony Wayne had been victorious over the Indians in 1794. The next day the army crossed the river, entering Michigan Territory and setting up camp in a small village near the abandoned British Fort Miami, only 30 miles from Frenchtown (today's Monroe).

Here Hull discovered the schooner *Cuyahoga* at anchor. Its presence presented Hull with a golden opportunity to speed up his march by having the ship carry the army's heavy baggage, musical instruments, medical supplies, and extra uniforms to Detroit. The *Cuyahoga's* captain, Cyrenius Chapin, agreed to make the trip for a fee of only $60. Also making the trip were several officers, officers' and enlisted men's' wives, two boys, and three regular troops. Unknown to Hull, his son and aide had inadvertently included with the baggage placed on the ship a trunk containing official government correspondence plus the muster rolls and records of the army.[23] The eventual loss of these papers would plague Hull throughout the campaign. Hull engaged a smaller boat to carry about 30 men who had fallen ill during the march.[24] Meeting with Chapin on the morning of July 1 as the army readied to head north, Hull recommended that the captain sail by way of the shallower western channel of the Detroit River rather than the normal deep-water route to avoid passing directly under the guns of Fort Malden, which guarded the eastern channel. Hull had not yet been informed that war had been declared, but he saw no need for Chapin to take unnecessary risks.

Free of the trials of the Black Swamp, the army now set out on the easiest stretch of its march to Detroit. That evening the camp was aroused by the arrival of a special messenger with a dispatch from the War Department. It carried the same date as the dispatch Hull had received five days previously at Fort Findlay but its news was of a more serious import. It read: "Sir, war is declared against Great Britain. You will be on your guard, proceed to your post with all possible expedition, make such arrangements for the defense of the country, as in your judgment may be necessary, and wait for further orders."[25] This dispatch reportedly had been sent to Cleveland with an order from the postmaster general to forward it immediately to General Hull. It took some time for the Cleveland postmaster to determine where Hull might be and arrange for someone to carry it to him, at which point it was discovered that the dispatch had disappeared. Someone suggested that it might have been placed by mistake with the mail set aside for delivery to Detroit. The postmaster was reluctant to open the Detroit mail, which was against the rules, but, having heard that war had been declared and remembering that the dispatch had come from the War Department, he overcame his scruples and sorted through the Detroit mailbag, where it was found. By now it was June 28. A young lawyer named Charles Sheeler volunteered to carry the message posthaste to Hull. When he arrived at the falls of the Maumee, where Hull was reported to be, he learned that the general had already moved on to Frenchtown. It was not until 2:00 a.m. July 2 that he finally caught up with the general. To his credit, Sheeler had made a remarkable ride of over 200 miles in less than four days on the same horse, not being able to secure a replacement en route.[26]

Hull had no way of knowing whether news of the war declaration had already reached the British at Fort Malden, but realized that the *Cuyahoga* might be in danger if Chapin had chosen to sail up the main channel instead of the western fork. He hastened to send word to Chapin, but the *Cuyahoga* had already sailed. Unfortunately, the news of the declaration of war had reached Fort Malden three days earlier on June 28, thanks to Major General Brock who, when informed by his sources in the Canadian fur trade industry, quickly passed the information on to his army units. Had the dispatch that Hull received from Eustis at Fort Findlay the previous week, also dated June 18, contained this vital news, he obviously would not have chartered the *Cuyahoga*. The reason for this disastrous omission in Eustis's first dispatch has baffled historians to this day.[27]

The unwitting Chapin further aggravated matters by choosing to ignore Hull's recommendation to proceed by way of the western channel. He considered it to be a more difficult passage. Having a fair breeze and no reason to believe that his ship was in danger—indeed, he had sailed past Fort Malden the day before without incident—Chapin opted to head to Detroit by way of the eastern or main channel.[28] As the *Cuyahoga* drew near to Amherstburg and Fort Malden, it was hailed by a longboat filled with military personnel that had pulled away from the British brig *General Hunter*. Puzzled, Chapin hove to and, to his surprise, was ordered to surrender. Off in the distance he could see a canoe filled with British reinforcements heading in his direction as well. The men in the longboat, led by the master of the *General Hunter*, boarded the *Cuyahoga* and declared all American military personnel on board prisoners of war. The master removed Chapin to the *General Hunter*, where he was ordered to surrender to the brig's officer of the day. The loss of Hull's muster roll, the army's medical supplies, and other baggage was a devastating blow. It also was a source of embarrassment to the country, one that could have been avoided had Eustis only informed Hull of the declaration of war in a timely fashion.[29] Not captured was the second, small boat containing sick members of the militia, the army's medical staff, and other miscellaneous items. It had avoided being taken by virtue of sailing upriver via the western channel, where it was shielded from Fort Malden by Bois Blanc Island.

Ignorant of the fate of the *Cuyahoga*, Hull's army proceeded northward, arriving that evening at Frenchtown, a small settlement on the Raisin River enclosed within a stockade and surrounded by isolated farms. En route Hull had met several travelers heading south who informed him that the Shawnee chief Tecumseh was known to be at Fort Malden with about 2,000 braves. When passing Brownstown, the main Wyandot village, 13 miles from Detroit, they also had seen 200 Sioux braves flying the British flag heading toward the river. They cautioned Hull to expect an attack when he arrived in that vicinity. Hull ordered Robert Lucas to scout ahead to determine if there were any truth in the information. Lucas reached Brownstown that same day but found only friendly Indians in the area. He reported back to Hull that the road was clear of hostiles.[30]

Hull had learned from another source that the British intended to surprise the army as it passed through a swamp above Brownstown. To forestall such an attack, Hull spread word that he planned to collect all the available boats along the river, request that cannon be brought from the fort at Detroit, and attack Fort Malden before proceeding any further. He saw that this false information made its way to Lieutenant Colonel St. George, Fort Malden's commandant, who assembled all of his forces within the fort and kept them on the alert. Thanks to this subterfuge, Hull's army was able to reach Detroit without incident. Hull's aide Robert Wallace later wrote that the general rode on as if he had "no sense of personal danger" although Wallace believed Hull certainly would have been killed if the British had ambushed the Americans while they were strung out along the trail.[31]

Getting an early start the morning of July 5, the army marched 20 miles to Spring Wells, three miles south of Detroit, where it bivouacked for the night. Hull rode ahead, however, to learn why heavy gunfire had erupted from the direction of Fort Detroit. Arriving at the town, he was informed by Captain John Whistler, Fort Detroit's commandant, that he had removed two 24-pounder cannons from the fort to the riverside to open fire on the British, who were attempting to set up a battery on the other side of the river. Hull ordered him to cease fire so as not to damage Canadian private property and thereby discourage Canadians from deserting the British cause.[32]

The following day Hull led the army into Detroit, where grateful citizens enthusiastically greeted them. Hull ordered Colonel Cass and Captain Hickman to cross the river under a flag of truce and request Lieutenant Colonel St. George to release the private baggage that had been confiscated from the *Cuyahoga*. Cass was highly indignant at the command, claiming that it was a violation of military diplomacy that he (a colonel) be ordered to carry a dispatch to an enemy officer inferior to him in rank.[33] St. George responded to the request that it was not a "custom of war" to return captured property. However, he added that he would be happy to discuss an exchange for the prisoners who had been taken from the vessel. (The Americans civilians involved had all been shipped to Detroit earlier.)[34]

On July 9 Hull received another dispatch from Secretary Eustis that finally ordered him to take offensive action against the British.

> Sir, By my letter of the 18th inst. You were informed that war was declared against Great Britain. Herewith enclosed, you will receive

a copy of the act, and of the President's proclamation, and you are authorized to commence offensive operations accordingly.

Should the force under your command be equal to the enterprise, consistent with the safety of your own posts, you will take possession of Malden, and extend your conquests as circumstances may justify.

It also is proper to inform you that an adequate force cannot soon be relied on the reduction of the enemy's posts below you [opposite New York].[35]

The last paragraph of the dispatch deeply concerned Hull. Poised to invade Canada as part of a three-pronged, simultaneous attack on Upper and Lower Canada, he now was given to understand that no attacks would take place in the Michigan–Lake Ontario area or Lower Canada in the foreseeable future. It was not clear whether the War Department had abandoned this strategy altogether or whether it had simply been delayed (and if so, for how long). These were legitimate questions that the dispatch did not address.

Eustis, in fact, seemed quite unaware of the difficult situation in which he had placed Hull. General Dearborn appeared oblivious to Hull's predicament as well, most probably because he was having difficulty of his own in raising a volunteer force from the northeastern states. They, being heavily Federalist and against the administration, were not overly enthusiastic about a war most of their representatives had voted against. Eight days after war was declared, Eustis wrote to Dearborn:

Having made the necessary arrangements for the defense of the seaboard, it is the wish of the President, that you should repair to Albany and prepare the force to be collected at that place, for actual service. It is understood, that being possessed of a full view of the intentions of the government, and being also acquainted with the force under your Command, *you will take your own time* [emphasis added] and give the necessary Orders to the officers on the Sea Coast. . . . It is altogether uncertain at what time General Hull may deem it expedient to commence offensive operations. The preparations it is presumed will be made to move in a direction for Niagara, Kingston, and Montreal. . . . On your arrival in Albany you will be able to form an opinion of the time required to prepare the Troops for action.[36]

One has to wonder what Eustis truly had in mind. On the same day that he wrote Dearborn to take his time in assembling his force, he authorized Hull to begin offensive operations in the northwest theater. The lethargy with which Dearborn approached his critical task of raising an army was inexcusable. In fact, two weeks later, as Hull prepared to cross the Detroit River and invade Canada, Dearborn still had not arrived in Albany. Eustis himself now became restless at Dearborn's slow response. On July 9 he wrote, "The period has arrived when your services are required at Albany, and I am instructed by the President to direct, that, having made arrangements for placing the works on the seaboard in the best state of defense your means will permit, . . . you will then order all recruits not otherwise disposed of to march to Albany or some station on Lake Champlain, to be organized for the invasion of Canada."[37] Thus, while Hull's troops were sitting on the doorstep of Upper Canada, ready to go into action, Dearborn still had not begun to gather an army!

[4]

THE INVASION OF CANADA,
JULY 12–AUGUST 2

The number of troops that General Hull had available at the outset of the invasion has been disputed for generations. No official list exists. The numbers offered by officers involved in the campaign, including Hull, all differ. Historian Alec Gilpin, after comparing the various accounts as well as other evidence, has come to what is probably the most reasonable conclusion. "[I]t seems likely that Hull had a force at Detroit of about 450 regulars, 1,450 militia [volunteers] from Ohio, and 200 militia from Michigan—a total, allowing for some errors in the above figures, of between 2,000 and 2,200 men, largely untrained and ill-equipped."[1]

He based his estimate on the following: on June 24 Hull wrote the secretary of war that he began his march to Detroit with 1,592 volunteers, but after detaching troops to garrison the five forts established along the trail from Urbana, no more than 1,450 probably made it to Detroit. Already on duty in Detroit were 200 members of the Michigan Detached Militia. Miller's Fourth Regiment of regulars added another 264 troopers, plus there were about 100 men of the United States Artillery and First Infantry within Fort Detroit. The combined total came to between 2,000 or 2,200 men.[2]

Arrayed against Hull across the Detroit River was a British/Canadian/Indian force of about 1,550. However, and more important, the number of British regulars matched those of Hull. In a dispatch to Lieutenant Colonel R. H. Bruyeres, Captain Dixon of the Royal Engineers at Fort Malden wrote on July 8, "Our force here consists of 300 Regulars, 850 Militia, and about 400 Indians, so that I think we have no reason to be afraid of our Yankee friends."[3] Dixon certainly was aware of the size of

Hull's army yet did not seem to be overly impressed. In the same dispatch, he also wrote, "Since we have received here news of the War with
the U.S. my attention has been wholly directed to the object of putting
the Fort [Malden] in a decent state: The S. and E. curtains [stockades]
have been formed and finished with the exception of the Timber Facing:
Twenty Pieces of cannon are mounted: the Platforms all repaired; Four
12dr Green Carriages made; the Four Bastions Fraized and the escarp
all around as much as possible deepened." He added, "The North Cur-
tain [the side that Hull would most probably attack] remains as it was,
and with Timber we are giving it a thickness of 14 feet to that side."[4] It
would seem that Fort Malden was not in a state of total disrepair, as some
have claimed, and would be a formidable obstacle to attack by troops not
backed by heavy guns.

If there was any factor that tipped the balance in favor of the British
force, it was the presence of the Canadian Provincial Marine, for which
the Americans had no counterpart. Guarding Amherstburg and Fort Malden at the riverside was the formidable sloop of war the *Queen Charlotte,*
armed with 17 guns, 14 of which were short-barreled, 24-pounder carronades, very effective in short-range firing. It also carried two long guns,
both 24-pounders. Also on hand was the brig *General Hunter,* which carried four 12-pounder carronades and two six-pounder long guns, and the
Lady Prevost, mounting 10 12-pounder carronades and two nine-pounder
long guns. This fleet was augmented by two lightly armed ships of the
British North West Company ordinarily used in its fur trade.[5]

It would be natural for Hull to have been concerned about their presence in Detroit waters. He had no means of counteracting their firepower
if he chose to attack Malden other than to construct several floating batteries, borrowing cannon from Fort Detroit, and ferry them across the
river. A secondary concern was that the ships could transport troops to
any point along the riverside trail to Ohio to interdict Hull's main supply
route to Ohio.

The Indians, with their countless number of canoes, represented a
floating force in themselves, and Hull did his best to keep them on the
sidelines of military action. On July 7 he held council with the principal chiefs residing on the American side of the river. Among them were
Crane of the Ohio Wyandots, Walk-in-the-Water of the 1,200 Michigan
Wyandots, and Logan Blue Jacket, head of a small group of Shawnee. The
majority of their followers advocated adopting a neutral stand. Lieutenant
Colonel St. George also attempted to win the chiefs over, urging them to

take up arms against the Americans—otherwise the British would cut off their usual supplies, a persuasive argument, to say the least. The Indian reaction was split, the most noteworthy of the chiefs objecting to taking up arms against the Americans being the influential Walk-in-the-Water.[6]

Two days later Hull wrote Secretary Eustis that he had been collecting boats to transport his troops across the river, but for the reasons described above as well as others he had doubts that the enterprise would succeed. "The British command the water and the savages; I do not think the force here equal to the reduction of Amherstburg [Malden]; you therefore must not be too sanguine."[7] The Indians indeed did present a problem, being a highly mobile force able to attack his army at any point.

Despite these concerns, Hull ordered the crossing to Canada to begin the evening of July 10. He hoped that darkness would mask the army's crossing from the British warships, which were anchored at Amherstburg, 18 miles south of Detroit, out of sight because of the curvature of the river shoreline. If alerted, they could sail up and wreak havoc among his small boats filled with troops. However, an indiscriminate firing of guns by exuberant militia ruined the element of surprise and forced Hull to postpone the crossing. A severe loss was Major Jeremiah Munson of Cass's regiment, who was severely wounded during the incident.[8]

Hull rescheduled the invasion for the evening of July 12, but another problem arose. When the new orders were posted, volunteer companies led by Captain Nicholas Cunningham and Captain David Rupe of McArthur's regiment refused to obey, as did about 70 men from Colonel Findlay's regiment. The majority of these men technically were both volunteers and members of the Ohio state militia who had been drafted into the volunteer ranks. They had good grounds for their refusal. As members of the Ohio Militia, under state law they could not be forced to fight outside the borders of the United States. Their being drafted into the volunteer force did not alter matters. Colonel McArthur used all the powers of persuasion at his command to change their minds, calling them cowards, traitors, and other derogatory names. This tactic cowed the men in Cunningham's company, who agreed to go, as did several of Rupe's and Findlay's men. About 100 militia members declined his colorful invitation and remained in Detroit.[9]

To deceive the British about his selected landing place, Hull had Colonel McArthur's regiment march three miles south along the river road toward the River Rouge late on July 11 to give the impression that he would attempt to cross the river at that point the next day. McArthur silently stole back later that evening. The feint apparently succeeded, as the British withdrew their militia from that area to Fort Malden.

On the morning of July 12 all was ready. The army marched about one and one-half miles above Detroit near Belle Isle and boarded boats that had been gathered to ferry them across the Detroit River. There were an insufficient number to carry the entire force in a single trip; Cass's Third Regiment and Miller's Fourth Regiment of regulars were the first to cross. As soon as they disembarked on the Canadian shore, they unfurled the American flag. Their boats then immediately returned to bring the First and Second regiments across. General Hull, who had been one of the last to set foot on the Canadian shore, was heard to say, "The critical moment draws near."[10]

The army met no opposition. Scouts who had been sent ahead reported that the Canadian shore was deserted as far as Sandwich, and the army quickly occupied the town. Hull set up his headquarters in a fine, new but still unfinished brick house belonging to Colonel Jacques Baby, head of the Kent Militia, who had retreated to Fort Malden shortly before the Americans had landed. Hull had brought with him copies of a proclamation he had printed before leaving Detroit, which his men circulated through the town (see appendix 2). In part it was quite conciliatory in tone: "In the name of my *Country* and by the authority of my Government I promise you protection to your *persons, property, and rights.* Remain at your homes, Pursue your peaceful and customary avocations." Unfortunately, he added the following comments: "If the barbarous and Savage policy of Great Britain be pursued, and the savages are let loose to murder our Citizens and butcher our women and children, this war, will be a war of extermination. The first stroke with the Tomahawk the first attempt with the Scalping Knife will be the Signal for one indiscriminate scene of desolation. *No white man found fighting by the Side of an Indian will be taken prisoner.* Instant destruction will be his Lot."[11]

Major General Brock considered Hull's proclamation an atrocious threat and roundly condemned it. Secretary Eustis approved the language, however, as did the president when a copy was forwarded to the War Department. Interestingly, though, when the United States signed the Treaty of Ghent ending the War of 1812, the U.S. government repudiated the proclamation, saying that it had never authorized Hull to release it. And curiously, after Hull's death, Lewis Cass wrote that he had authored the proclamation, although there is no evidence to support his claim, nor did Hull ever mention that some other person had been its author.[12]

Soon after organizing his headquarters in Sandwich, Hull held a council of war with his officers, who were eager to march on Fort Malden. Hull demurred. He told them that if they attempted to storm the fort without any heavy artillery it would be by bayonet, which to his mind would be suicidal. The officers agreed that it would be better to delay an attack until they could rig heavy guns to transport with them on their march.[13]

After the council Hull ordered Captain Henry Urey to lead a detachment of 40 men on patrol toward Fort Malden. At Turkey Creek, three miles below Sandwich, Urey discovered that the bridge had been partially dismantled and there was evidence that at least 200 Indians had hidden in ambush at the crossing the night before. A farmer who lived nearby claimed that a large body of Indians still lingered in the area, too many for the American's small detachment to overcome. Urey decided it would more prudent to return to camp and report the news to Hull.[14] Since there already had been another Indian alarm that evening, Hull put his troops to work building an earthen breastwork around their encampment, with an open side facing the river and defended by three six-pounder guns that had been ferried over by boat.

Having learned that he could obtain provisions at the Thames River, about 35 miles east of Sandwich, to augment his dwindling food supply, Hull had Captain James Sloan and his light cavalry ride out in that direction and bring back what supplies they could commandeer. When Sloan reached the Ruscom River, still over 10 miles from the Thames, he sighted a body of Indians and sent two men back to inform Hull. Hull ordered Colonel McArthur to assemble 100 men from his regiment plus a rifle corps of 15 men, join Sloan, and give chase to the hostiles. The men marched until dark, then, on the next day, July 15, made a brief halt at the Belle River, about five miles from Sloan's camp. There they purchased beef, flour, and whiskey since they had left Sandwich too quickly to be assigned rations. As soon as McArthur and his men reached Captain Sloan at the Ruscom River, the Indians fled in their canoes, one of which was captured.

McArthur received a dispatch from Hull ordering him to continue to the Thames River and forage for supplies along its banks. As he did so, he came across the home of Isaac Hull, William Hull's younger brother, who had been living in Canada for the past eight years. A Canadian militia captain and six others stood guard at the door, probably because Isaac had refused to take an oath of allegiance to the British government. McArthur disarmed the militiamen and ordered them to return home. He then continued foraging along both banks of the Thames River, accumulating 100 barrels of flour, 20 barrels of salt, five bales of blankets, three barrels of whiskey, and other assorted stores.[15] Rather than attempt to carry everything back to Detroit by land, McArthur confiscated all the boats he could find, filled them with the supplies, and sent them off by water along the southern shore of Lake St. Clair to the Detroit River and the town itself. By the evening of the 17th the detachment had returned to Sandwich.[16]

While McArthur was away, Hull ordered Colonel Cass to scout ahead and determine if there were enemy in the field between Fort Malden and his headquarters at Sandwich. Cass gathered about 280 men, made up of a company of regular troops and five companies of volunteers. Robert Lucas and Lieutenant Colonel Miller volunteered to accompany them. Cass found the way clear up to the bridge over the Canard River, 12 miles to the south. Blocking his path was Lieutenant John Clemow with a detachment of 50 British soldiers. As Cass approached, Clemow removed his troops to the south bank of the river. Two men, privates John Dean and John Hancock, did not make it in time. When ordered to surrender by Cass, they refused and opened fire. Hancock was killed and Dean taken prisoner, the first British casualties of the campaign.[17]

Instead of reporting this news to Hull as he had been ordered, Cass decided to circle behind the British to prevent their retreat to Malden. He left a 40-man company of riflemen hiding in the underbrush opposite the bridge with orders to commence firing once he had maneuvered the rest of his force behind the British on the far side of the river. As he later reported to Hull, after describing his crossing, "I then proceeded with the remainder of the force about five miles, to a ford over the river aux Canards and down on the southern bank of the river. About sunset we arrived in sight of the enemy. . . . After the first discharge the British retreated—we continued advancing. Three times they formed, and as often retreated. We drove them about half a mile when it became so dark that we were obliged to relinquish the pursuit."[18] It now being nightfall, Cass left a guard at the bridge and took his troops about one or two miles north and bivouacked in barns and farmhouses at Petite Cote village. Lucas claimed that there were 150 British troops and about 50 Indians at the bridge when Cass commenced his attack, but his numbers are probably suspect.[19]

A curious incident had occurred earlier as Cass marched toward the Canard River. Captain Brown of Miller's regiment, carrying a flag of truce, overtook him. Brown, not anticipating that Cass intended to do any more than carry out his reconnaissance and report back, explained that he was on his way to Fort Malden with a message from Hull to the fort's commandant, another request to Lieutenant Colonel St. George to return the personal baggage that had been captured with the *Cuyahoga*. Cass advised him to wait as he intended to attack the British on the other side of the bridge and it would be better if Brown did not proceed any further until the action was over. Brown agreed, but while attempting to stay out of harm's way he inadvertently exposed his flag of truce. Fort Malden signaled back that it had been recognized. Brown now felt obliged to continue on to Malden even as Cass made his way around the bridge preparatory to beginning his attack. Luckily for Brown, he managed to see St. George, receive his reply, and leave before the British were aware of Cass's activities. St. George again turned down Hull's request, citing papers he had found in the baggage: "They have upon examination, almost without exception, proved to be valuable public Documents," and therefore not subject to return. He also mentioned Hull's proclamation: "I regret to find in Your Excellency's letter, the words 'retaliation & avenge'— You must be aware, Sir, that retaliation can be carried to a great degree on both sides 'till there is no saying where it will stop."[20]

There is some suspicion that Hull was well aware that St. George would refuse his request again, but was using Brown's trip to gain information on the strength of the enemy he faced and how prepared the fort was to withstand attack.

After coming upon the British rear at the Canard bridge and putting them to flight, Cass wrote Hull what had taken place and asked permission to remain to solidify possession of the bridge. Cass may have assumed that its capture would compel Hull to bring the rest of the army forward. While awaiting Hull's answer, Cass had Lucas scout southward. Lucas came within two miles of Fort Malden, finding the way open, then quickly returned after sighting several boats carrying British troops heading upriver toward Sandwich. (Historian Gilpin has speculated that the lack of British resistance at this point was a deliberate strategy, an attempt to gull Cass and his troops into an ambush, knowing they could expect little help from the main army, which was too distant to provide immediate support.)[21]

On the next day the rest of the Fourth Regiment arrived with Hull's response to Cass's news. Merely reminding Cass that his troops were about 12 miles away from the main camp, Hull left it to his subordinate's judgment whether to continue holding the bridge or to return to Sandwich. Cass put the question to a council of his officers. All except Cass and Captain Snelling voted to abandon the bridge if they did not receive further support. Cass was angry, not so much at the council's vote to retreat but because Hull had left matters up to him rather than ordering him either to hold the bridge or to return.[22] His officers' vote may have been prompted by the realization that a sizeable number of British troops could pass up the river by boat and cut them off from the main camp whenever they chose.

Their retreat may have been providential. That evening news reached Hull that the *Queen Charlotte* had slipped her moorings and anchored across the mouth of the Canard River so that her guns could play on any Americans at the bridge crossing. As soon as Cass left the river crossing, the British ripped up the planks on the bridge and constructed a wooden breastwork across the trail.

The morning after Cass returned, Hull ordered Colonel McArthur to detach 150 men from his command, take up a station near the Canard bridge, and keep him informed of the enemy's activities. When within three miles of the bridge, McArthur sent Lucas and several rangers scouting forward. As they approached within 200 yards of the crossing, they came under fire from a gunboat concealed at the riverbank. They fell back until met by McArthur and the rest of the troops. When the entire command attempted to proceed, it came under severe fire from the same gunboat and was compelled to retreat. Later, as he attempted to return once again, McArthur's troops were confronted by a force of 40 to 50 Indians, which they drove back across the river. Having completed his reconnaissance, McArthur started back to Sandwich but had proceeded no more than two to three miles when he was met by Colonel Cass hurrying forward with his regiment and one piece of artillery. Cass convinced McArthur to make camp while he and his regiment scouted the bridge to see what damage they could do to the British with their small cannon. After a lively exchange, Cass returned, unfortunately after having lost four men.[23]

The next day, July 20, the persistent Cass and McArthur again returned to the Canard bridge to discover that the British now had brought up two pieces of artillery to face them on the far side. McArthur was reluctant to make an attack, but relented when Cass insisted. Things did not go well, and the troops were forced to retreat. Hungry and fatigued, the entire detachment marched back to Sandwich.[24]

On July 21 Hull recrossed the river to Detroit with Lieutenant Colonel Miller and a battalion from his regiment, hoping to speed up work on the construction of carriages for a pair of 24-pounder guns that had been removed from the fort for transport against Malden. He was told it would take two weeks to finish them, not very welcome news for an army anxious to go into action.[25]

That same day, at Fort George on the Niagara front, Major General Brock issued his own proclamation to the Canadian people to counter the one distributed by Hull. His intention was to woo back those Canadian militia members who had departed from Fort Malden and returned home when Hull occupied Sandwich. It was an exercise in political posturing and propaganda. Brock claimed that the American presence in Canada had "no other motive than to 'relieve' her ungrateful children from the oppression of a cruel neighbor: this restitution of Canada to the Empire of France was the stipulated reward for the aid afforded to the revolted Colonies. . . . Are you prepared Inhabitants of Upper Canada to be come willing subjects or rather slaves to the Despot [Napoleon] who rules the nations of Europe with a rod of iron?"[26] The proclamation served its purpose: the number of militia supporting Hull declined.

Hull's army had now been camped across the river for over a week. Except for several skirmishes at the Canard River, it had accomplished little. Even Cass's initial success was now regarded as having been suspiciously easy, as if the British indeed had attempted to lure the Americans further away from their main camp where they could easily be ambushed. Still, Hull was willing to wait longer before attacking Malden, content in the news he was receiving that members of the Canadian militia, many of whom he probably knew from his days as governor, were quitting the fight.

Before he crossed the river to Detroit, Hull placed McArthur in charge of all American troops on the Canadian side during his absence. He also requested McArthur to send out a party to find an alternate road to Fort Malden, one that would support heavy artillery and not expose the troops to gunfire from the *Queen Charlotte*. Captain McCulloch and his rangers rode out for this purpose only to return to report that they could find no other good road that would sustain the weight of heavy cannon.[27]

Having received a report from friendly Canadians that a large number of Indians were massing at the Canard bridge, McArthur ordered Major Denny to take 117 men and set an ambush for them as they attempted to cross. His order read: "You will place your men in ambush, near some road or trace where you expect the Indians to pass. I think it would be well to divide them into two parties, and suffer the Indians, or the enemy, to pass the first unmolested (unless the opportunity of taking them should be very good,) and let the second party commence the fire on them, and the first to prevent their retreat."[28]

Denny left the evening of July 24 and arrived within a mile of the Canard River at 3:00 a.m. He and his men rested for the remainder of the night in a wheat field. The next day, as the troops were positioning themselves for the ambush in a nearby orchard, they encountered a farmer who had come from the direction of the river. When accosted, he pretended to speak only French and said he was on his way home to cut his wheat. Through further questioning Denny learned that the man was actually Captain Bondy of the First Essex militia, under orders to spy on the Americans. Denny sent Bondy to Sandwich under guard and resumed his ambush, hiding the troops in a grove of trees.

By 2:00 in the afternoon the tired troops, having been up most of the night, began nodding off. Denny, alerted by a party of Indians moving in their direction, roused the attention of his men. The oncoming Indians, equally surprised, retreated about a half mile as Denny attacked; then the Indians regrouped, counterattacked forcefully, and attempted to outflank the Americans and reach the bridge over Turkey Creek before them, thus cutting them off from Sandwich. The right wing of Denny's troops set up a spirited fire as they quickly retreated, but when the left wing finally gave way, the entire detachment turned and fled despite Denny's repeated attempts to force the men to turn and make a stand. The Indians' pursuit finally broke off within a half mile of Turkey Creek when they discovered Lucas approaching from Sandwich, possibly with others behind him. Lucas, fortuitously, had been sent by McArthur to find the body of an American trooper reported to be lying on the road. It turned out to be that of Avery Powers, a ranger who had been with Denny but had taken ill and been sent back alone to Sandwich. It was not a good experience for Denny's detachment, which suffered six dead and two wounded as a result of the action.[29]

That same evening Colonel Henry Procter, the most senior of the officers under Major General Brock, arrived at Amherstburg to take command of Fort Malden. Brock had detached him from his post as commander of Fort George on the Niagara River and placed him in charge of all military operations in the western part of Upper Canada or, as it was termed, the "right wing" of the British army in Canada. Procter was 49 years of age and had 31 years of military experience. He had arrived in Canada in 1802 with Brock, who also held the rank of lieutenant colonel at that time. The two developed a close bond over the next 10 years. Procter, promoted to full colonel in 1810, was considered Brock's right arm.[30]

Reporting to Brock his safe arrival, Procter wrote, "I do not apprehend that this Post is in any immediate Danger, but I am fully convinced of the necessity of Reinforcement."[31] Brock, anticipating Procter's request, had already ordered Captain Chambers of the 41st Regiment to take 50 of its regulars and march to Moraviantown. There he was to recruit 200 Canadian militiamen to create a diversion on Hull's flank that would force him to retreat back to Detroit. Chambers's recruitment efforts were not met with much enthusiasm. The townspeople were concerned that if they answered Brock's call their settlement would be at the mercy of the Indians, whom they did not trust even though they professed to be on the British side.

On July 29 Hull received information that he had not anticipated, information that did not augur well for the campaign. Two Chippewa Indians traveling south by way of Detroit reported that Fort Mackinac on the southeastern end of Mackinac Island had surrendered to the British on July 17. The fort commanded the water passage between Lake Michigan and Lake Huron. Its primary purpose, like that of most other forts in the wilderness, was to protect settlers against the Indians as well as provide a base for the fur trade. The loss of Fort Mackinac meant that the northern tribes, who favored trade with the British, would now flock to Britain's banner and travel south to join in an attack on Detroit with the other tribes. The news prompted Hull to write immediately to Governor Scott of Kentucky requesting 1,500 volunteers from his state; Hull also put in a request for 500 from Ohio. He explained that the fall of Fort Mackinac would drastically affect the state of affairs in his area because it released the Indian tribes to descend upon Detroit in great numbers.[32]

The surrender of Fort Mackinac was inevitable. Its commander, Lieutenant Porter Hanks, had only 61 officers and men. When attacked, he had no idea that war had even been declared. However, the British on St. Joseph Island, 40 miles northeast of the American fort, had been alerted of the war's declaration as early as July 8 via a dispatch from Major General Brock. In command of the British post on St. Joseph was Captain Charles Roberts, with 46 officers and men. Brock had instructed him through a dispatch Roberts had received on July 15 to be prudent when deciding whether to attack Mackinac. Roberts opted to attack immediately, fearing that the Indians he had collected as allies during the past week would chafe at the lack of action and disappear if he dallied too long. Roughly 400 Indians and a volunteer force of 230 local residents who worked for the North West Fur Company augmented his 46 regulars. His force set out by canoe at 10:00 on the morning of July 16, landing on a secluded beach behind Fort Mackinac at 3:00 in the morning on the 17th. Well acquainted with the lay of the land, they dragged two six-pounder cannon to the top of a high bluff in the center of the island overlooking the fort. At 11:30 a.m. Roberts sent a message under a flag of truce demanding the fort's surrender; otherwise he would begin dropping shot down into the fort's compound from above. Thoroughly startled, Hanks consulted with his officers. They decided it would be impossible for so few of them to hold out very long, especially since they were completely exposed to fire from the guns on the hill.[33]

Ironically, on the previous day Hanks had noticed a large group of Indians heading toward St. Joseph Island and had become suspicious that it might be planning an attack on Mackinac Island. A Captain Dausman of the local militia volunteered to canoe to St. Joseph Island to investigate. Dausman had proceeded no more than about 15 miles when he encountered a flotilla of British canoes and was taken prisoner. Roberts kept Dausman with him as his force landed quietly on the opposite side of the island from the town, then paroled him with instructions to alert the island's inhabitants of the pending battle and tell them to silently rendezvous at the west beach, where they would be placed under British protection. He told Dausman to caution the townspeople that if anyone attempted to forewarn the fort, the Indians were prepared to massacre each one of them.[34]

Even had Hanks received prior warning of the war's declaration, he would have had no other recourse but to surrender, considering the number of British he faced. Roberts's terms allowed the American troops to march out of the fort with honors of war and elicited a promise from them not to fight again unless exchanged. Those who lived on the island were required to take the British oath of allegiance. Anyone who refused would be obliged to leave within the month.[35] John Askin, one of the Canadian volunteers involved in the attack, later wrote that it was providential no one had attempted to warn Hanks beforehand, because otherwise "not a Soul of them would have been saved [from massacre]."[36] Among the arms, equipment, and other items that Roberts captured were 700 packs of valuable furs, which he told the islanders were public property and therefore would not be returned to them, their rightful owners. A week later Roberts placed all prisoners of war and those American civilians who refused to take the oath of allegiance on one of the captured ships with instructions to sail down to Detroit. He had no desire to hold them on the island since they would have to be fed. He needed all the supplies he could obtain, not only for his own troops but for the Indians gathered to fight with him as well. Hanks arrived at Detroit on Tuesday, August 2, corroborating the news that Hull had received earlier from the Chippewas that Fort Mackinac had surrendered.

As tiny and obscure as Fort Mackinac was, its surrender had enormous implications for Hull—all having to do with the Indian menace, as testified by Governor Harrison. When he received the news of Mackinac's surrender, he wrote to the secretary of war from Lexington, Kentucky, prophetically observing, "I greatly fear that the capture of Mackinac will give such eclat to the British and the Indian arms, that the northern tribes will pour down in swarms upon Detroit, oblige Hull to act entirely on the defensive, and meet, and perhaps overpower, the convoys and reinforcements which may be sent him. . . . It is possible that the event may be adverse to us, and if it is, Detroit must fall."[37] According to all contemporary evidence, Hull certainly believed that he soon could be forced to fend off an enemy from the north as well as the south.

On the day that Hanks arrived in Detroit, Colonel Procter conducted a council with the Indian chiefs residing on the American side of the river. He gave the usual pledge of British support for the Indians' interests and informed them of the capture of Fort Mackinac. The council lasted four days, during which time the Wyandot chiefs succumbed to Procter's as well as Tecumseh's arguments. It was at this council that Walk-in-the-Water, the major chief the British were attempting to win over, agreed to support the British.[38] Fearing that he might change his mind, Tecumseh, Round Head, and Captain Muir, backed by a number of Tecumseh's Indians and 100 British troops, forced the issue by crossing over to Brownstown, where about 300 Wyandot and Shawnee had gathered, and escorted them across the river to Bois Blanc Island, where they set up camp. Years later the Wyandot averred that they had been captured by the British and carried off unwillingly. Their removal meant that no Indians, friendly or otherwise, now lived along the river in Michigan, and that their towns, through which the river trail to Ohio passed, were abandoned.

Two thousand miles away at Quebec City at roughly the same time period, Sir George Prevost, governor-general of Canada and commander of all its military forces, wrote to Major General Brock, "As I propose sending Colonel Baynes immediately into the United States with a proposal for a cessation of hostile operations, I enclose for your information the copy of my letter to General Dearborn, or the commander-in-chief of the American forces."[39] Baynes reached Dearborn in Boston on August 9 under a flag of truce. Although Dearborn recognized that he was not in a position to answer for the president, he agreed to forward Prevost's request to Washington. He and Baynes also agreed to an informal, interim cease-fire until Madison responded, which would remain in effect for four days beyond the date Prevost heard from the president. Dearborn's agreement to a temporary cease-fire was extremely ill advised. It applied only to the British troops in Lower Canada and American armies in the New York area. Hull's troops in Upper Canada were not included. In his dispatch to the president accompanying the cease-fire request of Prevost, Dearborn claimed that the United States had nothing to lose by the arrangement, a claim that Hull vigorously disputed later and throughout the remainder of his life. Dearborn argued that he could not include the North Western Army in the negotiations since Hull received his orders directly from the War Department and therefore was not under his command.[40] His thinking was somewhat disingenuous inasmuch as everyone had assumed that Dearborn was commander in chief of all American forces. Dearborn did write a dispatch to Hull outlining the terms of the cease-fire across the New York front, apologizing for not including him because "as you received your orders directly from the department of war, I could not agree to extend the principle to your command, but I agreed to write to you, and state the general facts; and propose to you a concurrence in the measures, if your orders and situation would admit of it." He naively closed his dispatch with the comment: "The removal of any [British] troops from Niagara to Detroit, while the present agreement continues, would be improper, and incompatible with the true interest of the agreement."[41]

The cease-fire itself was highly improper, and severely damaged Hull's position at Detroit, as attested by Prevost himself. As he immediately wrote to Brock,

> Since the return of Col. Baynes I have not received any further communication from the United States upon the subject of this mission, am happy however to find that the advantages to result from the ar-

rangement entered into by him with the Commander in Chief of the American Army, in the event of the Government of the United States persevering in their views of the conquest in Upper Canada are becoming every day more apparent. . . . A suspension of hostilities therefore on a considerable portion of the extremely extensive line of Frontier which I have to defend has enabled me rapidly to strengthen the Flank attacked . . . [and] has permitted me to move without interruption, independently of the arrangement, both Troops & supplies of every description towards Amhersterberg, whilst those for Gen Hull having several miles of wilderness to pass before they can reach Detroit, are exposed to be harassed and destroyed by the Indians.[42]

Thus alerted, Brock quickly assembled a force of 350 men and a number of Indians and sent them out by canoe along the upper reaches of Lake Erie toward Malden.

To make the waters even muddier, Dearborn neglected to send the notice of the cease-fire to Hull by special mail. When he finally received it, its import no longer mattered. Thus, although Hull did not realize it at the time, for the first two weeks of August he waged the war of 1812 entirely on his own.

[5]

TRAGEDY ON THE TRAIL TO
FRENCHTOWN, AUGUST 3–AUGUST 14

Word reached Hull on August 3 that a shipment of provisions for the army had reached the Rapids of the Maumee, only 30 miles from Frenchtown and the Raisin River. It was the most welcome news Hull had received in some time. Since July 9, the army had existed on the supplies that it had brought on the journey from Urbana, supplemented later by the food that McArthur had foraged during his journey to the Thames River. In the intervening three weeks the troops had used up over half their rations of flour and almost two-thirds of their salted meat.[1] What remained could, with care, provide subsistence for another 20 days. It therefore was necessary to bring those supplies safely to Detroit.

The fact that they were at the Rapids was a testament to Hull who, when he learned that the War Department had failed to make the necessary arrangements to feed his army, had privately contracted a Cincinnati merchant, John Piatt, to take charge of the matter. Piatt had begun gathering provisions as soon as the army had marched north from Urbana. By July 18 he had assembled 300 cattle and 70 packhorses, each of the latter carrying 200 pounds of flour, and forwarded them to Urbana. However, he did not believe that it was wise to send the provisions beyond Frenchtown through Indian country without an armed escort. A request to Governor Meigs resulted in the latter raising a company of 69 men, led by Captain Henry Brush, a Chillicothe attorney. Brush led the cattle and pack train out of Urbana on July 25, arriving at the Rapids on August 3, when he alerted Hull of his presence and asked for an escort from Detroit. To protect the supplies, he stored them in one of the blockhouses that Hull had constructed as the army marched north. He dared not move any further with so few men, having been alerted that the Indians were blockading the trail between the Raisin River and Detroit.[2]

Lucas made it a point to record in his journal that both Colonel McArthur and Cass had requested of Hull that he immediately dispatch a detachment of men to meet Brush and escort him to Detroit, but that Hull had repeatedly rejected their advice.[3] Considering the importance that Hull repeatedly attached to acquiring the necessary supplies for the army throughout the campaign, Lucas's claim about Hull on this date is open to question.

Hull's supply concerns were well founded. His supply base at Urbana was well beyond the distance over which an army could easily be provisioned. According to historian Kimball, the normal effective operational distance for packhorses between an army and its base of supplies was about 30 miles. The reason is that for packhorses to advance further, they also must carry their own forage. The longer the distance they are forced to travel, the more forage they consume, until a point is reached—about 45 miles—where they must carry more forage than supplies. Thus the transportation of foodstuffs by water to the location of an army camp was highly desirable, an option denied to Hull because the British controlled the river and lake traffic.[4]

On the day that the pack train had arrived at Frenchtown, Hull had convened a council of war to discuss whether the army should wait a few more days before attempting an attack on Malden, at which time the construction of the floating batteries for the heavy guns should have been completed. The immediate reaction of several of the officers, especially Cass, was that they should not wait but attack Malden immediately, even without heavy artillery. Most, however, were disposed to wait until the work on the floating batteries had been completed. Cass's professed eagerness to go against Malden was surprising, inasmuch as on July 13 he written to Senator Worthington in Chillicothe, Ohio: "We are in high spirits, but I doubt if we are adequate to the reduction of Malden."[5] Captain Dyson of artillery skewed the debate. He claimed that even should they be able to transport the heavy guns in sight of Malden, they still were faced with another problem. The area around the fort was so marshy that they would need to be remounted on solid platforms if their fire were to have any effect.[6]

Colonel Miller offered a counterproposal calling for an attack without artillery. He suggested that Hull form an elite attack group of about 800 to 1,000 men who would silently pass Malden at night and land on a beach below the fort at daybreak. This detachment then would form into two groups. The first would take up a position near the Canard River bridge and commence a raucous fire with small artillery to draw the British out of the fort to counterattack. As soon as they had done so, the second group would attack from the north, interposing itself between the British who had gone to the Canard and those who had remained within the fort. The officers voted down Miller's proposal because they considered it too complicated. As their debate continued, Hull settled the issue. The army would wait until the heavy guns were ready for transport even if it proved longer than expected.[7]

After the council of war, Hull ordered Major Thomas Van Horne to cross the river with all the army's riflemen and march south to French-town to meet Captain Brush. He also authorized Van Horne to order Captain Lacroix and 50 of his company to accompany them. Van Horne selected 150 riflemen from his own battalion, bringing his total force to about 200 men. Also accompanying them would be 18 to 20 mounted men who were in charge of conveying the army's mail to Ohio.[8] McArthur later claimed that he believed Van Horne's force was too small for the assignment and argued that it risked being defeated if attacked on the trail. He did persuade Hull to add a few more men after Van Horne had departed.[9] Volunteering were Captain McCulloch, with two select riflemen and Robert Lucas, who caught up with the main force by nightfall. Van Horne did not seem to be concerned about the size of his detachment. The troops left Detroit late that afternoon, and by evening had traveled 10 miles to the Ecorse River, where they bedded down for the night. A British force already was lying in wait. Alerted of the pack train's presence in Frenchtown, Colonel Procter had a drummer walk through Amherstburg calling for volunteers to join his British regulars under the command of Captain Adam Muir and Tecumseh's Indians in setting up an ambush at Brownstown. By nightfall they were concealed on both sides of the trail over which the Americans were expected to travel the next day.[10]

After Van Horne's detachment had left, Hull confided to McArthur that he had decided to remove most of the army back to Detroit until the supply situation could be resolved. He had selected McArthur's First Regiment for the task of manning a small picket fort on the Canadian side. McArthur responded angrily to the order, arguing that this would be tantamount to sacrificing the First Regiment. He told Hull that it was certain the regiment would immediately be attacked once the rest of the army left, resulting in inevitable defeat that would disgrace his men.

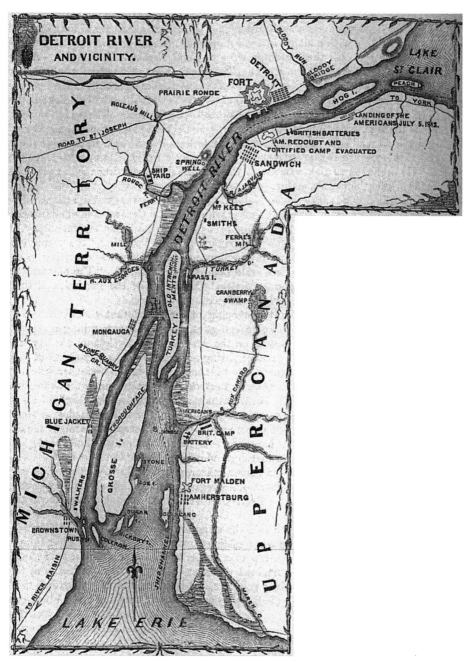

The Detroit river trail, 1812. (From Benson J. Lossing, *The Pictorial Field-Book of the War of 1812* [New York: Harper & Brothers, 1868].)

McArthur was also upset because he felt that Hull was insinuating that his, McArthur's, reason for objecting to the order was simple cowardice, which Hull denied. However, McArthur indicated that he would obey orders regardless of his feelings.[11]

Early morning on August 5 Van Horne's troops resumed their march. Captain McCulloch and Robert Lucas took the lead positions as the detachment's advance guard. Hull had warned Van Horne to take a back trail that would keep the detachment away from the river, but his scouts claimed that they could not find it. Van Horne instead took it upon himself to follow the main river trail. He forwarded a message to Hull indicating that he had changed his line of march but did not wait for a response. The troops met no resistance as they passed through the abandoned Wyandot village on the Ecorse River, nor did they encounter any British or Indians six miles beyond at Monguagon, the second-largest Wyandot town, which also was deserted. The trail then divided into left and right branches as it circled around a large cornfield. McCulloch rode down the left branch, Lucas the right. Suddenly a number of Indians hidden in the brush opened fire on McCulloch's flank, striking him in four places. Hearing the gunfire, the main body rushed forward, but before it could reach McCulloch's position, the Indians had already ripped off his scalp and disappeared into the forest. A short time later Van Horne encountered a Frenchman on the trail heading in the opposite direction, toward Detroit. The Frenchman warned him that 300 to 400 Indians were hiding near Brownstown, waiting in ambush for the Americans. Van Horne ignored the warning, which he considered to be just another of the many false alarms perpetrated by French settlers in the area.[12]

However, Van Horne did change the order of march, forming his men into two columns, each preceded by three cavalry and an advance guard of 24 men. The mail escort and the rest of the cavalry formed a rear guard. The two columns marched alongside each other, separated by a gap of about 100 yards. After passing through Brownstown the trail wound through a narrow, cleared gap bordered on one side by a creek and on the other by a thick stand of bushes. Directly before them also was a creek that they had to ford in order to continue. Just as the lead columns entered the water, Indians led by Tecumseh, dressed only in loincloths and painted for war, sprang up out of the bushes on all sides, setting up a withering volley of gunfire. Van Horne's first reaction was to charge them, but the Indians were so cleverly concealed it was difficult to focus on a worthy target. Unable to determine the size and placement of the enemy, and fearing that the detachment might be surrounded and cut off from Detroit, Van Horne ordered a retreat. Initially the troops responded in good order, stopping at intervals to form a line and set up a heavy fire of their own. But gradually panic spread through their ranks and they broke off in groups until the entire detachment was in flight. Their retreat was so rapid that the Indians were unable to circle behind them to prevent their escape. After three miles, they finally gave up the chase.[13]

A later head count revealed that Van Horne had lost 17 men. More significant, the British had captured the mail when its guards fled into the woods, and they now had a more accurate picture of what was taking place in Detroit.

Those Americans who were wounded and could not keep up with the fleeing columns or had been captured received no mercy from the Indians, who killed them and mounted their scalps on long poles along the trail. They also drove stakes through the bodies of the dead and left them exposed as a warning to Americans attempting to march down the same route in future. One of two young Americans who had been captured was being readied for torture when British major Adam Muir intervened and promised Main Poc, his captor, a barrel of rum and clothes for his family if he would spare the man's life and place him in his hands. As they discussed the terms, four Indians rushed into camp bearing the dead body of Chief Logan Blue Jacket, the only Indian killed during the skirmish. Muir knew immediately that his plea was in vain and no mercy would be extended to the American. A blow of a tomahawk to the head summarily executed the second captive as he was being taken to the Indians' council house.[14]

The number of the enemy that Van Horne faced before the retreat may never be known. Lucas thought that the attacking force was about three times that of the detachment, or 600 Indians. Van Horne reported a figure of 150 to 200. McAfee later wrote that "an American gentleman of high standing" confided in him that 40 British troops and 70 Indians were involved. A British account gave the number as 24 Indians led by Matthew Elliott.[15] The wide disparity in numbers is confusing, especially since one would assume that those involved should have been able to tell the difference in sound between a very large volley of gunfire and a small one. Since the pursuing Indians did not continue their chase after three miles, one would expect the number of Indians to be on the lower side—otherwise they would have made every attempt to cut the detachment off before it reached the Ecorse River.

The Ohio volunteers still at Detroit did not greet Van Horne's defeat too kindly as it besmirched their reputation. It also made Hull all the more skeptical of attacking Fort Malden with a force inexperienced in heavy battle, despite the volunteers' continuing clamor for an attack. Nevertheless, after convening his officers at his headquarters in Sandwich the next day, he told them that, notwithstanding his own reservations, he was willing to assault Malden without heavy guns and would be with them at the head of the troops. His decision led to much excitement among the volunteers, who were eager to attack immediately. Only two officers dissented, Captain Dyson and Lieutenant J. Eastman of the artillery. Both already had expressed reservations about transporting several 24-pounder cannons to a point where they could fire effectively against the fort. Despite their doubts, Hull told his officers to prepare to march from Sandwich on August 8. No doubt he already had learned that his officers were plotting against his command for not attacking sooner, and his marching orders would forestall their designs.[16] Even so, he continued to have strong reservations about leaving Detroit without adequate protection once the army's attack on Malden commenced. The fear that a large force of Indians, accompanied by many Canadian fur traders, was descending upon Detroit from the north and news reports indicating that Major Chambers had gathered a large militia force to approach Detroit overland from the east continued to plague him.

The next day Hull's preparations to march on Malden were interrupted when messages from the Niagara frontier arrived with totally unexpected news. In Hull's own words:

> At about one o'clock, an express arrived with letters to me from the commanding officers on the Niagara frontier—two from Maj. Gen. Hall, and one from Gen. P. B. Porter. These letters were sent to me by express to inform me that a large force from the neighborhood of Niagara was moving towards my army. But, what was more decisive in its influence on my measures was, that I learned from those letters, that I was not to expect that these movements of the enemy were to be checked, or that my army would be sustained by any operations against the enemy in any quarter. I found that the invasion of Canada and the whole war, were to be carried on by the 300 regular troops of Col. Miller, and the 1200 or 1400 militia which had been placed under my command.[17]

The news deflated Hull had and dissuaded him from moving against Fort Malden the next day. It seemed too risky under the circumstances. Instead, he ordered the army to prepare to cross the river back to Detroit, where they would wait until he received news that matters on the Niagara frontier had stabilized. "In making this movement, I had no design of relinquishing the attack of Malden. My intention was to take post at Detroit, and there to wait until events . . . afforded me some hopes of success, and of advantage from success."[18]

Hull indeed was faced with a conundrum. As head of the army, his duty was to attack the enemy with the forces at his disposal. He had reason to fear how they would react when they came under heavy fire from the fort, after Van Horne's retreat. "I commanded an army the troops of which except a few regulars of the Fourth Regiment, had no experience, and had never been tried; and this army was officered by men, the chief of whom had not hesitated to express, in the most indecent terms, his want of confidence in me."[19]

Hull also had to bear a second important duty in command. As governor of the territory, it was his responsibility to protect the citizens of Detroit. Should an assault on Malden fail and the Americans be defeated, the Indians would be free to descend on the town and wreak what havoc they chose. The British had no such similar concerns. They knew very well that if the Americans prevailed and Hull captured Malden, the citizens of nearby Sandwich and Amherstburg would not be harmed. The Indians would simply melt away into the forest.

Hull further questioned in his own mind whether acquiring Fort Malden would be worth the effort, and came to the conclusion "that if I had attacked Malden, and had been successful, it would have been a useless waste of blood. It would have been utterly impossible to have maintained the fortress. It must have fallen for want of supplies."[20] He based this assessment on the fact that the British would still control the water even if they no longer possessed the fort, and thus be free to harass his army's supply route along the river to Ohio at will.

Much to the great disappointment of the volunteers, Hull reversed his decision and ordered the evacuation of Canada. Left on the Canadian side in a small stockade opposite Detroit was Major James Denny of McArthur's regiment, with 150 Ohio volunteers along with Captain Joe Cook's regular troops and Lieutenant Gowie's corps of artillery. Their presence was meant to discourage the British from reprisals against members of the Canadian militia who had deserted to the Americans but now chose to remain on their farms in Canada.[21] Hardly had the army completed its crossing on the morning of August 8 when Denny sent word that his Ohio volunteers were in a state of revolt for having been left behind. Hull had no option but to let Denny handle the situation as best he could, for he dared not replace them with more of Miller's regular troops, which he considered to be the mainstay of his army.[22]

From a strategic standpoint, Hull favored removing the army to the Maumee River where it could more easily be supplied with men and food from Ohio. When he broached the subject with Colonel Cass, the response he received was anything but favorable. In Cass's own words, "I recollect a conversation with Gen. Hull, after the retreat from Canada, and before we went to the River Raisin, in which Gen. Hull suggested, that as he heard of no co-operation from below, it might be necessary to take a post at Miami [the Maumee]. I think I told Gen. Hull that if, under existing circumstances, he took such a step, the Ohio militia would desert him to a man. Whether I told Gen. Hull so or not, I am confident it would have been the case."[23] Once again his volunteer officers had placed Hull in an awkward position.

The need to convoy the supplies waiting for escort at Frenchtown had to be dealt with soon. To assure their retrieval Hull ordered Lieutenant Colonel Miller to assemble his regiment and together with selected companies from each of the three militia regiments make a new attempt to descend down the river road to reach Brush. Miller added to his force Captain James Sloan's cavalry detachment, a troop of Michigan cavalry under Captain Richard Smythe, and an artillery detachment under Lieutenant John Eastman. Several other officers volunteered to accompany Miller, the most prominent being Lieutenant James Dalliba with a six-pounder cannon and Majors Van Horne and Morrison. Miller's force now numbered about 600 men, virtually a third of Hull's entire army. As they prepared to set out, Miller paraded the troops in front of Detroit's citizens and regaled them with a spirited speech, closing with the words, "I shall lead you. You shall not disgrace yourself nor me. Every man who shall leave the ranks or fall back, without orders, shall be instantly put to death. I charge the officers to execute this order."[24]

Miller's command set off at late afternoon, August 8, and reached River Rouge, five miles below Detroit, by evening. There being no bridge crossing, the troops were ferried over by small boats. Not until 10:00 p.m. was everyone safely camped on the other side.

In hiding at Brownstown was Captain Adam Muir with 90 regulars, two companies of militia, and a large number of Indians, who had arrived the previous day in anticipation of Hull making another attempt to reach Brush. The following morning, August 9, nothing yet having occurred, Muir was on the verge of crossing back to Malden when Indian scouts excitedly reported that a large American force was descending down the trail and was no more than a few miles distant. The British hastily regrouped and took up a concealed position in a ravine near Monguagon. Having just been reinforced with 150 more regular troops, 50 members of the Essex militia, and about 200 Indians, Muir was ready for whatever American force he would encounter. He adopted the plan of attack suggested by Tecumseh. It called for the British troops to greet the Americans with a volley of gunfire when they appeared, bringing them to a halt, after which the Indians, hidden in an adjacent cornfield, would spring up and attack them on their right flank.[25]

Miller's order of march was for the infantry to proceed in two parallel columns 200 yards across on either side of the trail with the cavalry patrolling the road between. An advance guard of 40 men led by Captain Josiah Snelling scouted some distance ahead. About 4:00 in the afternoon, Snelling's lead detachment reached the ravine in which the British were concealed and were greeted by a heavy volley of gunfire, which cut down at least half its numbers. Hearing the sound of battle ahead, Miller immediately rode forward and formed his troops in a line of battle. Captain Snelling, despite his losses, continued to hold his advanced position until joined by the main body. Miller, who had been thrown from his horse at the outset, remounted and ordered his troops to charge ahead with bayonets, dislodging the British from the ravine. He met the attack of Tecumseh's Indians on his right with vigorous resistance as well, driving them back until they melted away into the woods. Captain Muir, although wounded, gathered his command together and retreated southward to Brownstown, where the troops boarded their boats and crossed back to Malden.

It was a shocking defeat for the British, although they later offered various excuses for its occurrence. One was that a group of grenadiers sent over by Procter to support Muir once the firing began mistakenly took Muir's bugle call, which was meant to signify a bayonet charge, as a signal to retreat. The grenadiers' abrupt departure disrupted the entire British line. Another was that the British had fired on the Indians by mistake, disrupting everything until they recognized their error.[26]

Miller's command took charge of the battlefield, where the troops made camp for the night, the British and Indians having fled across the river. But it was a hungry camp. When the troops had rushed forward at the beginning of the battle, they had discarded their knapsacks to gain greater freedom of movement. Those knapsacks still were scattered all along the trail. Miller for some reason feared that it would be too dangerous to retrieve them, though the trail now was clear. Instead he ordered Snelling to rush to Detroit, report the outcome of the battle to Hull, and have him dispatch new supplies.[27]

Losses on both sides are difficult to determine, given the typically extreme variation in reports. Colonel Procter reported that the British had sustained four dead and 15 wounded.[28] Miller's losses, more severe despite winning the battle, were listed as 10 noncommissioned officers and privates of the Fourth Regiment killed and 45 wounded; of the Ohio volunteers, eight had been killed and 13 wounded.[29] Other reports had as many as 40 Indian bodies being discovered at the scene of the action.

At nightfall Captain Maxwell, head of the spies, reconnoitered the trail several miles ahead. He returned to report that the road was completely free as far as Brownstown.[30] It has never been explained why Miller did not order Maxwell to proceed to Frenchtown and inform Captain Brush of the successful outcome of the battle. Since the trail between Monguagon and Frenchtown was clear, it would have been an excellent opportunity for Brush to join Miller with his supply train. The two detachments then would have constituted a force ample enough to reach Detroit without incident.

The next morning Hull, having received Snelling's report of the battle, ordered Colonel McArthur to gather a day's rations for Miller's men and freight them downriver by boats. These boats, once unloaded, would be used to transport Miller's wounded back to Detroit. Hull provided sufficient rations for one day, assuming that Miller would take up his march to Frenchtown the next morning and no more would be necessary. McArthur gathered 100 men and 12 boats and bateaux, but his departure was delayed four hours because of a dispute with David Baird, the supply contractor, over the number of rations required. As his troops prepared to leave, a drenching downpour began. Although inconvenient, its cover allowed McArthur to slip his boats unseen past the British *General Hunter* during daylight hours and into the western channel of the Detroit River, where they were shielded from the Canadian side by Grosse Isle. Arriving at Miller's encampment, McArthur quickly unloaded the army's rations and took aboard the wounded.

As they were leaving, McArthur could hear signal guns from the *Queen Charlotte,* the *General Hunter,* and Fort Malden alerting him of what was taking place on the other side of Grosse Isle. The *General Hunter* did not attempt to enter the western channel but continued to maintain a position at the northern tip of Grosse Isle, the point at which McArthur's boats would be out of the channel and in the open. Realizing the danger he was in, McArthur ordered all the boats beached before they reached the head of the channel and the wounded troops carried into the woods. Once they were hidden, he sent word to Colonel Godfroy of the Michigan Militia to bring up wagons for transport. His messenger had traveled only a short distance before he encountered Godfroy, who had taken it upon himself to set off as soon as he heard gunfire indicating that McArthur was on his way back. Unfortunately, the poor condition of the trail prevented the wagons from reaching the wounded. McArthur had them carried back to the boats to row them closer to where the wagons waited. It meant briefly exposing the wounded to gunfire from the *General Hunter,* but this could not be helped. What shelling there was did not prove to be effective, however, and McArthur returned the entire detachment and wounded to Detroit without further incident.[31]

The rain that had begun that morning continued throughout the day, making life dreary for Miller's troops at Monguagon. Miller had spent a good part of the day waiting for McArthur to arrive with his boats, then transfer the wounded into them for their return trip to Detroit. That being accomplished, Miller inexplicably made no effort to continue to Frenchtown. Instead, he sent another express to Hull that evening requesting two days' rations as well as reinforcements.[32]

Miller's actions after the end of the battle are puzzling. He had made no attempt to inform Brush of his victory. Perhaps his judgment was clouded by an attack of the "ague," a condition akin to malaria. If so, it would have been better had he turned command over to one of his senior officers.

Unknown to Miller, Colonel Cass with a detachment of his own was coming down the trail to help evacuate the wounded and was only a few miles away. Learning that Miller was ill (how is not known), he sent Hull a dispatch requesting permission to take over Miller's command (although there is no evidence to verify this). He later claimed that he never received an answer from Hull—therefore, he marched his detachment back to Detroit without communicating with Miller![33]

In an ironic twist of history, on the day after Miller's victory at Monguagon, Major General William Harrison wrote the secretary of war: "It appears to me, indeed, highly probable that the large detachment which is now destined for his [Hull's] relief, under Colonel Wells will have to fight its way. I rely greatly upon the valor of those troops, but it is possible that the event may be adverse to us, and if it is, Detroit must fall, and with it every hope of establishing our affairs in that quarter until next year." He doubted whether the supplies that a relief force could carry would be sufficient to sustain the troops in Detroit. This being the case, both forces would be forced to depend on small rather than large supply convoys "which can never reach their destination in safety, if the British and the Indians think proper to prevent it . . . commanding as they do the navigation of the lakes."[34]

While waiting for further word from Miller, Hull had second thoughts about the safety of the small garrison he had left across the river under Major Denny. On August 11 he ordered Denny to burn the fort and cross over to Detroit. It was a curious decision inasmuch as the fort was not in any danger at that moment, and it deprived those Canadians who had sided with the Americans of protection.[35] (Fortunately, when Major General Brock arrived at Malden he absolved all Canadian militia members who had gone over to the American side on the condition that they become active volunteers in the British army.)[36]

As soon as the last American had left the Canadian shore, Procter ordered the bridge over the Canard River repaired and had his troops occupy Sandwich. He also ordered Captain Dixon, his engineering officer, to site two artillery batteries on the Baby estate, about a half mile west of the small fort that Denny had just abandoned. Both the *Queen Charlotte* and the *General Hunter* moved in position on the river to mask what was taking place.[37]

The second request from Miller for supplies and reinforcements perplexed Hull. He could not understand why Miller continued to be immobile. His victorious battle had been fought two days previously, more than enough time for his troops to reach Brush at Frenchtown. The time it would take to assemble and forward more supplies and troops would further extend Miller's stay at Monguagon, allowing Procter to regroup and attempt a new assault. Finally, Hull ran out of patience. Concerned that Miller's inaction was playing into British hands, he ordered the detachment to return. Miller promptly struck camp on the morning of August 12, and had his troops back in Detroit by late afternoon. Had he gone in the opposite direction, he conceivably could have reached Brush that same day or the next. Miller's lack of action unsettled Hull, who had considered him the one officer in his army on whom he could rely.

That same morning, while idling at the river's edge near Detroit, Robert Lucas noticed a boat displaying a white flag descending downriver toward Fort Malden, where it remained briefly before returning to Detroit. He told McArthur what he had seen, and without checking any further wrote a letter to Major William Kendall of Portsmouth, Ohio, stating,

> Never was there officers more Solicitous, or more united than our Patriotic Colonels (and indeed the whole army) have been both of the Regulars and Volunteers, to promote the Public good neither was there ever men of talents as they are so shamefully opposed by an imbesile or Treacherous Commander as they have been—he has frequently Called the field officers to councill in which they have without an exception united in Sentiment, and have in every instance been opposed by Gnl Hull. Would to God Either of our colonels had the command, if they had, we might yet wipe off the foul stain, that has been brought upon us, We are now reduced to a perilous situation, the British are reinforcing, our Communication with the State are cut off, our Provisions growing short, and likely to be Surrounded by hosts of Savages.[38]

The Ohio colonels approached Hull after hearing from Lucas and demanded a reason for the flag of truce. Hull appeared puzzled by their request, saying that he was unaware that any such thing had taken place. They told Hull they would punish anyone they found to be involved. Hull asked them to wait a moment while he questioned his aide (and son-in-law) Captain Hickman. When he returned he explained that "Captain Hickman had conversed with Captain Rough [probably Ruff] on the subject but did not wish him to consider himself permitted to take a flag, but that the captain had probably considered himself authorized."[39] Ruff was captain of one of the merchant vessels that had descended from Fort Mackinac with prisoners after its surrender. Not quite certain what to make of this, the Ohio colonels left without inquiring further, but concluded that Hickman and Ruff may have discussed the possibility of a surrender, and that the ship captain had taken it upon himself to sound out the British. The truth of the matter was never known, but the Ohio colonels were disturbed enough to talk of removing Hull as the army's commander. By day's end they had determined that Colonel Cass should pen a letter to Governor Meigs of Ohio urgently requesting that he not only send reinforcements but lead them himself to Detroit.

> Dear Sir—From causes not fit to be put on paper, but which I trust I shall live to communicate to you, this army has been reduced to a critical and alarming situation. We have wholly left the Canadian shore, and have abandoned the miserable inhabitants, who depended on our will and our power to protect them, to their fate. Unfortunately the general and our principal officers could not view our situation and our prospects in the same light. That Malden easily might have been reduced I have no doubt. That the army was in force and in spirits enough to have done it, no one doubts. But the precious opportunity has fled; and instead of looking back, we must now look forward. The letter from the secretary of war to you, a copy of which I have seen, authorizes you to preserve and keep open the communication from the state of Ohio to Detroit. It is all important that it should be kept open; our very existence depends upon it. Our supplies must come from our state. This country does not furnish them. In the existing state of things, nothing but a large force of 2,000 men at least, will effect the object. It is the unanimous wish of the army that you should accompany them. Every exertion that can, must be made. If this reaches you safely by Murray [a courier], he will tell you more than I can or ought to insert.

Before Murray left, Cass added a postscript:

> Since the other side of the letter was written, new circumstances have arisen. The British force is opposite, and our situation has nearly reached its crisis. Believe all the bearer will tell you. Believe it, however it may astonish you! As much as if told by one of us. Even a ——— is talked of by the ———! The bearer will supply the vacancy. On you we depend.
>
>   Signed by—CASS, FINDLEY, M'ARTHUR, TAYLOR & E. BRUSH[40]

Cass and the others took quite a risk in sending this letter. It could easily have fallen into the hands of the British; the army had been having difficulty moving the mail to Ohio over the past several days. If captured, it would have revealed the mutinous state of the American army to Brock, who would have made good use of it.

Brock arrived at Amherstburg just before midnight, August 13. With him he brought 300 reinforcements, 50 of them regular troops. Hearing of his arrival, the Indians camped on Bois Blanc Island across from Malden celebrated by repeatedly firing their guns. Brock sent Colonel Elliott, head of Indian affairs, to order them to forego any further noisy displays to conserve their ammunition. Elliott returned within the half hour, accompanied by Tecumseh, whom onlookers described as a finely proportioned man of about five feet ten, dressed in a tanned deerskin jacket and long pants edged in fringe. Tecumseh was delighted to meet Brock and agreed to a council on Bois Blanc Island in the morning.

Tecumseh, famed Shawnee warrior. (From Benson J. Lossing, *The Pictorial Field-Book of the War of 1812* [New York: Harper & Brothers, 1868].)

About 1,000 Indians assembled to greet Brock when he arrived. Brock told them that he had come to drive the Americans out of Detroit and off their lands. After the usual array of speeches, Brock took Tecumseh and a few other chiefs aside. Through an interpreter he explained how he intended to use them in the attack on Detroit. Returning to Malden, Brock issued a general order dividing his army into three brigades. Lieutenant Colonel St. George would command the First Brigade. Major Chambers with 50 regulars of the 41st Regiment and three militia detachments would head the Second Brigade. The Third Brigade under Major Tallon would consist of the rest of the 41st Regiment. Finally, he placed Colonel Procter in charge of the entire force, subject to his orders.[41]

Brock then moved a good part of his army to Sandwich. En route they were protected from surprise attack by a screen of Indians who roamed along their flanks. The *Queen Charlotte* and the *General Hunter,* accompanied by small gunboats, patrolled the water. Because of the bend in the river, none of this activity could be seen from Detroit.

On August 14 Hull received a dispatch from Captain Brush indicating that he would move his pack train from Frenchtown to the upper road crossing of the Huron River, the site of Colonel Gabriel Godfroy's trading post (today's Ypsilanti). It was an area in no immediate danger, being 30 miles west of Detroit. The news invigorated Hull. At noon he ordered McArthur and Cass to select 400 men from their regiments and meet Brush at Godfroy's. Brush felt that these forces, combined with the Ohio men coming to meet him at the Huron River, would represent a formidable detachment that should be able to deal with any problems they might encounter, especially since they would be so far removed from the river road.[42]

Hull was shocked later that afternoon to learn that McArthur and Cass still had not left Detroit. He demanded an explanation. McArthur said they were waiting to receive provisions from quartermaster general James Taylor. When confronted by Hull, Taylor said that he had provided packhorses for carrying the rations but had not checked whether they had been loaded. An exasperated Hull ordered McArthur and Cass to assemble their men and march down the trail immediately without rations, which he personally would see were drawn, loaded onto the packhorses, and sent after them. McArthur and Cass duly left the town, but bedded their troops down for the night no more than three miles from Detroit. At that distance the packhorses should have reached them easily, but they never did. The drovers later claimed that they had got lost on the trail.[43]

One other event of significance took place that day. Lieutenant James Dalliba, commanding the battery on Bartlett's Wharf at the water's edge, became concerned about the activity taking place across the river from his post. He reasoned that if the British set up guns to bombard Detroit, his own battery, being at the shore of the river, would be in a vulnerable position. With Hull's permission he relocated it to higher ground inside the town where he could provide it with better protection.

[6]

FROM CRISIS TO SURRENDER, AUGUST 15–16

Saturday morning, August 15, ushered in the weekend that would bring a sad closure to military events in Detroit as well as in Fort Dearborn on the opposite, or western, portion of the Territory of Michigan. Before it was over, the entire territory would be in the hands of the British.

For lonely Fort Dearborn, now the site of Chicago, the day would prove disastrous. Over two weeks before, on July 29, General Hull had written an urgent express to Captain Nathan Heald, the fort's commandant, after receiving news of the fall of Fort Mackinac. He ordered Heald to distribute the fort's stores to the neighboring Potawatomi Indians, abandon the fort, and remove the garrison to a new location, either Detroit or Fort Wayne, as quickly as possible. Hull had forwarded the dispatch through a friendly Potawatomi chief who subsequently warned Heald to leave as soon as he could. News of the orders for Heald to turn over the fort and its supplies to the Indians spread rapidly. When Heald dallied, the Indians became impatient, for they were anxious to claim the fort's excess guns—and its whiskey. Heald, however, wasted several days by calling the Indians to council to explain what they already knew. During the council he promised to leave all the stores that the garrison would not need during its march to Fort Wayne. He then proceeded to destroy all the surplus arms and ammunition, and the liquor as well, rather than leave them behind. He assumed that if the Indians acquired them while the garrison was still in the area, he would have trouble on his hands. It was a wrong decision. The Indians believed he had broken his promise and turned hostile. Before they could act, however, Heald received a surprise visit from Captain William Wells, accompanied by 27 Miami

Indians. Wells, an Indian agent based at Fort Wayne and a chief of the Miami as well, had come to reinforce Heald's garrison. He also was the uncle of Heald's wife. Wells readily agreed to Hull's orders for the fort's evacuation.

Heald's party marched out of the fort at 9:00 in the morning on August 15, heading toward Fort Wayne, some 165 miles to the southeast. For protection, Wells placed several of his 27 Miami Indians at the head of the column and the rest at its rear. Heald's group of soldiers and civilians otherwise consisted of 53 regular troops, 12 militia volunteers, nine women, and 15 children. The trail initially tracked along the shore of Lake Michigan, with the water on their left and a high sandbank 100 yards inland to their right. Heald noted that a large group of Indians trailed them on the other side of the bank. Fearing that they were preparing an attack, he ordered his regulars to disperse them, only to discover that other Indians had circled around and enveloped the rest of his train. A fierce fight erupted, during which 26 of the regulars and all of the militiamen were killed, including Captain Wells. When the Miami Indians learned of Wells's death, they defected to the Potawatomi side.

Heald and his remaining men plus the women and children retreated to a small elevation in the center of the prairie between the lake and the sandbank. They continued to beat off new attacks but lost two of the women and 12 children. Meanwhile the Indians made off with their horses, baggage, and provisions. At a pause in the fighting, one of the Potawatomi chiefs, Black Bird, made signs for Heald to approach. Heald bravely did so, alone. Black Bird promised him that he would spare the lives of all survivors if they would surrender. Confronted by several hundred Indians, realizing that further fighting would lead to the death of the rest of his party, Heald reluctantly agreed. The Indians took the survivors captive and distributed them among themselves.

Heald and his wife, both severely wounded, were conveyed by canoe to an Indian camp at the mouth of the St. Joseph River. There an Indian trader named Burnett took them under his protection. A few days after they had arrived, all of the Indians in the vicinity unexpectedly departed for Fort Wayne. Heald immediately arranged for a local Frenchman to take him and his wife by canoe 300 miles along the Lake Michigan eastern shoreline to Fort Mackinac, where Heald surrendered to the British commandant for protection from the Indians.[1]

On the eastern side of Michigan territory, August 15 would signal the beginning of the end of Detroit under American rule. British general Brock, impatient to go against Fort Detroit and having learned that Colonels McArthur and Cass were off in the woods with a very large detachment of troops, placing Hull at a distinct manpower disadvantage, decided to attack immediately. He also was aware that the fragile truce to which General Dearborn had agreed in the Niagara area could be dissolved at any time, forcing him to leave Fort Malden before having settled matters in the Detroit area.

In the early morning of the 15th he placed his troops on the trail toward Sandwich, from where they would cross the river and proceed to Detroit. He also positioned artillery directly across from Fort Detroit, shielded by a high bank: an 18-pounder, two 12-pounders, and two five-inch howitzers.[2]

Although Hull was aware that something was happening on the other side of the river, there still was no indication that Brock planned an attack in the foreseeable future. He had placed his forces at the fort on alert, but otherwise military business continued to take place in usual fashion, including the scheduled court-martial that Lieutenant Hanks had requested regarding his culpability in the surrender of Fort Mackinac.

About 1:00 p.m. a sentry rushed into the fort to announce that a small boat was approaching from the Canadian shore under a flag of truce. Miller, the officer presiding over Hanks's court-martial, temporarily adjourned the proceedings to investigate. Captain Snelling and Captain Fuller met the boat at the Detroit River landing and were greeted by British officers Lieutenant Colonel John McDonell and Major John Glegg. They informed the two Americans that they had a message for Hull from Brigadier General Brock. McDonell and Glegg were blindfolded and escorted to a house about 100 yards from the fort, where they remained awaiting General Hull's reply. Under the circumstances Brock's letter was not only surprising but totally audacious. He wrote:

> The force at my disposal authorizes me to require of you the immediate surrender of fort Detroit. It is far from my intention to join in a war of extermination, but you must be aware, that the numerous body of Indians who have attached themselves to my troops, will be beyond controul the moment the contest commences. You will find me disposed to enter into such conditions as will satisfy the most scrupulous sense of honor. Lieut-colonel M'Donell and major Glegg are fully authorized to conclude any arrangement that may lead to prevent the unnecessary effusion of blood.[3]

Hull delayed his response for two hours, hoping during the interim to hear from the courier he had dispatched to McArthur and Cass ordering their return, which would factor into his decision. Finally, about 3:00 in the afternoon, Hull gave the two British officers his reply to Brock's demand: "Sir, I have received your letter of this date. I have no other reply to make, than to inform you that I am prepared to meet any force which may be at your disposal, and any consequences which may result from any exertion of it you may think proper to make."[4] If Hull thought Brock was bluffing, he was disabused of that idea at 4:00 p.m., when the British batteries on the opposite shore opened fire on Detroit. Because of the distance and the erratic nature of artillery in that era, the damage was not as severe as the noise would indicate. Nevertheless, the din frightened the townspeople, who snatched up whatever belongings they could and fled to the safety of the fort, but not before pausing long enough to bury their silver and money somewhere on their property.

Hull responded with counterfire from his three shore batteries, each of which consisted of three 24-pounder guns. These were located at the riverbank because the town's Main Street (now Jefferson Avenue), extending along an elevated plateau near the river but across the front face of the fort, and being bordered by houses, obstructed cannon fire from the fort proper. The shore battery west of the town and outside its perimeter originally had been designed to halt water traffic, and therefore was not sited very well for firing across the river. The center battery, located just south of the Citadel, was in the weakest position of the three, being lower in height than the British guns and thus exposing its gun crews to the British fire; therefore, it could be manned only sporadically. The third battery was located within the town on the south side of Main Street across from St. Anne's Catholic Church. Lieutenant Dalliba had hastily constructed it just the previous day.[5] He had chosen this location because it placed the battery at a height roughly level with the British guns on the other side of the river.

Before the British bombardment had begun, Dalliba had requested permission to open up on the British batteries. Hull's response confused him. "Mr. Dalliba, I will make an agreement with the enemy, that if they will never fire on me I will never fire on them." He added, "Those who live in glass houses must take care how they throw stones."[6] Dalliba had no idea what Hull meant by this remark, unless it were not to entice the British to respond until they had declared their intentions. This they did beginning at 4:00 p.m. The American batteries immediately replied with equal vigor. Despite all the shells that both sides fired at each other, little actual damage was done, although one errant shot did pierce the roof of Augustus Langdon's two-story house. It smashed through the table around which the family was seated and landed in the cellar. The family fled instantly, just before the shell exploded, wrecking their home.[7] Captain Snelling volunteered to ferry 100 to 150 men across the river, attack the British redoubt, and spike its guns, but Hull refused his suggestion. The British guns were not having a critical effect on the fort, and the possible loss of a 100- to 150-man detachment if the attack failed could have serious future consequences.

Near sundown Hull ordered Captain Snelling to take 40 to 50 men with a four-pounder cannon and take a position near Spring Wells, which would be directly across from Sandwich on the Canadian side. Hull asked to be alerted immediately if the enemy made any movement suggesting an attack; otherwise, Snelling was to return at daybreak and report what, if anything, he had learned. Colonel Taylor and Lieutenant Jessup joined the troops on their march. When they arrived at their post at Spring Wells, they noted that the *Queen Charlotte* was anchored on the river, which at this point was three to four miles wide, across from them. The three officers evaluated the situation and came to the conclusion that if they had a 24-pounder cannon they might be able to drive the brig away. Jessup had visited this position earlier and had noted that the British appeared to be collecting boats as if they intended to cross the river. The 24-pounder could deal with them as well. Snelling forwarded a message to Hull requesting that one of the large cannon be hauled over to them for this purpose. Hull discussed his request with Captain Dyson of artillery, who advised the general that the wooden bridges over two intervening creeks could not support the heavy weight (over a ton) of a cannon that size. On the advice of Dyson, therefore, Hull turned down Snelling's request. Nothing further occurred that evening during Snelling's watch, although he did detect what he believed were the sound of oars.[8] That Snelling's suspicions of what was taking place across the river were not aroused is curious inasmuch as the British force then was preparing to land at daybreak near where his force was stationed.

Although Hull was not certain of Brock's immediate intentions, he did suspect that an Indian attack would take place that same evening, and allocated his troops accordingly. He posted Colonel Findlay and his entire regiment behind a row of pickets west of the Citadel, where they commanded the trail. The troops who remained from McArthur's and

Cass's regiments he combined with the Michigan Detached Militia and placed at the rear of the fort. The First Michigan Militia under Colonel Elijah Brush guarded the northern perimeter of the area outside the fort. Miller's regiment was dispersed throughout the fort and commanded its batteries.[9]

Brock took great care to conceal his activities through the night. After dark 600 Indians led by Matthew Elliott, the British Indian agent at Amherstburg, stealthily crossed over to the eastern shore of the River Rouge, about one and one-half miles below Spring Wells, and advanced silently toward Detroit. Their objective was to enter the town and create all the havoc they could while Brock assaulted the fort from the west. They made their way forward with great restraint, not harming anyone in the settlements they passed, although they could not resist plundering homes and making off with every horse they could find.[10]

Shortly after daylight on the 16th Brock began ferrying his men across the river at Spring Wells. He later claimed to have had only a small force of 730 troops, of whom 400 were militia volunteers. Brock's accuracy is questionable. According to the British prize pay list of regulars and militiamen who were entitled to a share of the property captured at Fort Detroit, there were 117 officers, 131 noncommissioned officers, and 1,112 privates who qualified, or a total of 1,360 men who received prize money for having participated in the attack in one form or another.[11] Subtracting the attack force from this number meant that Brock held 630 men in reserve as he began his assault, which is highly improbable.

That Captain Snelling and his men, camped directly across the river from Brock that night, had no suspicion of the mustering of the British troops is either a credit to how well Brock masked his forthcoming actions or an indication that Snelling was incredibly naive. Snelling and his troops left their post shortly before dawn, claiming to have received an order from a Colonel Wallace, whom no one recognized, to return to Detroit. Snelling reached the town at dawn. He dropped off his four-pounder cannon at the gate of the Citadel and marched his men into the fort. He then asked for Hull's whereabouts, but no one could give him an answer. Not knowing what else to do, he simply went to bed, only to be awakened at dawn when British batteries began shelling the town.[12]

Brock began to ferry his troops across the river as soon as his batteries opened their bombardment of Detroit. In his own words: "I crossed he river with an intention of waiting in a strong position the effect of our fire on the Enemy's Camp, and in the hope of compelling him [Hull] to meet us in the field. But receiving information upon landing that Colonel McArthur, an officer of high reputation, had left the Garrison three days before with a detachment of five hundred men, and hearing soon afterwards that his Cavalry had been seen that morning three miles in our rear, I decided on an immediate attack."[13]

Most ironic is the fact that Brock knew exactly the location of the McArthur/Cass detachment, but that Hull, who soon would have desperate need of it, had no idea that the force was within a few miles of the fort. Had he been so informed, it is conceivable that the events of that day may have turned out entirely differently.

Unanswered is why the McArthur/Cass detachment was so close to Detroit that morning since, according to Cass's account of their return march, the troops should still have been on the trail, miles away, at dawn. If, as Cass later testified, the detachment had marched until midnight on the 14th, the men had probably covered six to seven miles. Again according to Cass, they were on the trail the entire next day. At a conventional hiker's walking pace of two and one-half miles per hour, with time added for rest stops, they should have covered another 20 to 22 miles before they bivouacked for the night, which would have placed them within four to five miles of Godfroy's post on the Huron River.

At dark a courier from Hull hurriedly rode into their camp with an urgent order to return to Detroit as quickly as possible, as Brock had demanded the fort's surrender, which Hull had rejected. Again, according to Cass, the men were too tired to leave immediately, and so they did not set out until very early the next morning, the 16th. If they had been about 25–27 miles from Detroit when they began their return march, as Cass indicated, they could not have reached the fort until well past noon. Why, then, did Brock's Indian scouts discover them only two to three miles from Detroit at daybreak?

Cass claimed that when he had come within two miles of Detroit the troops had met a Frenchman who informed them that the fort had surrendered. They therefore decided to retreat to the River Rouge to camp until they could confirm the news.[14] If the fort indeed had surrendered, the meeting with the Frenchman could not have taken place until well after noon.

McArthur's recollection of the same march, oddly enough, varies substantially from what Cass later reported. According to his account the detachment marched 24 miles the first evening and proceeded still further the next morning before making camp. If the troops had covered

24 miles the previous evening and continued further the next day, they should have arrived at the Huron River, but they apparently did not. According to McArthur, he ordered the detachment's guides and dragoons to ride forward to the trading post and confirm whether Captain Brush had arrived. They returned about six hours later that evening and reported that they had seen Indian tracks but no pack train. Under the circumstances the officers voted to return to Detroit, especially since the provisions that Hull had forwarded never arrived. They had proceeded no more than one-half mile when a courier from Hull met them and requested that they return to Detroit as soon as possible. That night the men were allowed to rest while the officers stood guard. How far they were from Detroit at this point is not known. McArthur did say that shortly after resuming their march on the morning of the 16th they could hear cannon fire. They subsequently crossed the River Rouge, then "halted for refreshment" at the spot they had camped the night before, which certainly could not have been 24 miles outside of Detroit, the distance McArthur had claimed they had traveled the first evening. McArthur then sent three or four mounted dragoons into town to learn why the cannons were being fired but neglected to order them to report the detachment's whereabouts to Hull. When McArthur came within three or four miles of Detroit, he met the returning dragoons, who informed him that the American flag still flew over the fort but they had heard from "some person" that General Hull had surrendered.[15] They did not report seeing a white flag flying over the fort. McArthur claimed to have learned (from whom?) that Hull would surrender at noon, which convinced him to retreat to the River Rouge, kill and roast an ox, since the troops had not eaten since leaving Detroit, then hold a council of officers to decide upon their next move.

McArthur's description of the detachment's march begs the same question asked of Cass: just how far down the trail did the detachment proceed before turning back to Detroit, since it is highly unlikely that it could have reached the River Rouge by early morning on the 16th unless it had marched the entire night. Regardless, if the dragoons that McArthur sent to town had communicated with Hull, they might have been able to coordinate an attack on Brock, who feared that such a situation might develop. A flank or rear show of force by the 350 men in the McArthur/Cass detachment could have created sufficient disturbance to force Brock to pull back from his intended attack on the fort.

By 8:00 a.m., still not having heard from McArthur and Cass, Hull was in a serious predicament. Brock was approaching, and despite the large number of fighting men that others have claimed he had to defend the fort that day, Hull himself could count no more than about 800 effective troops, although between 1,000 and 1,100 is a more accurate number.[16]

As the morning progressed, the British bombardment resulted in a few fortunate hits. One stray shot bounced off the parapet of the fort, struck Lieutenant Porter Hanks in the chest, then ripped into the legs of Cass's surgeon mate, Dr. James Reynolds, killing them both. It also seriously wounded Dr. Hosea Blood of Miller's regiment.[17]

Hull was forced to slacken his own cannon fire since Captain Dyson reported that they could soon run out of ammunition if they continued their bombardment at its present rate. Captain Brown reported also that they had only one box of cartridges remaining for the 24-pound guns.[18] Both reports were moot inasmuch there were only 5,625 pounds of powder on hand. At the high rate of powder required for each cannon shot, this amount would last only a few more days before the big guns would fall silent.[19] Should Brock's attack turn into a siege, the lack of heavy cannon fire could prove pivotal.

In preparing for Brock's oncoming attack, Hull stationed Colonel Findlay's regiment and the remaining troops from McArthur's and Cass's regiments in a line about a quarter of a mile below the fort perpendicular to the river. In their midst he placed two 24-pounder cannon loaded with grapeshot facing the trail over which Brock should approach. As the British came into view, Hull, it was later said, ordered Lieutenant Anderson, who was in charge of the battery, to hold his fire. Robert Wallace, Hull's aide, who was standing at the battery, maintained that Anderson had received no such order. He was delaying his fire until it could achieve maximum effect. The leading British officer coming down the trail, perceiving the trap into which his troops were marching, immediately informed Brock, who dispersed the column within the woods on either side as Anderson waited.[20] Before they appeared again and Anderson could bring his guns to bear, his battery as well as Colonel Findlay's volunteers and all others stationed at the Citadel were recalled into the fort.

Hull realized that he could not challenge Brock in the open field primarily with volunteers. Indeed, he found himself faced with another conundrum: as commanding general he was expected to defend the fort at all costs, even if it led to his ultimate defeat. As governor of Michigan territory, however, he was responsible for the lives of the people of Detroit. If his troops outside the fort (which is where Brock preferred to fight them) were defeated, he risked their loss. The only troops remaining then (besides the McArthur/Cass detachment, whose whereabouts were unknown to him) would be Miller's regulars, penned up in the fort with all the men, women, and children of the town, including his own daughter and grandchildren.

Captain Charles Askin, who had accompanied Brock in the campaign and kept a journal of what was taking place, wrote that "most of us wished I believe they should not [fight]—to spare the effusion of blood and for the sake of the poor Women and children who we knew would not be spared by the Indians should an action once commence."[21]

Hull now decided that his best option was to bring the volunteers into the fort and wait for McArthur to contact him with a report of his whereabouts so that he could formulate a strategy that would drive Brock back across the river. After several hours with still no word from McArthur, and with Brock deploying his forces around the fort, Hull made his decision: he would open negotiations in the hope of buying still more time to hear from McArthur. It was a vain hope.

Finally, at 10:00 a.m., he ordered that his bombardment of the Canadian shore cease and that a white flag be flown at the top of the wall of the fort. He then ordered his son and aide, Captain Abraham Hull, to cross the river under a flag of truce with a message for Brock, unaware that Brock was with the British attacking force on the American side. The message simply stated, "I propose a cessation of hostilities for one hour to open negociations for the surrender of Detroit."[22] Brock, for his part, noted the white flag flying over the fort and saw that an American was crossing the river under a flag of truce. He told Lieutenant Duer to ride up to the fort under his own flag of truce and ask the meaning of both. Receiving Duer, Hull composed a new dispatch, which he asked to be personally delivered to the British general. He also ordered Captain Snelling to accompany Duer and wait for Brock's reply. The second message read, "The object of the Flagg, which passed the river, was to propose a cessation of hostilities for one hour, for the purpose of entering into a negociation for the Surrender of Detroit."[23]

Although Captain Snelling initially had no knowledge of the content of Hull's letter, it became known to him when, when after reading it, Brock asked if he (Snelling) had been authorized to negotiate the terms of a surrender. Snelling replied that he had not. Brock then ordered his aides, Lieutenant Colonel Macdonell and Major Glegg, to ride back with Captain Snelling to negotiate the terms. After the three reached the town, the two British officers were conducted to an open-sided tent outside the fort where Lieutenant Colonel Miller and Colonel Brush were waiting. After discussion the four drew up the details of surrender, which they completed between 10:00 and 11:00 a.m. Miller was so ill with fever that he was scarcely able to participate; as soon as he had signed the articles he went into the fort and took to his bed.[24]

When the terms were shown to Hull, they were not entirely to his liking, but the designated officers had already signed them. A separate set of supplemental articles was formalized, to which the British officers agreed. These then were added to the document and signed during a meeting in Captain Dyson's quarters within the fort.[25] As the negotiations were taking place Hull was informed that the two companies of militia guarding the rear of the fort were deserting to the British, and that the First Michigan militia defending the eastern side of the town also was deserting, which left this sector completely open to Indian attack. Hull's options for defending Detroit had become all the more constricted.

The Articles of Capitulation read:

1st. Fort DETROIT, with all the troops, regulars as well as Militia, will be immediately Surrendered to the British forces under the Command of Maj. Gen. BROCK, & will be considered prisoners of war, with the exception of such of the Militia of the MICHIGAN Territory who have not joined the Army.

2d. All public Stores, arms & all public documents including every thing else of a public nature will be immediately given up.

3d. Private Persons & property of every description shall be respected.

4th. His excellency Brigadier Gen. HULL having expressed a desire that a detachment from the State of Ohio, on its way to join his Army, as well as one sent from Fort DETROIT, under the Command of Colonel Mc ARTHUR, should be included in the above CAPITULATION, it is accordingly agreed to. It is however to be understood that such part of the Ohio Militia, as have not joined the Army, will be permitted to return to their homes, on condition that they will not serve during the war; their arms however will be delivered up, if belonging to the public.

5th. The Garrison will march out at the hour of twelve o'clock, & the British forces will take immediately possession of the Fort.

CAMP at DETROIT 16 August 1812.

CAPITULATION for the Surrender of Fort DETROIT, entered into between Major General BROCK, commanding His BRITANNIC MAJESTY's forces, on the one part; & Brigadier General HULL, commanding the North-Weſtern Army of the UNITED-STATES on the other part.

1ſt. Fort DETROIT, with all the troops, regulars as well as Militia, will be immediately Surrendered to the Britiſh forces under the Command of Maj. Gen. BROCK, & will be conſidered priſoners of war, with the exception of ſuch of the Militia of the MICHIGAN Territory who have not joined the Army.

2d. All public Stores, arms & all public documents including every thing elſe of a public nature will be immediately given up.

3d. Private Perſons & property of every deſcription ſhall be reſpected.

4th. His excellency Brigadier Gen. HULL having expreſſed a deſire that a detachment from the State of Ohio, on its way to join his Army, as well as one ſent from Fort DETROIT, under the Command of Colonel Mᶜ ARTHUR, ſhould be included in the above CAPITULATION, it is accordingly agreed to. It is however to be underſtood that ſuch part of the Ohio - Militia, as have not joined the Army, will be permitted to return to their homes, on condition that they will not ſerve during the war, their arms however will be delivered up, if belonging to the public.

5th. The Garriſon will march out at the hour of twelve o'clock, & the British forces will take immediately poſſeſſion of the Fort.

APPROVED.	{ (Signed.) J. Mᶜ DONELL Lieut.
(SIGNED) W. HULL, Brigr.	Col. Militia, P. A. D. C.
Genl. Comg. the N.W. Army	J. B. GLEGG Major A. D- C.
APPROVED.	JAMES MILLER Lieut. Col.
(SIGNED) ISAAC BROCK,	5th. U. S. Infantry,
Major General.	E. BRUSH Col. Comg. 1ſt. Regt.
	Michigan Militia.

A true Copy;

ROBERT NICHOL Lieut. Col. & Qr. M. Genl. Militia.

Facsimile of Detroit surrender document of August 16, 1812. (Courtesy of the Burton Historical Collection, Detroit Public Library.)

To the signatures of Macdonell and Glegg for the British, and Miller and Brush for the Americans, Hull and Brock added their own, giving the document official status.[26]

Of the Supplementary Articles that Hull negotiated, the first stipulated that the officers and soldiers of the Ohio militia were free to leave for their homes on condition that they would not serve in the army again unless exchanged. The second permitted all officers and soldiers serving in the Michigan militia under Major Witherell to return to their Detroit homes under the same conditions.[27]

At 12:00 noon, after stacking their arms, the American troops marched out of the fort and assembled on the common, at which time Lieutenant Jessup read to them the terms of capitulation. Despite Hull's objections Brock refused to allow the Americans the customary honors of war: that is, to retain their colors. The British entered the fort after it was evacuated, lowered the American flag, and replaced it with the Union Jack. As they raised the flag, their cannon fired a rolling salute and their band played "God Save the King." After 16 years, they once again possessed Fort Detroit.

In recognition of Hull's concern for the safety of the women and children of Detroit Brock ordered his Indian allies to refrain from annoying the militia volunteers or any of the people living in the town. However, as soon as they were out of sight of the town, the Indians became particularly obnoxious to those living on farms in the outlying areas, plundering their property, stealing their livestock, ruining their crops, and setting fire to their buildings.[28]

Later on the day of the surrender, Brock located a printing press in Detroit and published copies of a proclamation promising the protection of American property and declaring that the laws then in existence under American rule would be continued. The proclamation stated:

> Whereas the Territory of Michigan was this day by Capitulation ceded to the Arms of His Britannic Majesty without any other condition than the protection of private property—And wishing to give an early proof of the moderation and justice of the Government, I do hereby announce to all the Inhabitants of said Territory, that the laws heretofore in existence shall continue in force until His Majesty's pleasure be known, or so long as the peace and safety of the said Territory will admit thereof—And I do hereby also declare and make known to the said Inhabitants, that they shall be protected in the full exercise and

General Hull surrenders Fort Detroit to British Major General Brock. (Courtesy of the Burton Historical Collection, Detroit Public Library.)

enjoyment of their Religion, Of which all persons both Civil and Military will take notice, and govern themselves accordingly.

All persons having in their possession or having any knowledge of any Public Property, shall forthwith deliver in the same or give notice thereof to the Officer Commanding, or Lieutenant Colonel Nichol, who are hereby duly Authorized to receive and give proper Receipts for the same.

Officers of the Militia will be held responsible that all Arms in possession of Militia Men be immediately delivered up, and all Individuals whatever, who have in their possession, Arms of any kind, will deliver them up without delay.[29]

After the surrender, General Hull retired to the home in which he had lived as governor, now occupied by his daughter and her family. Brock ordered that a guard be stationed outside its front door to make certain that the Indians did not bother them. Brock himself moved into a house nearby on Main Street.

In his reports of the capitulation, Brock made much of the fact that his "small army" had been faced by 2,500 American troops on the day of surrender. This was a gross exaggeration of the numbers he faced at the time of the attack, possibly calculated to impress his superiors. According to the historian Alec Gilpin, Brock included in his count just about every regular soldier and militia member that could have been found in the Territory of Michigan on the day of the surrender. This exaggerated number, in such stark contrast to what Brock claimed was the size of his attacking force, has been handed down for generations, leading some historians (McAfee for one) to claim that Hull surrendered to an enemy whose army was only half the size of His own. In truth Hull opposed Brock with an effective American force that numbered fewer than 1,100 men not the 2,500 that Brock claimed. Historians Gilpin, Quimby, and Rauch agree that Hull's effective force was greatly outnumbered. Jessup, Hull's own adjutant general, estimated at the time of the surrender that only 1,000 men were fit for duty, while Cass gave the number as 1,066.[30] Clarke through his own analysis came up with an estimate of 840 effectives, and Van Duesen does not believe that Hull had more than 600 men available.[31]

As for the British numbers, Brock informed Prevost, his superior, that he had engaged Hull with 330 regulars, 400 militiamen, and 600 Indians, a total of 1,330 men. This number did not include the troops attending the guns across from Detroit nor members of the Provincial Marine manning the British ships on the river. A more accurate report of the size of Brock's army can be found in the official report of the number of British and Canadians who were to share in the prize money for being involved in the surrender (not including Indians), which came to 1,360 men. In essence, Hull probably was confronted with an effective attacking force almost double that of his own.[32]

While the surrender negotiations were taking place, McArthur and Cass continued to remain in camp at the River Rouge and made no attempt to learn why the cannon fire from Detroit had ceased. Late in the day Captain William Elliott of the Essex Militia approached carrying a flag of truce. He showed the two officers a copy of the Articles of Capitulation that had been signed by both Brock and Hull. After reading them, McArthur surrendered the detachment.

Having learned from McArthur that Captain Brush and his supply train probably still were at Frenchtown, Elliott had McArthur write a message on the back of the copy of the Articles of Capitulation ordering Captain Brush to surrender. Elliott gave command of the American detachment to Major Dixon with orders to convey it to Detroit.

According to an account kept by a William Willis, a private in Cass's regiment, General Brock met the detachment when it entered Detroit, whereupon Cass broke his sword "out of indignation and mortification" rather than give it to Brock.[33] Other anecdotes from Ohio volunteers told of their officers breaking their swords. Such responses seem highly unlikely—there was no mention of them in any of the official accounts of what took place.

After leaving McArthur and Cass, Captain Elliott continued on to Frenchtown, arriving at 2:00 the following afternoon. When he came within a half mile of the small fort protecting the town, and despite carrying a flag of truce, he was confronted by 12 Ohio men, disarmed, blindfolded, and taken to Captain Brush. Elliott gave him the copy of the Articles of Capitulation to read, on the back of which was McArthur's note. Brush refused to believe that the document was genuine. Instead he locked Elliott up in the fort's blockhouse and said that he would provide him with an answer in the morning. About midnight Elliott awoke to the noise of departing men and wagons, and immediately realized that Brush was taking the supply train back to Ohio before more British arrived.

After they were gone Lieutenant Colonel John Anderson, head of the local militia, released him and surrendered his 120-man detachment with the provision that the men be permitted to return to their homes. It was well that they did, since there were no British troops on hand to protect their families from the Indians, who had begun harassing the townspeople. A large British party arrived from Amherstburg under a Major Chambers the next day and made every effort to restrain them. Chambers was especially mortified by what took place. Writing to his superior, he said, "I feel compelled to state, that notwithstanding every Effort on my Part, to Insure it [protection] to them so strong was the disposition on the Part of the Indians in particular the Wyandotts, to Pillage, Ravage, and destroy, that I could not Succeed, scarcely a House in the Settlement having escaped Pillage. Indeed it was one universal scene of desolation."[34] Chambers's orders were to burn down the blockhouse at Frenchtown, then proceed to the small settlement at the Foot of the Rapids on the Maumee River, receive its surrender, and fire its blockhouse as well. When he arrived, he found it virtually deserted except for 25 American soldiers who were ill. Indians already had begun to remove all the abandoned property they could find.

On Monday, August 17, Hull, his staff, and all officers and men of the regular army were taken aboard the *Queen Charlotte* preparatory to removing them as prisoners of war to Quebec, where they would be lodged until they could be exchanged for captured British prisoners.[35] When detained at Fort George en route to Quebec on August 26, Hull wrote his official account of the Detroit campaign, which the British forwarded to the U.S. secretary of war. In it he graciously wrote that no censure should be leveled against McArthur, Cass, Miller, or any of the militia officers, as they had faithfully discharged their duties. His letter was received in Washington with little fanfare, in stark contrast to an inflammatory account written by Cass two weeks later. (The complete text of Hull's letter is in appendix 4.)

Hull and his troops arrived in Quebec on September 16. Sir George Prevost, governor-general of Canada, released Hull on parole to his home in Massachusetts. He also released on parole all married regular officers. Single officers remained on parole in Charlesbourg. The rest of the men were confined to two transports on the river until they could be exchanged.

A week after the surrender the British had commercial ships carry members of the Ohio militia to the Cleveland area, where they were released to make their own way to their homes. McArthur worked especially hard to facilitate the return of militia members who were without money or horses.

On August 25, at the urging of McArthur, Cass departed for Washington, DC, with the expressed intent of providing the administration with a letter he had written giving his account of the events that precipitated the surrender of Detroit (see appendix 5). Cass was aware of the negative influence that the surrender could have on their future political careers of the Ohio volunteers and their officers; his account can be construed as an attempt to deflect blame from them and place it squarely on the shoulders of Hull. In his letter he defended the dilatory movements of the detachment on the day of the surrender, claiming that Hull had surrendered before his detachment could come to his assistance. He did not mention that he and McArthur had failed to notify Hull that their troops were less than a two-hour march away on the morning of the surrender.

To Secretary of War Eustis's credit, he declined to make Cass's account public despite the urging of Comptroller Richard Rush, who had written an editorial for the *National Intelligencer* at the president's request in which he quoted Cass as saying he never saw such a sight in his life, nor did anybody—so many "men in tears, the officers and privates crying with guilt and indignation. . . . The suspicion of treason gains ground."[36] Rush also argued that the publication of Cass's letter was imperative: "The fate of the general is and must be sealed. The issue is made up between him and the nation, and this letter will promulgate the true and righteous decision."[37] President Madison, who had been in Virginia when the letter was brought to Washington, permitted its release when he returned to the capital on September 12. It subsequently was picked up and reprinted across the nation, inflaming public indignation against Hull as a coward or even a traitor, accusations that continued to persist even after his death.

Anyone reading Cass's letter would assume he was relating an eyewitness account of the events he described. However, Cass was not in Detroit on the 15th and 16th, and therefore his graphic descriptions of the indignation that the Ohio men felt over the surrender are hearsay, and no doubt dramatized after the fact. For example, he wrote, "To see the whole of our men flushed with the hope of victory eagerly awaiting the approaching contest, to see them afterwards dispirited, hopeless and desponding, at least 500 shedding tears, because they were not allowed to meet their country's foe and to fight their country's battles, excited sensations, which no American has ever before had cause to feel, and which, I trust in God, will never again be felt, while one man remains to defend the standard of the Union."[38]

Whether this account is true or not, it is certain that Cass was not actually present during the surrender, and therefore was not in any position to write these words. Yet his account created enormous bitterness against Hull, especially in Ohio. Many felt as did one American, who said, "Everybody pronounces him a traitor and a coward and if he was to pass this way he would be hunted and shot like a mad dog. . . . The poor fellows who were out with him . . . all say that if Hull had not betrayed them they could have beaten the British and the Indians united."[39]

In his letter Cass also took great pains to explain why the detachment remained outside Detroit on the morning leading up to the surrender: "Had a firing been heard, or any resistance visible, they [the detachment] would have immediately advanced and attacked the rear of the enemy. . . . With his [the enemy's] raw troops enclosed between two fires and no hopes of succor, it is hazarding little to say, that very few would have escaped."[40] Brave words, but after the fact, a fact that ignored reality. As Brock himself attested, Cass and McArthur were several miles south of his forces when they crossed the river, and they had made no move against him. There is no evidence either to indicate that they had conferred with Hull about coordinating an attack on the rear of Brock's army. And it is difficult to believe that they did not hear the firing of cannon at Detroit when they were only about 10 miles away.

The universal acceptance of Cass's description of the surrender and his condemnation of General Hull gave President Madison the scapegoat he needed. The war was not going well. General Dearborn had yet to make a strong military effort on the Niagara front and at Lake Champlain, and his foolish truce with the British had contributed in no small way to Hull's surrender. The administration had yet to figure out how to conduct a war properly, and perhaps as much as a quarter of the nation, if not a third, was against it, especially the New England states, where requests for militia volunteers were being ignored. If nothing else, the letter helped shift the focus of blame away from Dearborn and the administration to Hull. Politically Madison meant to keep it that way. Elections for his second term would be taking place in two months, and the surrender came at a most inconvenient time. Opposing Madison was DeWitt Clinton, who claimed to be the candidate of the "peace party." Madison's fear that the national uproar over the surrender might affect his reelection was not realized. The electoral vote tilted 128 to 89 in his favor. Nevertheless, he lost three of five New England states plus the states of New York, New Jersey, and Delaware, states in which raising militia quotas became an arduous task.[41]

Madison never forgot the embarrassment caused by Hull's surrender. Long after finishing his term as president he wrote, "With such qualifications and advantages which seemed to give him [Hull] claim above all others to the station assigned to him, he sunk before the obstacles at which not an officer near him would have paused, and threw away an entire army."[42]

THE TRIAL OF BRIGADIER GENERAL WILLIAM HULL

The Court's Accusations and Hull's Rebuttals

After he was paroled by the British in September 1812, Hull went to his home in Newton, Massachusetts, and waited to be exchanged for British prisoners of war so that he could return to active duty. Despite General Dearborn's repeated overtures to Governor-General Prevost regarding Hull's exchange, the British were in no hurry to act. Dearborn argued that since an exchange was in the process, Hull no longer was on parole. The British denied his claim.[1] Despite the arguments over Hull's status, on January 19, 1813, now almost five months after the surrender, Secretary of War Eustis issued the following General Orders:

> A general court martial of which Brigadier General Wade Hampton is appointed President and Alexander I. Dallas Esqr., Judge Advocate, will sit in such place in Philadelphia as may be provided for the purpose, on the 25th day of February next at 12 o'clock for the trial of Brigadier General William Hull. Brigadier Generals Joseph Bloomfield, Henry Burbeck and John R. [P.] Boyd, Colonel George Izard, Alexander Macomb, James Burn, Jacob Kingsbury, Jonas Simonds, Thomas Parker, Peter F. Schuyler, William H. Winder and Hugh Brady, Lieutenant Colonels Winfield Scott, John Christie and Richard Dennis are to attend as members and supernumeraries.[2]

No doubt those selected to serve on the court, each an experienced officer, could be expected to conduct a fair trial. They were not "closet soldiers"—that is, soldiers who had never tasted battle. Wade Hampton, the court's president, had fought with distinction during the Revolutionary War and after retiring had returned to the army in 1808. Joseph Bloomfield, another Revolutionary War veteran, had since been elected governor of New Jersey. General John Boyd had served under Harrison during the battle of Tippecanoe. Colonel Kingsbury had been in command of Fort Detroit prior to the outbreak of the war and originally had been selected to head the North Western Army, until taken ill. Colonel Izard eventually would become a major general in charge of American forces at Plattsburg, Colonel Macomb also would become a major general and defeat British forces at the battle of Plattsburg in 1814, and Colonel Winder would be captured in the battle of Stoney Creek. Winfield Scott, another career army officer, would win fame at the battle of Lundy's Lane and also become major general. Indeed, the court-martial board was a stellar cast of professional army men, not political appointees, and could be expected to be more understanding of the problems Hull faced that led to the surrender of Detroit.

As ordered, Hull appeared in Philadelphia on the 25th of February and his trial was begun. Scarcely a week later, before any charges were filed against him, the court received a surprising General Orders from the secretary of war dated March 1. Eustis wrote: "The meeting of the General Court Martial for the trial of Brigadier General Hull is postponed until further orders, and the President and members of the said court martial will return to duty." A second General Orders dated the same day stated, "The meeting of the General Court Martial of which Brigadier General Hampton is President, ordered to sit in Philadelphia on the 25th of February last, for the trial of Brigadier General Hull, having been postponed indefinitely, the attendance of the witness summoned for this trial will not be required, until further notified."[3]

No explanation for the postponement was given. The administration was silent on the matter. Hull was left in limbo—under arrest but with no indication as to when the court would be reconvened again, during which time his reputation continued to be exposed to public scorn.

The only rationale for the postponement that seems likely is that the administration came to the conclusion that the officers selected to the board might be sympathetic to Hull's plight and find him not guilty of the charges brought against him, whatever they might be. Each member was experienced in the responsibilities of command (two were fellow Revolutionary War officers), and therefore would have a more realistic understanding of the problems Hull faced in the Detroit campaign. One member who might be particularly sympathetic to Hull's situation was Colonel Jacob Kingsbury, who had commanded Fort Detroit when Hull was governor and who did not think too highly of the militia that made up the majority of the North Western Army he had originally been asked to command.

Another factor that may have affected the trial date was the widespread revulsion the country experienced at the massacre of 80 American wounded prisoners of war by the Indians after the defeat and capture of General Winchester at Frenchtown. The massacre took place on January 18, just before the General Orders for Hull's first trial were released. (It will be discussed in greater depth later.) Winchester found himself in a position similar to Hull's but had fought first before surrendering, which had raised the blood lust of the Indians. As soon as the American prisoners were left unguarded by the British, most were slaughtered or beaten by the Indians, a situation that had haunted Hull as the possible fate of Detroit's men and women had he fought and lost. It is a distinct possibility that if Hull's trial had proceeded as scheduled, with the Frenchtown massacre still on the public's mind, he would have been exonerated.

By the end of summer 1813, the trial still had not been reconvened. However, on September 24 the British and American armies finally agreed to an exchange of 185 prisoners of war and their release from parole. Hull was exchanged for 20 British prisoners of war, Colonels McArthur, Cass, and Findlay for 15 each, and Lieutenant Colonel Miller for 10.[4] All the Americans were immediately placed on active duty, although Hull continued to be under arrest.

Not until November 7, 1813, did the War Department reconvene Hull's court-martial, scheduled to open on Monday, January 10, 1814, in Albany, New York, almost a year after the first trial was canceled. The War Department kept only Brigadier General Joseph Bloomfield from the original trial membership, selecting 12 new members: colonels Peter Little, William Irvine, J. B. Fenwick, and Robert Bogardus and lieutenant colonels James House, William Scott, William Stewart, Richard Dunn, Samuel Connor, S. B. Davis, John Livingston, and J. G. Forbes. Only Fenwick, House, and Connor had held a military rank at the time of Hull's surrender, and the regiments they represented had not even existed then. Other than Bloomfield, none had ever distinguished himself to this date during the war. Most were civilians, political appointees of the administration and friends of General Dearborn. Lieutenant Colonel Samuel Connor was not only General Dearborn's aide but also a member of his family.[5] It would be fair to say that the composition of the second court, so weighted with political appointees, was not intended to be as favorably inclined toward Hull as the previous court when it came to rendering a verdict.

This became all the more obvious when the president selected Major General Dearborn as president of the reconvened court-martial. To remove a senior officer from active duty in the midst of a war so that he could preside over a trial which, because of its political implications, might last for several months, was very unusual. It suggests that the administration was concerned that if Hull were exonerated the blame for the surrender of Detroit might then be attributed to the War Department, even General Dearborn himself. Dearborn in fact had his own reputation to salvage. The public had not been too happy with his military leadership of the past year. His army had little to show for its efforts on the Niagara frontier. The War Department finally reassigned him to administrative duty in New York City.

Hull thus was to be judged by a president of the court who many felt had betrayed him during the campaign and a cast of officers who, for the most part, had little or no military experience.

As Hull later reflected,

> When . . . I saw the commander in chief of our armies at the head, and when I beheld a majority of the members young Lieutenant Colonels, very lately promoted to that rank, and some of whom, I knew had been his [Dearborn's] Aides-de-Camp, and introduced into the army by his patronage, and others, whose names I never had heard, until they were called on that service, I thought it a strange organization of a court martial for the Trial of a General officer . . . when invariable custom and the articles of war provided, that officers should be tried by those of at least as high a rank as themselves, when such officers could be obtained.[6]

Before the trial began Hull requested that Robert Tillotson and C. D. Colden act as counsels in his behalf. Both counsels expected to be able to cross-examine each witness for the prosecution as well as the defense, and asked that they be allowed to address members of the court over any questions of law that might arise. The court agreed to their representing Hull—but not in the courtroom! The two lawyers were informed that the opinion of the court was "that the communications by the prisoner's counsel should be made in writing through the accused."⁷ They would not be permitted to cross-examine witnesses in court nor discuss questions of law with its members. As a result, Hull was forced to act as his own defense attorney, something he certainly did not expect and for which he was not prepared.

Arrayed against him were two of the leading lawyers in the country: Philip S. Parker and Martin Van Buren, the latter a future president. Both had been hired by the administration to conduct the trial, Van Buren taking the role of special judge advocate with the assistance of Parker. Having civilians in charge of a military trial again was a departure from the norm. Of more significance, both Parker and Van Buren were free to question the witnesses at any point during the trial; Hull's attorneys were not. If a question of law arose in Hull's mind, he had no other recourse than to ask the judge advocate to give his explanation of its ramifications. Parker and Van Buren drew up the charges against Hull, developed the list of witnesses, took their pretrial testimony, and directed the questioning. Without the direct benefit of his own counsel, Hull was relegated to being a spectator at his own trial.

Hull's defense further was hindered by his lack of the necessary documents to counter the claims made against him. Many of these had been packed in trunks and shipped with his daughter when the British allowed her and her family and other Americans to leave Detroit and sail to Buffalo via a civilian schooner, the *Caledonia*. It arrived in Buffalo under a flag of truce, and the civilians were allowed to disembark, but it was too late to send a boat back to retrieve their trunks and baggage. Later that night the ship was captured by the U.S. Navy and removed to Black Rock, but the ship's officer refused to allow the civilians their baggage. The *Caledonia* had been accompanied by a second sailing vessel, the *Detroit*, which also was captured, then set on fire by the Americans when the British attempted to retake it. It was later believed that the trunks with Hull's papers had been stowed on the *Detroit* instead of the *Caledonia* and perished with the ship.⁸ Gone were his daily reports, letters he had received from the War Department and the governors of Ohio and Kentucky, his daily journal of army operations, and all the communications he had penned to his officers.

To compensate for their loss, he requested that to be allowed to personally view the War Department files and have copies made of the documents he needed for his defense. He was refused full access, but was told that War Department clerks would copy specific documents that he requested. But when he did so, most could not be found, and Hull was left primarily with the documents that had been provided to the prosecution, which certainly would not be favorable to his case. As Hull later wrote, "In my repeated applications to the government, I requested to be furnished with all the copies which had any relation to the campaign. None were furnished, excepting such as it was thought would operate most strongly against me."[9] Thus Hull had no access to any of the messages that pertained to the August 8, 1812, armistice made by Dearborn that affected his own campaign. After the trial had ended, Hull asked at least for a certified copy of the proceedings. The secretary of war never responded. It was not until John Calhoun became the secretary of war in 1817 that Hull received any favorable response relative to the documents he could have used during the trial, such as his correspondence to and from other departments and copies of the orders sent each day to his officers.

As a former judge himself, Hull was aware of the irregularities in court procedure that were taking place. He was particularly disturbed to learn that the witnesses for the prosecution would be allowed to sit in court and hear the testimony of other witnesses, which could not help but frame their own testimony. Hull considered it a rule of both civil and military law that a witness should not be questioned in the presence of other witnesses. When one of the members of the court agreed and questioned the propriety of examining witnesses in this fashion, Dearborn replied "that it was not necessary in his judgment to examine them apart from each other."[10]

Hull also objected to the fact that none of the witnesses were required to testify under oath—a fundamental rule of any court trial. They were free, therefore, to say whatever they pleased without fear of being punished for perjury should their testimony be proven false. Thus the court was essentially hearing nothing more than opinions or allegations against Hull without attesting to their veracity.[11]

Hull made all of his concerns known to the court, but the members, especially the judge advocate, a trial lawyer in his own right, acted on none of them. Hull might have made a greater effort to force the issue, but he chose not to do so; since "all the proceedings of the court were regulated by his [Dearborn's] opinion . . . it would have been a useless waste of time to have discussed the question. His judgment was pronounced in a positive manner, and the court at once acquiesced in it."[12] As Hull later reflected, most of the members of the court-martial board depended on the administration for their recent promotions in the military ranks.

Although they realized the direction in which Dearborn and the judge advocate were taking them, they were not about to jeopardize their careers.

The charges brought against Hull finally were read to him in court on Monday, January 17, 1814, the fifth day of the trial, 17 months after the surrender of Detroit. The prosecution leveled three charges against Hull: treason, cowardice, and neglect of duty. Each charge carried several counts or, as the court referred to them, "specifications."

Looking at the transcript of the trial, the charges seem incredibly naive given all that was known of the Detroit campaign. Either that or they were politically motivated, intentionally brought against Hull to embarrass him and lay the entire blame for the surrender on his shoulders.

Also, the testimony of the participants as printed in the trial transcript presents a difficult problem in itself. The witnesses rarely if ever identified the charge they were responding to in their testimony, nor did the court specify the charge being addressed in its questioning of the witnesses. The result is a trial transcript that reads like a tangled skein of yarn, with no apparent beginning or end. To make matters more difficult, the court often allowed the witnesses to continue their testimony even when it had no bearing on any of the charges. The author has done his best to extract those comments made by the participants that can be related to a specific accusation.

The First Charge: Treason

Under the charge of treason, the court gave three specifications. The first was that under the guise of transporting the army's sick soldiers and hospital stores to Detroit as the army marched northward, Hull deliberately placed a trunk carrying his official correspondence on the unarmed boat he had hired, knowing that war had been declared and the vessel would be captured by the British.

In his testimony Duncan McArthur did his best to incriminate his superior, suggesting that Hull had been informed that war had been declared before he chartered the boat in question, and for that reason he himself refused to have his own baggage placed on board. He claimed that on June 26, the date on which Hull had received a letter from the secretary of war in which the declaration of war was not mentioned, he (McArthur) had also received a letter, from Ohio senator Worthington, that contained a postscript he asked Hull to read: "Before this reaches you, war will be declared." Hull in turn gave him the letter from Secretary of War Eustis to read, which made no mention of impending hostilities. McArthur could not recollect the exact words, but the substance of the letter was that "circumstances had occurred there [Washington] which rendered it necessary for General Hull to proceed to Detroit with all possible expedition, prepare for defense and wait further orders."[13] Hull disputed McArthur's remembrance of the exact wording of the first letter—and he was correct. Whether by intent or from loss of memory, McArthur radically misquoted the contents of the first letter. It did not contain the words "prepare for defense and wait further orders." These words can be found in the letter he received on July 2: "Sir, war is declared against Great Britain. You will be on your guard, proceed to your post with all possible expedition, make such arrangements for the defense of your country, as in your judgment may be necessary, and wait for further orders."[14] The first letter merely told Hull, "Circumstances have recently occurred which render it necessary you should pursue your march to Detroit with all possible expedition." The court made no effort to correct McArthur's testimony, which gave the impression that Hull should have known war had been declared before hiring the *Cuyahoga* to carry the army's baggage.

James Taylor attempted to support McArthur in his testimony, in which he stated he thought the appearance of Captain Chapin at the Miami River when the army arrived was too fortuitous to be believed. He said that he had warned Hull to use wagons for transport of the heavy baggage, not Chapin's ship, the *Cuyahoga*, but that Hull did not agree. He did recall, however, that Hull told Captain Chapin to use the western channel as a precaution, to avoid sailing by Fort Malden.[15] Chapin chose to ignore Hull's advice, thinking there was no danger to his ship. Had he had any forewarning, he certainly would have avoided selecting a route that would lead to the capture of his ship, his source of livelihood.

The rest of the army apparently did not agree with McArthur's and Taylor's accounts regarding the two dispatches. Cass, who was aware of the contents of the first letter from Eustis, clearly had no reason to believe that the country was at war, for he had his servant and his baggage placed on the *Cuyahoga* before it sailed.[16] Hull also reminded the court that as soon as he received the second letter telling him that war had been declared, he had made every effort to have the *Cuyahoga* recalled but was unsuccessful.

In the second specification the prosecution charged that Hull had conspired with enemies of the United States "whose names are unknown" to recross the river back to Detroit and abandon any attempts to attack

Fort Malden. Cass testified that after he had captured the bridge over the Canard River, Hull declined to bring the army to that point and left the decision as to whether it should be held or not to the discretion of the officers in the field, which they thought was unfair. Cass also believed that most of the officers were in favor of attacking Fort Malden immediately with or without heavy guns, and did not agree with the assessment of the artillery officers that the terrain was such that it would be extremely difficult to transport them past the Canard River. In response to a question from Hull, Cass replied that he could not recall Hull having said he would lead the attack on Malden without the assistance of heavy cannon if the troops insisted. Nor did he recall telling Hull that the Ohio volunteers would leave his command if they were ordered to retire to the Raisin River and regroup. However, Cass did add that "[h]e never believed Gen. Hull guilty of treason; never was in action with him, and knows nothing of his courage; but considered him an inattentive officer."[17]

McArthur testified that after the army crossed the Detroit River, the officers had urged Hull to march against Malden as soon as possible. However, the general insisted that transport for the heavy cannon had to be arranged if they were to breach Malden's walls and make their attack successful. McArthur was all for storming the fort immediately after crossing into Canada regardless: "There was no doubt that they [the Canadian militia] would leave Malden upon the first appearance of our army."[18]

Miller agreed with McArthur in principle. "I never had any doubt of the success of an attack at any time . . . that I would answer for my men; that they would attack the fort and not fall back in disorder."[19] He told the court that when Hull asked the heads of the other regiments if their troops would do the same, they replied that they could not answer for their men but assumed that they would "behave well" under fire. As for Hull's view, continued Miller, "[t]he general said he had no doubts as to the regulars, but that he had some as to the militia, who were inexperienced, against a fort."[20]

Major Munson told the court that the majority of officers were not in favor of crossing the river back to Detroit or falling back to the Raisin River to await reinforcements when Hull proposed these alternatives. However, they were inclined to wait for the floating batteries to be constructed before attempting an attack on Malden.[21]

Taylor commented that the officers urged Hull not to retreat from Canada. He was aware that the general's decision to return the army to

Detroit and forego the attack was based on the news that some 5,000 to 7,000 Indians and 200 employees of the North West Company had embarked from Mackinac to descend on Detroit.[22]

In rebuttal Hull reminded the court that during the intervening months since the surrender, General William Henry Harrison had assumed command of a new North Western Army four times the size the one he commanded. Even with this large number Harrison had not been successful in invading Canada until Commodore Perry cleared Lake Erie of British naval vessels, something he had advocated himself at the outset of the war. He argued that his orders did not specifically command him to attack Fort Malden. Nor did he any longer believe that his army had been in a position to mount an assault on the fort and at the same time deploy enough men along the trail to keep his supply line to Ohio open. He told the court that ordering the army into Canada before it was prepared to attack a fort like Malden probably was his mistake. It would have been better to have stayed on the Detroit side until the carriages of the heavy cannon had been prepared and to have used that time to train the militia for an assault on an entrenched, guarded fort. But at the time, despite his better judgment, he had decided that the only way he could curb the impatience of his officers was to get the troops across the river. He claimed that it was only after he had learned that Fort Mackinac had surrendered and that he could expect no diversionary help from Niagara that he began to doubt he could succeed in capturing Malden. It was then that he ordered the army back across to Detroit.[23]

The third specification under the charge of treason was that Hull willfully conspired with the enemy to surrender the fort. The witnesses scarcely addressed this point. Hull did, however. He told the court that if a conspiracy did exist, it was that of his officers directed against him. He maintained that he had surrendered primarily to save the lives of the people of Detroit. "It was a sense of what I owed to the protection of the inhabitants of the territory I had so long governed."[24] He admitted that the possibility of his daughter and her children falling victim to the tomahawks of the savages should the army fail did weigh upon him. He added that even had the army continued to resist, his chances of being reinforced and resupplied would gradually have diminished to nothing since the British controlled the waterway and were able to cut the overland trail to Ohio at will.

The Second Charge: Cowardice

The next charge brought against Hull was that of cowardice, to which four specifications were attached. The first accused him of retreating from Canada out of fear and the apprehension of danger. This specification will be addressed with Hull's defense to the fourth specification. The second specification was that Hull had registered great fear and apprehension of personal danger during the bombardment of Detroit on Saturday, August 15. The accusation hung entirely on the suppositions of the witnesses. Lieutenant Jessup, Hull's brigade major, for example, said that the general had passed on horseback late that afternoon and "he appeared to be agitated. Mr. Dougan or I observed that the general was frightened; and it was also observed by one of us (I do not recollect which) that 'we must cheer him up.' We approached him, and noticed that he was pale and very much confused."[25] Lieutenant Peckham told the court that he saw Hull frequently during the bombardment and "he appeared to me to be much agitated; and the impression made upon my mind was, that he was under the influence of personal fear."[26] On the other hand, Captain Maxwell and quartermaster general Taylor both reported that they had seen Hull several times during that day and did not notice anything that gave them the impression he was agitated or frightened. Maxwell said that he had paid close attention to Hull's appearance because he had heard rumors that the general was intimidated by the British cannonade.[27] Yet Hull and the rest of the army in reality had little to fear from the exchange of shellfire. Second Lieutenant Dalliba reported that the British fire was principally directed at the three American batteries, which were located at the river's edge; therefore, there was minimal risk of injury from the bombardment except from an errant shot in other areas of Detroit.[28]

The wording of the third specification regarding cowardliness accused Hull of showing "great fear and apprehension of personal danger" when the British landed at Spring Wells. More specifically, he made no effort to prevent the landing, raised a flag of truce to arrange for a capitulation, and ordered his artillery not to fire on the British column when it approached Detroit.

Witnesses made a point of describing Hull's demeanor as cowardly on the morning of the 16th. When the court asked Captain Whistler if Hull's appearance had led him to believe he was under the influence of personal fear, Whistler responded that it did.[29] Captain Fuller told the court that he had seen Hull several times before the surrender and in his judgment

Hull was frightened. Questioned by Hull as to whether his appearance might have had something to do with the anxiety of command, Fuller replied that he presumed so, but "I have no doubt of your appearance on that occasion [the 16th] being the effect of personal fear; I had none then, I have none now."[30] Captain John Eastman agreed. "The general's whole conduct, on the evening of the 15th and the morning of the 16th, was such as to impress the witness with the conviction that he was under the influence of personal fear."[31] Lieutenant Philips testified that he saw Hull sitting on a tent that lay on the ground behind the fort's parapet and "that he appeared to be very much agitated, and witness then supposed that he was under the impression of fear."[32]

The testimony of Captain Snelling has been the most often quoted by Hull's detractors as evidence of his cowardice on that fateful Sunday morning. According to Snelling, "I have always understood that the passion of fear is indicated by certain looks and actions; and, judging from past knowledge on the subject, I thought him under the impression of fear: his whole conduct made the impression on my mind at the time." He went on to describe how Hull "unconsciously filled his mouth with tobacco, putting in quid after quid, more than he generally did: the spittle coloured with tobacco juice ran from his mouth on his neckcloth, beard, cravat and vest." He added that Hull had selected the safest place in the fort for his seat, and that "his voice trembled when he spoke."[33] Quartermaster Taylor agreed, testifying that "witness saw the tobacco spittle which was rubbed over his face, and that he thinks General Hull was under the influence of personal fear"[34]

In responding, Hull pointed out that others had a different opinion. Miller acknowledged that Hull had a habit of chewing tobacco and without thinking would sometimes remove it from his mouth with his fingers, then replace it.[35] He could not say whether any agitation Hull may have felt on the 16th had to do with the weight of his responsibilities or from personal alarm. Lieutenant Bacon added that "General Hull appeared engaged as usual, and agitated more than usual, on the morning of the 16th, but [he] does not know the cause—he had no suspicion that it proceeded from personal fear; neither did he hear any officers at the time express an opinion that it did."[36] Bacon also testified that the cannon fire from the British guns was directed primarily at the American battery that was situated 200 yards in front of the fort, although one shot did hit inside the fort. It is difficult to believe, as some of the witnesses implied, that Hull spent the majority of his time on the 15th and 16th cowering inside the fort during a bombardment that was directed primarily at the southern edge of the town near the riverside.

Relative to the first and fourth specifications accusing Hull of abandoning Canada and surrendering, several witnesses were of the opinion that he did so out of fear. Captain McCormick recalled that when at mid-morning Colonel Findlay asked Hull why he and his regiment were being ordered into the fort, Hull replied "in a low trembling voice . . . that a surrender would be best—that he could procure better terms from General Brock at that time than if he waited a storm . . . that the general appeared much agitated, and in as great a fear that I ever saw in a person."[37] Lieutenant Jessup told the court that after the white flag had been raised, he met Hull in the fort and thought that he looked very frightened. He asked Hull if he was thinking of surrendering, suggesting that they could hold out at least until Cass and McArthur arrived, but Hull responded, "My God! What shall I do with these women and children!"[38] Captain Baker claimed that Hull looked embarrassed on the morning of the 16th and as if at a loss how to act. He could not testify how Hull may have felt at that time, "but could account for the surrender no other way than by supposing him under the influence of personal fear."[39] Major Van Horne offered that after Hull had called the officers together and informed them that he had surrendered the town and the fort and was arranging terms, "from his whole appearance, [Van Horne] was immediately impressed with the idea that he was under the influence of fear."[40] This begs the question of why Hull should still appear to be afraid of an enemy with whom he had just arranged a surrender.

Other witnesses had a contrary view of Hull's demeanor on the 15th and 16th. Major Munson testified that he "saw nothing in his conduct but what might be accounted for without recurring to personal fear."[41] Captain Dyson recalled that Hull had passed his battery on horseback several times on the morning of the 16th. "I perceived nothing unusual in his voice."[42] To this Lieutenant Colonel Joseph Watson of the Michigan militia added that when he saw Hull that morning, he "appeared perfectly tranquil and collected."[43]

It is obvious from this litany of contradictory testimony that the issue of whether Hull showed cowardice was dependent on the subjectivity of the witness and on his feelings about Hull's command. Regardless, none of the witnesses offered any hard evidence that Hull had vacated Canada or surrendered because of cowardice. As Hull frequently told the court, he surrendered not out of fear for his personal safety but out of fear of what the Indians might do to the people of Detroit if the army fought and lost.

Hull said that much had been made of his hiding within the fort during the British bombardment, giving the impression that he had remained in its shelter during the entire two-day cannonade. He pointed out that various witnesses had testified to seeing him out and about on horseback both days, and that virtually everyone had at one time or another taken shelter within the fort during the bombardment. Were they all guilty of cowardice or personal fear? His most telling response to the charge was "[t]hat there never has been, and in justice, never can be conviction under the charge of cowardice, but when a want of courage is indicated by the *omission* or *commission* of some act in violation of the duty of the person against whom the charge is made."[44] Even as he said these words he probably realized that no one was listening.

The Third Charge: Neglect of Duty and Unofficerlike Conduct

The final charge against Hull was that he had neglected his duty. To this charge there were seven specifications. The first was that he had failed to inspect, train, exercise, or review his troops between July 6 and August 17. Snelling, for one, claimed that Hull had never issued an order of march as the army proceeded to Detroit. Several witnesses said that he had never held a review of the troops, and Colonel Cass and others told the court that they could not recall seeing Hull discipline, review, or conduct maneuvers with the men when on the trail or at Detroit. In rebuttal Hull said that his order of march also was his order of battle, the same as that adopted by General Anthony Wayne the previous decade when marching through Indian country. When cross-examined by Hull, Lieutenant Jessup testified that the order of march generally was forwarded to him by Hull's aide-de-camp and he in turn communicated it to the rest of the regiments.[45] It vexed Hull that none of the officers of the regiments had seen fit to bring their orderly books to the trial, which would have substantiated Jessup's testimony.

As far as being accused of never having reviewed his troops, Hull maintained that it would have been ridiculous for him to halt the men as they were building the road simply to hold a military parade in the midst of a wilderness crawling with Indian tribes. "There was neither time nor opportunity for that sort of discipline and exercise, which under other circumstances, would have been proper."[46] Lieutenant Colonel Miller, a trained professional soldier, agreed. "At Urbana the troops were drilled part of an afternoon: from thence to Detroit there was no opportunity for disciplining them. The fatigue of cutting the road, with the march, was as much as they could endure."[47]

One can argue that perhaps Hull should have conducted a thorough battle-training program for the raw militia once they had arrived in Detroit. However, it also must be said the Ohio militiamen were in such a fever to attack Malden immediately that they would not have responded too favorably to an enforced military training program before invading Canada.

The second specification under this charge related to the capture of Hull's papers on the *Cuyahoga,* which was treated sufficiently above in the discussion of the charge of treason.

The third specification accused Hull of not making any effort to repair and strengthen Fort Detroit against attack. One questions why such an ill-founded accusation should ever have been made. As Hull pointed out, Second Lieutenant Dalliba of the Ordnance Department, who had been assigned to the fort in 1811, told the court that even then the fort was in good order. The cannon had been mounted and most of the embrasures repaired. He added that between July 4 and August 8 "the field artillery was put in good order and many improvements were made in the implements, gun carriages and ordnance stores, for the purpose of moving into Canada and attacking Malden. On the arrival of General Hull at Detroit, the greatest exertions were used to put the regiment in a state of defense."[48] Captain Dyson of the First Artillery echoed Dalliba's testimony. He said that three or four days after Hull arrived in Detroit he was told to "put in order, repair and mount the heavy artillery, and that he made use of all the means in his power that circumstances admitted of."[49] He added that the carriages for the howitzers had been broken in an experiment and new ones had to be made after the army crossed into Canada.

The fourth specification was that Hull had wasted so much time preparing the guns and gun carriages for operations in Canada that he ultimately was forced to recross the river and cancel any attack. It was a specious argument. Hull had no idea that once the army crossed the Detroit River it would be so difficult to transport the cannon to a point where they could fire on Fort Malden. He could not have foreseen that the road from Turkey Creek to the Canard River, a distance of five miles, was, according to his artillery officer, too marshy to carry the weight of the heavy guns, which meant an alternate means had to be devised to get them as far as the river. The best solution developed was to mount them on wooden platforms and float them down to the Canard River, then transfer them back to land for the march to Malden. The officers agreed to wait until the platforms were ready before going any further. Hull went back and forth across the river several times in an attempt to expedite the process; he even had planks taken off his own home for that purpose. Taylor overheard Hull "express his anxiety to have the heavy cannon prepared as fast as possible."[50]

As time passed the Ohio officers had difficulty curbing their impatience, some even willing to make an immediate attack without the guns. If it should come to that, Hull said, he would be there to lead them. As he was the only member of the army who had experienced the storming of an entrenched fort and seen the sacrifice in lives that was entailed, especially if heavy cannon were unavailable to breach the walls, he was reluctant to issue such an order without the support of cannon. Whether he could have succeeded even with artillery became moot when news from the north and from Niagara caused him to pull the army back across the river and call off the attack he had scheduled for August 8.

Turning to the fifth specification, the court charged that Hull had allowed the enemy to interrupt and cut off communications between Detroit and the Raisin River. That Hull should have been held responsible for the failure of three attempts to reach Captain Brush at Frenchtown between August 5 and August 16 only reveals the bias that the court had against him. For example, despite evidence to the contrary, McArthur and Cass blamed Hull for not providing Major Van Horne with sufficient troops in the first of these attempts. McArthur testified that he had argued with Hull that Van Horne's detachment had too few men and would ultimately be defeated. Yet Van Horne himself, even though privy to this alleged conversation, did not share their concerns. His orders were to form his detachment of 150 riflemen and those members of the Ohio militia who had refused to cross over into Canada. Hull also had given him permission to deviate from this head count if he thought it was necessary but Van Horne did not do so—not that it would have mattered since the entire detachment of 250 to 300 men was completely routed by only 24 Indians. Had his troops stood their ground, they in all probability would have been able to proceed to the Raisin River and Frenchtown.[51] Although the court had full knowledge of how the militia acted, it made no attempt to ask Van Horne to explain why the failure of his men to stand fast under fire should be attributed to Hull.

The court also accused Hull of failing to provide Miller with the nec-essary supplies to enable him to proceed further after the battle of Mon-guagon. In his defense Hull explained that he could not understand why Miller requested further rations inasmuch as the detachment had left De-troit with each soldier carrying two days' rations in his knapsack, enough food to last until he would reach the Raisin River. That the troops had cast aside their knapsacks at the onset of the battle was understandable, but Hull was not aware that Miller had made no attempt to retrieve them afterward. Miller told the court that he felt it was "imprudent" to return along the trail to do so, although it is not clear why this should have been so since the trail would have been open back to Detroit as well. Equally puzzling is why Miller, only one day's march from the Raisin, had made no effort to continue on even if short of rations, which he could easily have obtained from Captain Brush at Frenchtown. Also puzzling is why Miller did not send word to Brush to bring the pack train forward to his camp since the way was clear. Miller also requested a reinforcement of more men from Hull before proceeding. As Hull told the court in his defense, "It did appear to me not less than extraordinary, that when Colonel Miller advised me that when he had gained so decisive a victory, that he consid-ered his road to the river Raisin as opened; and that he had ascertained that there was no enemy between him and Brownstown—that he should, at the same time, have made a demand for a reinforcement of 150 or 200 men."[52]

Since Miller had made no move in either direction at the end of the third day and had not given Hull any indication of when he would resume his march, Hull, fearing that time was being wasted while the British might regroup for a counterattack, finally ordered Miller back to Detroit. Miller had the temerity to tell the court that he would have gone on to Frenchtown had Hull not ordered his recall. "Neither myself nor my men were in as good a situation as we had been in; but we were able to pro-ceed, and should have proceeded if we had not been ordered back."[53] Miller never gave Hull a good explanation for his prolonged stay at Mon-guagon. He never understood that his delay in continuing to Frenchtown precipitated his own recall.

Hull was further accused that because of the lack of provisions, the detachment commanded by McArthur and Cass was unable to reach Brush and fulfill its mission. In his defense Hull explained to the court that on the 14th, when he discovered the detachment had been waiting half a day to be issued its rations without informing him of the delay, he commanded it to move out, explaining that he would arrange for the necessary supplies to follow. He then had ordered Taylor to send the necessary rations by packhorses in the detachment's wake. Taylor claimed that he had done so, yet none ever reached the troops. No one on the court saw fit to ask Taylor why the detachment had been kept waiting for six hours without being furnished with the necessary rations, nor why McArthur failed to inform Hull of the problem. For the remainder of his life Hull believed that the delay was part of a conspiracy on the part of the Ohio colonels and others to take over his command, and that his ordering the detachment to connect with Captain Brush when he did may have disrupted their plans. As Hull told the court, "If General M'Arthur was on trial for misconduct in relation to these transactions I am pursuaded that his testimony ought rather convict him than me."[54]

Never convincingly answered during the trial was why McArthur and Cass failed to inform Hull that they were camped within two hours' march from Detroit in the early morning hours of the 16th. Had Hull known of their proximity he could well have altered his decision to surrender. As Willard Klunder, the able recent biographer of Lewis Cass, wrote, "Colonel Cass joined in the condemnation of Hull, but his own conduct deserves scrutiny. . . . No explanation was ever given by Cass to account for this [not reporting the detachment's whereabouts], although political supporters later postulated he and McArthur hoped to avoid being included in the surrender terms. This is an insufficient defense; Cass had no way of knowing Hull was about to capitulate." Klunder added, "In the heat of subsequent political campaign, Democratic apologists emphasized that Cass broke his father's sword rather than surrender it to the British. . . . If Cass did break his sword (and it is doubtful such an event took place), it was one of the few times in the entire campaign that he drew his weapon in anger." Klunder then put this matter to bed with the comment, "Cass's rage was directed at Hull, but his own actions directly contributed to the ignominious surrender of Detroit. And in a broader perspective, the loss of Detroit was due more to the manner in which the Madison administration conducted the war than to the faults of any individual."[55]

Under the sixth specification of neglect of duty, Cass told the court that he had sent two messages to Hull stating that it was the opinion of his officers that his detachment should retain possession of the Canard River bridge. When Hull's response was that he left the decision to their discretion, they then reversed their vote and favored abandoning it, seeing as it was only three miles from Malden but about 12 from the main army at Sandwich.[56] Quartermaster Taylor, who was with Hull when Cass's first message reached him regarding the capture of the bridge, reported "that the General was very much displeased and irritated at their conduct, and said he was surprised that gentlemen would attack the enemy at this time, when he had not his heavy artillery ready, that he had only sent them down for observation."[57]

In responding to this specification Hull argued that it would have been absurd for him to maintain a post that was so far in advance of the army unless it was with the intention of immediately attacking Fort Malden, which he was not as yet prepared to do. He reiterated that Cass's orders were to reconnoiter the ground between Sandwich and the Canard River, not precipitate armed action with the British forces.[58] To Cass's second request, Hull had written, "It will probably be a week before the cannon will be mounted. I am sensible of the advantage of holding the bridge. I would not, however, hazard too much for the purpose. The enemy may pass the ford [Canard] above and come in the rear. I will however leave to your discretion . . . to do what you judge most expedient."[59] Hull later came to believe that the bridge held little importance to the British, for repeated forays by scouting parties in the days to come found it lightly occupied. Ignored by the court was the fact that Cass had disobeyed his orders when attacking the British at the river, and that his actions should have warranted a court-martial. Hull had been reluctant to bring charges, however, realizing that the Ohio militia probably would be up in arms if he did so.

The final and last specification of all three charges was that Hull made no attempt to halt the British from erecting an artillery battery opposite Detroit, nor did he fortify the riverbank at Spring Wells in anticipation of a possible British landing at that spot should Brock decide to cross his army to the American side. Hull admitted that he had made an error in judgment when he did not attempt to stop the British from setting up their battery across from Detroit. He at first had believed their guns were meant for defensive purposes only and therefore would not constitute a threat. Later, after he had determined otherwise, he had to limit his own shelling of their emplacement because his artillery officers reported that the ammunition for the heavy guns was running low.[60]

As far as fortifying the banks of the river at Spring Wells against a threatened invasion, Hull told the court that had he done so the British would merely have selected another landing point. Also, the Indians had landed further downstream at the Huron River and he would not have been in a good position to cover both sites as the army already had been reduced considerably with McArthur and Cass not having reported their whereabouts. He said that even had he agreed to Snelling's request for a 24-pounder cannon and found some way to transport it to him, the *Queen Charlotte* would merely have moved to another position. However, he claimed that he did consider Snelling's request a possibility until his artillery officers told him that they did not believe the bridge between Detroit and Spring Wells could bear the weight of a heavy 24-pounder gun.[61]

Hull concluded his defense on Friday, March 18, 1814. Thus, after over a month of testimony, the trial came to an end. Six days later General Dearborn gave a lengthy reply to Hull's impassioned defense, after which the court adjourned. On Friday morning, March 25, it met to deliver its verdict. It acquitted Hull of the charge of treason, which probably was no surprise since there was not a shred of evidence to indict him on this count. The real question was why it should have been brought against him in the first place.

However, the court found him guilty of cowardice on the following counts:

1. Retreating from Canada without plausible cause;
2. Displaying great fear during the bombardment of Detroit;
3. Surrendering Detroit out of fear for his personal safety.

Regarding the charge of neglect of duty, the court judged him guilty of:

1. Failing to discipline his troops;
2. Neglecting to ensure the guns and gun carriages were in proper order;
3. Allowing the British to disrupt his communications with Ohio;
4. Failing to secure the Canard River bridge;
5. Failing to prevent Brock from landing at Spring Wells and failing to prevent the British from setting up their artillery across from Detroit.[62]

Hull had asked for a fair trial. Reading the trial transcript and noting the court's irregularities, it is extremely difficult to believe that he received one. The verdict suggests that his own testimony usually was ignored while that of the Ohio militia officers, not delivered under oath, was accepted as fact against him. Curious also is the fact that the administration had promoted each of the leading witnesses against Hull just prior to the trial. Both McArthur and Cass received commissions as brigadier generals in the regular army. Captain Snelling became a major, Major Van Horne a lieutenant colonel, Lieutenant Jessup a major, and Captain Eastman a lieutenant. None had accomplished anything that would warrant their promotions. In a letter dated January 31, 1813, only five months after the surrender, Cass had written to Senator Thomas Worthington, "Perhaps I have no right to expect it, but I must confess, if a Brigadier General is to be appointed in this state [Ohio], I should be most happy to receive the appointment."[63]

Hull thought it was ironic that the officers who had served him so poorly had merited promotion soon after the surrender. "I must say that it appears to me my expedition was more prolific of promotions than any other unsuccessful military enterprise I ever heard of."[64]

On Saturday morning, March 26, 1814, the court convened one last time to announce its sentence.

> The court in consequence of their determination respecting the second and third charges and the specifications under those charges, exhibited against the said Brigadier General William Hull—and after due consideration, do sentence him to be shot to death, two-thirds of the court concurring on the sentence.
>
> The court in consideration of Brigadier General Hull's revolutionary services, and his advanced age, earnestly recommend him to the mercy of the President of the United States.[65]

One month later, after Hull was told to go back home and wait to hear further, President Madison commuted the court's sentence of execution. Nevertheless, he did approve the findings of the court. On the very next day, April 25, 1814, the adjutant and inspector general's office issued the following General Orders: "The roll of the army is not to be longer dishonored by having upon it the name of Brig.-Gen. William Hull. The General Court Martial of which Major General Dearborn is President is hereby dissolved. By order: J. B. Walbach, Adjutant General."[66] The adjutant general had no authority to issue these General Orders, and none ever were issued by the president, the War Department, or the court-martial board.

That a sentence of execution could have been pronounced on the basis of whether Hull's appearance seemed fearful or in the belief that untrained militia had more expertise on the leading of an army than its commanding general is egregious. The trial was devoid of any hard evidence to support the verdict and such an extreme sentence. The legal irregularities under which the trial was conducted alone hint of a preordained outcome. Hull himself believed that the court sentenced him to be shot primarily to humiliate him, knowing in advance that the president would remit the sentence.[67]

Many years later, Major General "Fighting Joe" Wheeler of Civil War cavalry fame, who had married Hull's daughter, Julia, took it upon himself to examine the War Department archives regarding the Detroit campaign and visit the Detroit area to seek out any other information he could. Wheeler, who became a historian after his retirement from the army, came to the conclusion that although Hull had made errors in judgment, the charges leveled against him by the court and by his personal enemies were exceedingly unfair. He considered the court-martial itself to be "an outstanding bit of legal perfidy."[68]

WAS HULL'S SURRENDER JUSTIFIED?

Given the circumstances that Hull faced in conducting the Detroit campaign, his surrender should have been foreseen. William Henry Harrison had made that very prediction to the secretary of war, but the administration was too enamored with the conviction that Canada could be captured easily. Initially it seemed that would be the case—Hull's march to Detroit in very difficult conditions had been conducted so effectively and efficiently that it held promise for an early victory. Perhaps that is why the news of the surrender came as such a shock to the nation and the condemnation of Hull grew so bitter.

Yet consider the conditions in which Hull found himself conducting his campaign, conditions not normally faced by military commanders: an extremely difficult supply transportation problem exacerbated by the British control of the river and lake, a fort that was inextricably nested within a town and burdened with the defense of a civilian population, an Indian threat that was a physical as well as a psychological menace, and junior officers who disputed virtually every command he issued.

Hull's fear of not being provided with sufficient supplies to weather a campaign was justified. The War Department lacked the organization to forward the necessary food, medical supplies, and arms once Hull arrived in Detroit. The contractor it had selected to arrange for the supplies never followed through, forcing Hull to make his own piecemeal arrangements. Simply providing sufficient rations to maintain an army of 1,500 to 2,000 men in a country chronically short of food was no small matter.

Not being able to transport supplies to Hull by water created enormous difficulty for his Ohio contractor. It forced him to move them down

200 miles of wilderness trail by pack train, which at any point could be assaulted and captured by roving Indian bands unless it were heavily guarded. Historians who fail to recognize negative impact this had on the campaign do Hull a disservice. The actions of British Brigadier General Procter, for example, testify to the vital importance of controlling the waterways in supplying the Detroit area: when Commodore Perry took command of Lake Erie and shut down the shipment of supplies from Niagara to his command by water, Procter immediately abandoned Fort Malden. Nor was the urgency of maintaining a reliable supply system lost on General Harrison when he was given the responsibility of recapturing Detroit in the fall of 1812. Understanding the difficulty of being forced to maintain a supply route by land once his army was in motion, he set about setting up supply depots along his intended line of march. No doubt from experience, he was aware that the maximum distance that a wagon train could be extended from its base was about 90 miles, or six to seven days' travel time if road conditions were good. Without such depots a supply train could travel nor more than about 135 miles without having to carry food for its animals as well as for the troops.[1] Harrison further pointed out to Secretary of War Eustis at the outset of his campaign that it would take an army twice the size of the British force at Malden to hold Fort Detroit, and another equal to its size to guard the 200-mile overland supply route from Ohio against Indian and British attack.[2] Hull had none of the resources Harrison considered requisite at his disposal; therefore, it is conceivable that the shortage of food would have forced his surrender not too long after the British besieged the fort—but only after untold military and civilian casualties had been suffered.

Fort Detroit itself was an anomaly. It was originally designed to withstand Indian attacks by land and to protect the citizens of Detroit from them, which is why the town's homes and other buildings were located between the south side of the fort and the river. But in that position they obstructed the fire from the fort's guns. In fact, those structures that had been built along Main Street (Jefferson Avenue) sat on a rise that placed them in jeopardy of being struck by the fort's own guns. Even had the buildings been torn down to give the fort's cannon a clear range of fire over the river into Canada, the guns' effectiveness would have been questionable. Although capable of launching a cannonball 2,000 yards, a 24-pounder cannon was unlikely to hit a target at a distance farther than 200 yards, which was the distance between the fort and the river.[3] For this reason among others, three 24-pounder gun emplacements had been constructed at the river's edge so that their fire could reach the British across the river; however, in these locations they could easily have been overrun and captured had the British laid siege to Detroit.

Another factor not to be overlooked is the presence of the civilian population—ensuring the safety of noncombatants was a high priority to Hull as military commander. The Ohio militia officers operated under no such constraints; they had no ties to the community, and in fact they held the civilians, because of their French descent, in disdain. At no point in their journals or in their testimony do they express an interest in their defense. This was not true of Hull, whose own daughter and grandchildren were part of the civilian population. Brock, commanding on the other side of the river, had no such concerns for the Canadian civilian population. With the Indians pledged to his support, he knew that a massacre of the men, women, and children living in Amherstburg or Sandwich was not likely should his army be defeated, and he knew that Hull would have treated them with compassion. While one can argue that the duty of a military commander is to win a battle regardless of potential danger to the citizenry, it must be remembered that Hull was also governor of the territory; he, unlike the Ohio colonels, had two conflicting duties to reconcile.

Hull's fear of a civilian massacre should his troops be defeated was not groundless speculation. Nor was such apprehension lessened by consideration of the role that Indian tribes might play in the conflict. The American and British governments took very different tacks regarding Indian involvement in warfare. American government policy called for Indian tribes to be persuaded to remain neutral, while on the British side, the governmental decision had already been made to enlist their services in military campaigns. Members of the House of Lords had debated the question as far back as 1777, at which time one of its members justified the employment of Indians in warfare with the argument that the British had the right to use those means that God and Nature had given them. Despite strong objections by William Pitt and an appeal to the sensibility of the bishops who sat on the bench, the vote was overwhelming in support of employing savages in war against the Americans.[4] The Indian tribes, for their part, inevitably chose the British over the Americans since the former were lavish in supplying them with guns and food when doing so served British goals. For example, Harrison was cognizant of the British policy of sanctioning Indian attacks on innocent settlers during wartime. In a letter he wrote to Major General John Vincent late in 1813, he cited three instances in which Indian war parties from Fort Malden had attacked American families on U.S. soil. Those men, women, and children they did spare often were taken back to Malden as prisoners, even though they were not involved in any military actions. In no uncertain terms Harrison urged Vincent to stop the operation of small Indian parties crossing over from Canada.[5]

In his letter to the secretary of war after the surrender (see appendix 4), Hull wrote that fighting Brock in the open or undergoing a siege within Fort Detroit without adequate supplies were not viable options. The only solution was to surrender—an option that he feared, but for which he had no other alternative:

> I have dared to adopt it—I well know the high responsibility of the measure, and I take the whole of it on myself. It was dictated by a sense of duty, and a full conviction of its expediency. The bands of savages which had then joined the British force, were numerous beyond any former example. Their numbers since have increased, and the history of the barbarians of the north of Europe does not furnish examples of more greedy violence than these savages have exhibited. A large portion of the brave and gallant officers and men I commanded would cheerfully have contested until the last cartridge had been expended, and the bayonets worn down to the sockets. I could not consent to the useless sacrifice of such brave men, when I knew it was impossible for me to sustain my situation.[6]

Hull could not have anticipated the continual challenges the three Ohio volunteer regimental heads made to his authority. He simply was unable to establish a rapport either with them or with their men. They resented him because he was an easterner, and therefore not one of them. More significantly, they had joined the volunteers for political purposes as well as patriotism. Each had raised a volunteer regiment and been awarded its command by Governor Meigs. Their expectations were that the Detroit campaign would be successful and therefore give a substantial boost to their future political aspirations. To protect themselves, whenever a failure in operation occurred, they did not hesitate to shift the responsibility to Hull. For example, after Cass had disobeyed orders and captured the bridge over the Canard River, he requested permission to hold it while Hull brought the rest of the army to that point. When Hull replied that Cass and his officers should make the decision since they were on the scene, they not only refused to do so but were indignant that

Hull placed the responsibility in their hands. It meant that if the British returned and recaptured the bridge, the failure would have been attributed to them, not Hull.

The volunteers lacked any sense of discipline, despite their fiery ardor. Hull never knew what to expect of them and came to distrust them. For example, despite their bravado, the militia volunteers did not fare very well in the skirmish at Brownstown, when Van Horne led them down the trail to rescue the supply train at Frenchtown. They fled at the first sound of gunfire, although their attackers were a grossly inferior force. On the other hand, Miller's engagement at Monguagon proved that they could fight well when bolstered by Miller's regiment of regulars, who refused to give ground when they came under attack. Such inconsistency made it extremely difficult, if not impossible, to develop a strategy for military success.

Hull's command problems suffered further from the command structure he had inherited. The three Ohio colonels were adamant in their belief that they outranked Lieutenant Colonel Miller, even though they had absolutely no military experience to warrant their ranks. This did not sit very well with Miller, a veteran of the battle of Tippecanoe. It created an awkward situation for Hull, who often was forced to give command responsibilities to the Ohio colonels rather than the much more capable and experienced Miller. It also led to Miller's reluctance to take the lead in developing attack strategy, depriving Hull of the one person whose advice he valued in military matters.

Despite these many obstacles Hull encountered in his leadership, he has been reviled, not only by his contemporaries but by historians through the years, for not achieving the victory that fell to his successor, General William Henry Harrison. Harrison has been described as being everything that Hull was not: forceful, aggressive, and in complete command of his troops when he formed the North Western Army to recapture Detroit. In his study comparing Hull's Detroit campaign with Harrison's, Steven Rauch maintains that Hull has been unfairly judged. He points out that prior to Perry's victory over the British fleet on Lake Erie, Harrison's own overland campaign had come to a virtual standstill. His subsequent victory over Procter at the Thames River, though laudable, was a direct result of Perry's success in taking command of the lake, thus forcing Procter to abandon Fort Malden and flee eastward. Given the same circumstances, Hull probably would have achieved a similar success. "Hull had assumed command at a time when Washington was overly optimistic about the chances of success; Harrison assumed command in an atmosphere of disbelief and shock at Hull's surrender. Hence Harrison was determined to take every precaution to avoid another defeat. It would be difficult to equal Hull's disaster, but Harrison came close on a number of occasions. The two generals' military performances were much more similar than historians have noted in the past."[7]

In reality, the conditions Harrison faced at the outset of his campaign were scarcely different than those Hull encountered. Neither, for example, had much of a staff to aid them with the decisions they had to make regarding personnel, intelligence, operations, or logistics. As a result, they were personally involved in responsibilities that more properly belonged to a staff officer.

They also were forced to rely upon subordinates who lacked the experience and skills necessary to provide them with sound advice or even assure them that their orders had been followed. The need to rely on unreliable subordinates led to significant setbacks to both generals, Harrison by the defeat and capture of General Winchester at Frenchtown, and Hull by the failure of both Van Horne and Miller to reach Hull's supply train. Hull in particular suffered from challenges to his authority made by officers who had no military experience—nor did he have confidence that orders to them would be obeyed. He lacked the luxury of being able to replace them, a luxury that Harrison, in command of a substantially larger body of troops, had at his disposal, permitting him to replace a poorly performing subordinate with one who was more capable.[8] However, while this argument is persuasive, it does not absolve Hull of the charge of not trying harder to take his officers into his confidence.

Both generals had to answer to a War Department that lacked the professionalism necessary to conduct a war. Secretary Eustis never quite understood the value of supporting Hull's campaign in the West along with parallel action by Dearborn on the eastern frontier. His late-arriving dispatch notifying Hull of the declaration of war and his refusal to correct the disparity in rank between Lieutenant Colonel Miller and the Ohio colonels also gave Hull serious problems. The Ohio men informed Hull that if he attempted to reduce their rank to that of lieutenant colonel, the same as Miller, they would disband their regiments and return to Ohio. Hull never should have accepted Eustis's decision regarding Miller's rank; he should have insisted that Miller be named his second in command, with a rank commensurate with that position. Most galling to Hull was the fact that by continually debating his decisions, the Ohio colonels

William Henry Harrison. (Courtesy of the Burton Historical Collection, Detroit Public Library.)

acted as if they knew more about strategy and fighting than did their commanding general.[9]

The War Department's lack of leadership had a profound influence on Hull, who was never certain what was expected of his army, especially in defining his dual responsibilities in the military and civilian spheres, as general and as governor of the territory. Hull naturally expected Eustis to provide him with the help he needed and the necessary orders to conduct his campaign. Eustis did very little of either. After Hull's surrender, when Harrison took command of a new North Western Army, he recognized the War Department's weak leadership and took complete control of requisitioning men and supplies for his forthcoming campaign, although this situation changed when the strong-willed John Armstrong replaced Eustis as secretary of war and asserted extensive control over military operations. When Harrison complained that bad weather hampered his attempts to reach Detroit, Armstrong ordered him to disband most of his volunteers and call off the winter campaign. Harrison continually chafed under Armstrong's attempts to manage his part of the war.

Unlike Hull, Harrison placed great faith in his volunteers; that is, in his Kentucky volunteers, with whom he was comfortable and who had his trust. He was not particularly fond of the Ohio volunteers, whom he considered too independent to be relied upon, an outlook shared by Hull, except that Hull had no other troops upon whom he could depend other than his regiment of regulars.

The most challenging problem that both generals faced was providing their armies with food and military essentials like ammunition and clothing over a prolonged period. Without command of Lake Erie, both had to rely on wagon trains or packhorses to transport supplies. If the trail was firm, wagons were preferred because each was capable of carrying 1,500 pounds. If the trail turned muddy the army had to resort to packhorses, whose load-carrying capacity was limited to 150 to 200 pounds each. A good part of the supplies consisted of forage for the animals pulling the wagons in order that they might maintain the strength to continue. To travel a distance of 135 miles, for example, each wagon had to carry more forage than supplies; otherwise the animals would break down.[10]

Considering that Detroit was 200 miles from its supply base at Urbana, the acquisition of supplies for Hull's troops was a major operation. When his army marched to Detroit, for example, 300 head of cattle accompanied it, along with 120 teams of horses carrying 14,000 pounds of flour and a large amount of forage to feed the horses each day.[11] When his troops arrived in Detroit after one month on the trail, Hull reported that he had enough flour left to last two months and sufficient meat for one. By August 16 his need for more supplies had become critical, which was why he placed so much emphasis on sending troops to Frenchtown to convoy the waiting supply train to Detroit.[12]

Harrison, on the other hand, not having been instructed by the the War Department to march to Detroit immediately, as Hull had been, was able to take whatever time was necessary to prepare his army for a similar march, and he planned three separate routes over which to supply his army once it arrived at the Rapids on the Maumee River. Despite his caution, his army still faced serious supply problems. General Winchester, in charge of Harrison's main force, which reached Fort Defiance late in September 1812, was the first to suffer from unanticipated difficulties. For over three months the troops camped at Defiance, awaiting winter clothing and other supplies. By December 10 they were completely out of flour because the incessant rains prevented even packhorses from reaching them. Winter clothing finally arrived—not from the government but from the women of Ohio, who made clothing in their homes for shipment to the troops. On December 30, when finally ordered to leave Fort Defiance and march the 40 miles to the Falls of the Maumee, the troops were so weak that it took them 11 days to cover what should have been a three-day journey.[13] In this area Harrison's advantage over Hull lay in the fact that it was unnecessary for him to detach a large number of troops from his army simply to protect his supply route as he moved away from his home base.

Comparing Hull's campaign to Harrison's (excluding the latter's success created by Perry's victory), Rauch came to the conclusion that Hull made more headway against the British (prior to the surrender) than did Harrison with a force between three to five times the size of Hull's army. Harrison's troops never succeeded in reaching Detroit via the overland route through Michigan along the river. By contrast, Hull advanced from Ohio to Detroit in slightly over one month with a much inferior force that had to create its own road through the wilderness.

Hull's image has been clouded because he surrendered without a fight, but his march to Detroit indicates that he was not the fearful, incompetent general that some historians have accused him of being, and that he "conducted his campaign as efficiently as any commander, including Harrison, could have done."[14] If Hull exhibited any fault in his campaign, it was in not storming Fort Malden when his army first invaded

Canada. The British were still in the process of preparing their defense and acquiring more troops. Even so, Hull's chances of success in attacking an entrenched fort without the assistance of heavy guns would by no means have been assured, especially considering the Ohio volunteers' poor performance when they did meet the enemy later.

In reply to critics who maintain that Hull should have made a stand at Fort Detroit and not surrendered to Brock, Rauch concluded that "the forces Hull had available were clearly inferior to the enemy in both quantity and overall military condition. If a battle had occurred I believe that it would have been a bloody defeat for the U.S. with a cost in lives perhaps equal to those of Frenchtown and Ft. Meigs."[15]

Rauch's assessment stands in direct contradiction to many others, including those of some who were at the scene, such as Robert Lucas, who in his journal wrote that Hull surrendered his army "to an inferior force of an inferior quality, without their being allowed the liberty of firing a gun in their own defense."[16] Recent military historians, however, tend to agree with Rauch. Elting, for example, believes that Hull could have repulsed Brock's assault but that "he would have been eventually starved and bombarded into surrender, with great loss of life among citizens in Detroit."[17] Quimby echoes Rauch and Elting: "Even if he [Hull] could have repelled Brock's assaults, he could not have withstood a siege for more than two weeks . . . and even if a first assault was repulsed, a second would be quite likely to succeed." He adds, "Hull had good reason to know what would happen to them at the hands of the Indians."[18]

Despite these observations, several historians, as indicated in the preface, continue to ignore the reality of Hull's situation in Detroit. They prefer to base their conclusions on the unreliable testimony of his Ohio officers, who characterized him as a coward unfit for command, a man who betrayed his country and his men by ignoble surrender. But whether those Ohio officers realized it or not, that surrender, I believe, most probably allowed them to live to see another day.

DETROIT UNDER BRITISH RULE,
1812–14

While Hull may have saved Detroit from a massacre of its civilians, the situation after the surrender remained grim. On the very next day following the surrender, August 17, General Brock left Detroit on board the schooner *Chippewa* bound for Niagara. He was anxious to return to the eastern theater of the war in case the truce negotiated with Dearborn had been rescinded during his absence. (This did not occur until September 5.)[1] Before he sailed he placed all military and civilian responsibilities for the now British-held Territory of Michigan into the hands of Colonel Henry Procter. When Procter asked him what he should do about Fort Detroit, whether it should be evacuated or destroyed, Brock told him to leave it intact and provide it with a garrison—otherwise, he believed, the people of the town would be vulnerable to massacre by the Indians.[2]

Procter considered Detroit to be a nuisance to his command, as it involved the care of the civilian population. Strategically Fort Detroit meant very little to him, as his base of operations was Fort Malden and he saw no reason for change. Consequently he stripped Detroit of all its military supplies, which he transferred to Malden. As far as the citizens of Detroit were concerned, he expected them to return to their previous way of life—but according to British rule. Although he did not demand that they pledge allegiance to England, he did issue a proclamation setting the parameters for a civil government, which he distributed on the Friday following the surrender, August 21. In it wrote that the American laws that had governed Detroit before the surrender would still be in force until he heard otherwise from his own government, and that he would be acting as civil governor of the territory. He added that the courts would be open as usual. He was astute enough to ask former justice Augustus B. Woodward's advice on what land made up the Territory of Michigan and how the territory's government was constituted. He then issued a "Regulation for the Civil Government of the Territory of Michigan."[3]

Procter appointed Woodward as his secretary, which meant that the latter would have the power to rule in his place, acting as lieutenant governor when Procter was out of the territory.[4] Woodward realized that Procter had no intention of becoming involved in the day-to-day governance of the territory; that would be left to him as secretary. Procter's selection of Woodward for this office was natural, for he was the only former U.S. territorial official still in Detroit. Gone were Governor Hull, who had been sent east as a prisoner of war, Justice John Griffin, who had left Michigan before the war began, and Justice James Witherell, also head of the Michigan Detached Militia, who had been taken prisoner. When placed on parole Witherell had left the territory as well. Woodward had been inclined to follow them after the surrender but then decided that Detroit's citizens could use what leadership he was able to provide against British incursions on their lives and property.

He filled this role admirably, but not as Procter's secretary, having refused the appointment. He was concerned that if he accepted the position, it could be construed as an act of treason against his own government, even though he would have done so for humanitarian reasons. Procter than attempted to force matters by issuing another proclamation calling for the Michigan Supreme Court to assemble on the third Monday in December at the home of George Meldrum. Since Woodward had been the chief justice, Procter assumed that he would continue in this office. When Woodward refused, Procter moved the court date to February 21, 1813, so that he would have ample time to persuade Woodward to resume his position on the bench.

To remove himself from the pressure that Procter was applying, Woodward told him that the Constitution of the United States forbade him to accept any office, honor, or pay from a foreign country. Procter allowed Woodward to write a letter to Washington explaining his dilemma and requesting instructions. He addressed the letter to the secretary of the treasury, Albert Gallatin, and Procter had it passed through the British lines. In the letter Woodward explained that Procter desired him to act as secretary for the territory, which meant that he would be in charge of the civil affairs of Detroit but under British rule. He asked what, under the circumstances, the government wished his role to be. He also explained

Augustus Woodward, judge, Michigan territory. (Courtesy of the Burton Historical Collection, Detroit Public Library.)

that he felt it was his duty to remain in Detroit "to intercede for my suffering countrymen; to save their lives, their persons, from the victorious
and insulting savages; to preserve the remnants of their little properties
from pillage; to aid, in the means of departing, those who will go to find
the standard of their country where her power is yet readministered, and
her glory untarnished, and to uphold and comfort those whom stern necessity compels, or hardier resolution prompts, to bear the full fury of the
storm."[5]

Gallatin never replied. Woodward's concerns over how Washington
would view his actions in Detroit notwithstanding, he continued to do
what he thought best for its citizens in an unofficial capacity. He performed services as a private citizen, not acting in any way on behalf of the
British government. He continued to refuse Procter's invitation to serve
as secretary of the territory and made no attempt to resume his duties as
chief justice, never holding a single session of court as long as the British
were in control of Detroit.

He also did what he could on behalf of the men, women, and children
who had been captured by the Indians. Not long after the Fort Dearborn
massacre, the Indians brought those who had survived to Detroit and
paraded them though the streets, offering to spare their lives for a stiff
ransom. They made a show of scalps they had already taken to demon-
strate the captives' fate if ransom was not forthcoming. Woodward formed
a relief organization to raise money to meet the ransom demands, realizing
that otherwise the Indians would return to their villages, where many of
the captives would be tortured and/or put to death. The British made no
effort to intervene. Their official position was not to interfere with the
Indians' actions to avoid offending the tribes, their allies in a war still being fought.[6] Captives not ransomed were sometimes removed to Indian
encampments far to the west. Robert Dickson, the British Indian agent
for the remoter British territories, tells of liberating 17 American soldiers,
four women, and several children whom he had discovered among the
Indians on the western side of Lake Michigan.[7]

Raising money to ransom captives was only one of many difficulties
that faced Detroit citizens during this turbulent time. Acquiring sufficient
food to feed the population became an even greater challenge than before
the war as people living on surrounding farms fled to town to escape the
hostility of the Indians, who engaged in unbridled plunder of their property. Because of the attack on Detroit before the surrender, members of
the Michigan militia, most of whom were local farmers, were not able to

work their farms, through no choice of their own. Abnormally high rainfall had rotted the crops left in the field. The fall wheat harvest produced only half a normal year's yield and the yield of Indian corn and potatoes was only a quarter of the usual amount. Meat supplies were scarce as well because the Indians continued to pilfer or kill what livestock still remained.[8]

Antoine Dequindre's experience is a perfect example of what Detroit citizens had to endure. On one occasion two Indians entered his store, snatched up a roll of cloth, and began to leave without paying. Dequindre leaped over his counter, snatched the cloth out of their hands, and forced them out of the building. The Indians reacted by yelling out their war cry. Anticipating trouble, Dequindre locked the door of the store and ran to the fort for protection. A horde of Indians surrounded the building, breaking down the front door and smashing windows. The British garrison told Dequindre that there was nothing it could do to help. Hearing the commotion, Colonel McKee, the British Indian agent, had the presence of mind to impound several barrels of whiskey. He placed them on the ground in the common before the fort and invited the Indians to join him in a drink. Soon all were too inebriated to concern themselves any longer with Dequindre's store. McKee appointed those who were still reasonably sober to sit on the doorsteps of nearby homes to prevent any further harassment.[9]

On another occasion the townspeople were surprised to hear loud shouting as an Indian war party entered Detroit sporting a woman's scalp on a pole and herding along nine white children. One Detroiter, J. E. Hunt, went out to meet the children, took them to his home, and fed them. He promised that he would ransom them the next day, which he and his brothers did for the sum of $500, a truly magnanimous bit of charity considering the dollar value of that era.[10]

The Indians had even become brazen enough to steal the pipes of the organ in St. Anne's Catholic Church. They marched through the town blowing on them as if they were horns, creating a noisy din they did not cease until informed that the tubes belonged to the Great Spirit, whom they had angered with their racket. A short time later the pipes were found back in the church where they belonged.[11]

By early January 1813, still not having heard from Secretary Gallatin regarding his responsibilities in an American city under British rule, Woodward decided that it would be best if he left the territory to remove himself from a potentially compromising situation with Procter. When word of his decision reached the citizens of Detroit, they drew up a memorial, signed by 30 French and Americans, thanking him for his efforts on their behalf. It read: "We feel it a duty incumbent on us to acknowledge that your stay in the country since the Capitulation, together with your exertions in favor of its inhabitants, has contributed in an eminent degree towards the preservation of their lives, their liberty, and the property of perhaps every individual in the Territory."[12]

Woodward was so touched by the memorial he changed his mind about leaving. In a letter he wrote to Secretary of State James Monroe he explained that, not having received any specific instructions from the administration to the contrary, he thought it best to stay and provide what help he could to the citizens of Detroit.[13]

It was good that he did. His services soon would be needed as a result of events that would develop at Frenchtown 35 miles to the north. The man who precipitated these events was General William Henry Harrison, who in September 1812 was appointed major general commanding the North Western Army of the United States, charged with the primary purpose of recapturing Detroit. Immediately after his appointment Harrison began to gather a large strike force of over 6,000 men, consisting of 1,500 militiamen from Pennsylvania, 1,500 from Virginia, 2,000 from Kentucky, and 1,200 from Ohio. He selected the Rapids of the Maumee River (Perrysburg, Ohio), about 10 miles from where the river empties into Lake Erie, as their gathering place.

Before an army of this size could become operational, Harrison had to accumulate a huge stock of provisions, food as well as winter clothing. Harrison did not intend to find himself in the same position as Hull when it came to supplying his troops.[14] Not having command of the waterways over which to carry his supplies once he reached the Michigan border, he was faced with the necessity of using wagons or pack animals, an extra burden since animals had to carry their own feed as well as food for the troops. The difficulty of supplying an army on the frontier the size of Harrison's cannot be exaggerated. A good example is the exhausting experience of assistant quartermaster Joseph Wheaton in his attempt to reach Harrison's forward supply base in Upper Sandusky. On November 22, 1812, Wheaton left Pittsburgh on his 250-mile trek with a train of 37 wagons, eight gun carriages, and 304 horses. Because of rain, snow, hail, poor roads, bad bridges, and difficult river crossings, the convoy was able to travel only six miles each day. On December 8 Wheaton reached Canton, Ohio, where the train was forced to remain for one week as eight blacksmiths and four wagon masters repaired the wagons and scoured the neighborhood for forage for the animals. Fourteen miles on, the train ran out of road and the Pennsylvania militia went to work cutting a new 12-mile road through the wilderness to Wooster, where the train rested for a day. By December 27, 36 days since leaving Pittsburgh, Wheaton's supply train reached Mansfield, Ohio, where it collected animals and stores that had previously been left for it in small forward depots. By this time his train consisted of 690 horses and 15 oxen, which added to the supply burden since one-third of the supplies carried by the horses was their own forage so that they could endure the distance of the march. The 36-day trip was all the more remarkable because previous trains had averaged 62 days. Wheaton finally reached Harrison's base the following week.[15]

By mid-October Harrison's state militia groups still had not arrived in camp. Then it began to rain. It rained all through the remainder of October and on into November. Streams that had to be crossed had overrun their banks; roads became a quagmire that submerged wagon wheels. It seemed as if the entire landmass of upper Ohio was underwater. The march of the state militias toward the Rapids soon turned into a nightmare.[16]

Harrison wrote Eustis on December 12 that he would have to delay the movement of his army toward Detroit until the winter when the ground had firmed up. Once that occurred he believed that it would take only six days to proceed from the Rapids to a point opposite Fort Malden. If the river were frozen the troops would cross over on the ice and attack Malden before proceeding to Detroit. If not, and the odds were in favor of this being the case, there would be a delay as he gathered boats from the settlers along the river and built what more were needed to ferry the men over to the Canadian side. In that scenario he would not be able to mount an attack on Malden until late February or March.[17]

Harrison had already made it clear to Eustis that he had no intention of proceeding to Detroit without first capturing Fort Malden. He wrote Eustis that should he attempt to rescue Detroit first, he would need an army twice the size of the opposing British force at Fort Malden to retain it while at the same time fending off counterattacks by the British to sever his supply line to Ohio. He offered to proceed with a winter campaign only if the administration insisted that he do so, but he preferred that the government first attempt to take control of Lake Erie. Once this had been accomplished he expected the capture of Fort Malden, Fort Detroit, and Fort Mackinac to be foregone conclusions.[18]

Washington, however, now intruded upon his plans. Secretary of War Eustis had resigned on December 3. His temporary replacement, James Monroe, wrote Harrison that the expense of feeding an army that would do no more than sit in camp for the next several months created a problem. Moreover, the wait would exhaust the militia members' six-month terms of enlistment, which would terminate in February before they had experienced any action. He suggested that Harrison dismiss as many of the militia troops as possible, then recall them when he was ready to march.[19] Harrison agreed, but the weather unexpectedly improved. He decided to proceed with his original plans before the volunteer enlistments expired. On December 30 he ordered General Winchester, whose troops were camped on the Auglaize River a mile from where it joined the Maumee, to take his army to the Rapids. There he was to construct an armed post to serve as a launching place for the entire army as it gathered for its march into Michigan. He wrote Winchester that he expected the rest of the states' volunteers to reach the Rapids by January 20, 1814.[20]

Winchester was only too happy to oblige. He and his army had been camping at Fort Defiance for the past 10 weeks waiting for marching orders. The weather had wreaked havoc on the delivery of their supplies. Discipline had weakened. Especially exasperating was their lack of winter clothing. Even firewood had become a problem since the troops had been in the same camp for so long they had cleared out the adjacent forests. Winter clothing and shoes finally reached them, encouraging Winchester to give the order to march on December 29, though the troops had to march through two feet of snow. Eighteen hundred strong, they reached the Rapids on January 8 and immediately began constructing the post Harrison had ordered, which they named Fort Deposit.

Their work was interrupted on January 13 when Winchester received a letter from one Isaac Day, a civilian in Frenchtown. Day claimed that he had hidden away 50 barrels of flour and 200 bushels of wheat, and that he thought there were another 3,000 barrels of flour and other supplies hidden in the village. There also was a rumor that the British were planning to evict the villagers now that the Americans were within a few days' march. Only 40 to 50 British and 100 Indians stood guard—Frenchtown could be taken if Winchester moved quickly enough.[21]

Frenchtown at this time consisted of 33 families. Several of their homes were grouped behind a picket fence with one open side that faced the river. All told, there were about 120 families strung out along a 12-mile stretch of the Raisin River.[22] Although Harrison had warned Winchester against taking any overt action against the British until he arrived at the Rapids, Winchester's volunteer officers voted to move immediately to the village's rescue. The one senior regular officer present, Colonel Wells, who commanded the 17th U.S. Infantry, opposed the move, but Winchester decided to proceed regardless.[23]

Lieutenant Colonel William Lewis led the march to Frenchtown on the morning of January 17 with 550 Kentucky volunteers, followed at noon the next day by Lieutenant Colonel John Allen with another 130 men. The two detachments represented half of Winchester's army. To mask their approach, they avoided the main trail and took to the ice over the frozen Raisin River. They arrived within a quarter mile of Frenchtown at 2:00 p.m. on the 18th, but a surprise attack was not possible. Indian scouts had spotted them within six miles of Frenchtown and warned the British of their coming. Their command consisted of 100 Canadian militia members augmented by up to 400 Indians. When the Americans arrived, they immediately made a determined assault that slowly drove the Canadians and Indians out of the village, backing them into the forest where they waged a furious tree-to-tree fight before giving way.[24] Regrouping at Sandy Creek several miles to the north, Major Ebenzer Reynolds, commanding the British contingent, immediately crossed over to Fort Malden to inform Procter what had taken place, arriving at 2:00 a.m. on the 19th.[25]

Elated by the Americans' victory, Colonel Lewis sent word back to Winchester that he had successfully freed Frenchtown. Winchester, who intended to use Frenchtown as a base, ordered Colonel Samuel Wells and his regiment of regulars to join Lewis. He himself would follow a short time later, leaving only 300 men at the Rapids.

With Colonel Wells's arrival the number of American troops at Frenchtown had grown to about 1,000 men. Since the victorious volunteers already had found billets within the village, Wells thought it prudent to set up a temporary camp for his regiment out in the open several hundred yards downriver. He did not favor his regulars fraternizing with the more rowdy volunteers, even though Lewis invited them to camp alongside the volunteers within the confines of the picket fence.[26] Wells, Winchester, and Lewis examined the surrounding area for a new camp for the regulars the next day but found nothing suitable for a natural defense.

Wells was becoming concerned with Winchester's casual approach to the defense of the village. Several of the Frenchtown inhabitants had warned that Procter had landed with troops near Brownstown, but Winchester was convinced that such reports were merely the result of overactive imaginations.[27] Wells later wrote: "By that time I began to think our situation very precarious. A man had just arrived from Fort Malden, informing us that the British and Indians would attack us on Saturday the 23rd in the morning. Among other things I asked the Genl if it would not be advisable to send out Spies to Brownes Town Sixteen miles toward Malden. He answered that he would do so tomorrow."[28] Wells asked permission to return to the Rapids, ostensibly to retrieve his baggage. In reality he intended to inform Harrison, who had just arrived there, of the poor disposition of the regular troops at Frenchtown and Winchester's lack of concern for their safety.

Wells's premonition of danger proved correct. On January 19 Procter crossed over the iced-up river from Malden with 336 regulars and 212 Canadian militia, plus 600 to 800 Indians under chiefs Roundhead, Splitlog, and Walk-in-the-Water. They carried three three-pounder cannon and three howitzers. Landing near Brownstown, they marched 12 miles south to Swan Creek, about two to three hours from Frenchtown, where they bedded down for the night. At Frenchtown all was serene, but the freezing weather had immobilized the troops. Because of the cold, pickets had not been posted to guard the approaches to the village, nor had any sentries been stationed, which Winchester later admitted was an oversight on his part. He had assumed that the volunteer colonels would have enough sense to make certain men were on guard.

Up before dawn at Swan Creek, Procter's force reached Frenchtown at daybreak and immediately attacked, his Canadian militia on the right, Indians on the left, and the regulars with their cannon in the center. Just as they began their assault, as luck would have it, reveille was being sounded inside the village, rousing the Americans, who reacted quickly when they heard the rumble of cannon. Wells's regulars, having camped out in the open, bore the brunt of the initial attack. For at least 30 minutes they held their ground, but when the Indians had worked their way around and behind them, they were forced to give way toward the river, at which time they also began to run low on ammunition. (They had had only 10 cartridges per man when the attack began.) Seeing the precarious position of the regulars, Lewis and Allen charged out from behind the village's picket fence to their aid with 100 volunteers.

Winchester, unfortunately, had lodged overnight in the home of Francis Navarre across the river, three quarters of a mile away. Awakened by the sound of battle, he hastily threw on his heavy overcoat, sans uniform, mounted his horse, and galloped off to take command. His attempts to rally the regulars were of no avail. As the fight progressed the regulars realized that their only recourse to safety was to retreat along the river to the open side of the pickets and join the volunteers, but the Indians prevented them from doing so. They had no choice but to flee down the road toward the Rapids in hopes of reaching Harrison. As they struggled through two feet of snow in their flight, the Indians systematically brought them down or took them captive. Only two officers and about 30 enlisted men succeeded in reaching Harrison.[29]

The Kentucky volunteers, shielded by the picket fence, continued to hold their own for the next two and one-half hours, thanks to the accurate fire of their Kentucky rifles, although they too were running short of ammunition. Realizing that his attempts to get inside the village were not succeeding and that the battle had reached a stalemate, Procter was on the verge of terminating the action and returning to Malden when Chief Roundhead approached, bringing with him the captured General Winchester, who with Lewis and several others had retreated as far as three miles from Frenchtown when the Indians caught them. Procter told Winchester that he intended to set fire to the village and that his troops inside would be massacred if he did not order them to surrender. Winchester replied that he did not have the authority to give such an order but would send a message recommending that they do so.[30] Major George Madison, now in command, consulted with his officers, who voted that further resistance would be difficult since they were low on ammunition and the British cannon were beginning to score. Madison, with only five men and 20 wounded, was in no mood to give up the fight but it seemed the more prudent decision. He did not do so until Procter agreed to his terms: to respect his troops' private property, help remove the sick and wounded to Malden, and treat them as prisoners of war. The battle finally came to a close between noon and 3:00 p.m.[31]

When news of the battle reached Harrison that morning, he dispatched about 900 men under the command of Colonel Wells toward Frenchtown. When still 18 miles from the village, Wells learned from his scouts that Winchester had already surrendered, and that if he continued forward he could be facing an attack on his own force. Having no artillery and with his troops already tired, he decided it would be best to return to the Rapids. Wells had no way of knowing that Procter was anxious to leave Frenchtown before Harrison could bear down upon him. He preferred to avoid the confrontation and return to Malden immediately with his troops, the wounded, and the prisoners he had taken. The number of American prisoners was substantial: 33 officers and about 462 enlisted men, which left as many as 325 missing.[32] Left behind were 80 American wounded or sick whom Procter promised to transport by sled to safety the next day. For the time being they were lodged in the homes of the villagers. Whether Procter intended to follow up on this promise will never be known. He left them under the protection of Major Reynolds, Captain Elliott, and several guards and interpreters, plus 50 supposedly friendly Indians. Within an hour after the surrender, Procter was on his way back to Brownstown to begin crossing his troops, prisoners, and his own wounded over to Malden. His own troops had suffered dearly as well, especially the regulars, with 18 killed and 127 wounded. The Indians and Canadian volunteers counted five dead and 34 wounded.[33]

At dawn Indians who had remained entered the town, brushed aside the guards, and broke into the building, formerly a tavern, in which Major Graves, Captains Hart and Hickman, and the Reverend Thomas Dudley were sheltered. They forced their way into its cellar and carried away many barrels of whiskey, which they soon pierced, drinking and raising a great commotion in the process. About 200 other Indians who had come back from Malden vowing vengeance on all Americans soon joined them.[34] They invaded the homes of Jean Jeraume and Gabriel Godroy, in which many of the wounded were lodged, then set the premises on fire. Any wounded who attempted to escape were either tomahawked or pushed back into the flames, about 30 perishing in such a manner. Those who survived were carried off to Detroit to be ransomed.[35] News of the massacre outraged the American public. For the rest of the war U.S. troops adopted the cry "Remember the Raisin!" when they went into battle.

Winchester's defeat severely crimped Harrison's plans for a winter campaign. Not happy with the fort that Winchester had constructed at the Rapids, which he considered to be on the wrong (north) side of the river and too difficult to supply, he temporarily moved his headquarters to the Portage River at the Upper Sandusky. On February 2, however, he moved back to the Rapids and began work on the construction of a strong new fort on the south side of the river. This effort effectively consumed what time still remained for a possible winter campaign in the Michigan area.

For the citizens of Detroit, Harrison's change in plans was tragic. Instead of the liberating army they had hoped to see was the sight of Indians parading their prisoners from Frenchtown through the streets like herds of sheep, bargaining for their ransom or auctioning them off like slaves for $10 to $80, even hawking American scalps for whatever price they could bring while the British stood idly by.[36] Detroiters made every attempt to raise the captives' ransom and take them into their homes, saving as many as 34 in this manner. Some of the British violated official policy and attempted to do the same. Colonel Elliott, the British Indian agent, bartered successfully for seven prisoners and Colonel Francis Baby, head of the Canadian militia, ransomed one.[37]

At Malden and Amherstburg the Indians presented the Canadian people with a grisly scene. They had cut off the heads of Americans killed at Frenchtown and mounted them on top of a high picket fence, where they could be seen with different expressions of death frozen on their faces. The Indians also found it amusing to parade through Amherstburg carrying poles to which were attached scalps: some painted red, some of young children, some of women and men of middle age or older.

Oliver Bellair, a young boy living with his parents at Amherstburg, later recalled that about 300 to 400 American prisoners were brought across the river from Frenchtown and kept in an open courtyard with no kind of shelter to help them endure the bitter cold of the January night. The strong guard posted around them was more to keep the Indians from assaulting them than to prevent their escape. Amherstburg villagers crowded around the perimeter in great numbers attempting to provide them with aid and may even have been instrumental in the escape of several.[38]

In reporting the outcome of the Frenchtown battle to his superior, Major General Sheaffe, Procter made no comment about the hardships the Indians caused the American prisoners other than a brief mention that he "had much difficulty in bringing the Indians to consent to the sparing of their Lives."[39]

On January 31 Woodward wrote an angry letter to Secretary Monroe describing his views of Winchester's conduct in the Frenchtown battle:

> In the Battle of "La Riviere aux Raisens" of the 22d of this month, and which terminated in a complete victory on the part of the British Commander, the American General evidently committed four Military errors.
>
> First, his troops were posted on the left bank of the River Raisin; when they should, unquestionably, have been on the Right.
>
> Second, they were posted at the extremity of a public road; when,

if posted on the left bank at all, they should have been in a situation, that either fences or woods might have presented some obstructions to the approach of cannon.

Third, He slept a mile and a half from his men; and the next to him [Wells] being absent they in fact had no commander.

Fourth, He received intelligence of the march of the attacking army in the evening; but would not credit it.

He went on to say that "the American Soldiers fought like Lions, but the British commander held a superiority in generalship."[40]

Reports of the massacre at Frenchtown and the manner in which the Indians were treating the survivors created uproar in Detroit, so much so that Procter felt it necessary to send a follow-up letter to Sheaffe on February 1 in an attempt to defend himself. He claimed that the Americans had been equipped with tomahawks and knives and had made every effort to use them. In addition, he wrote, "They fired at the [British] wounded as they lay on the ground, themselves behind enclosures, and in buildings. Every art, every means have been employed to prejudice and influence these misguided People against us, There have been some instances I am sorry to say of Indian barbarity, but the example was set by the Enemy, and they came to seek them, I know we shall be villified for the truth is not in them. I have nothing to accuse myself of."[41]

Procter had other concerns on his mind. As long as Harrison was at the Rapids, he worried that the leading citizens of Detroit were plotting against him, perhaps even planning an attempt to take over Fort Detroit and then urge Harrison to come to their assistance. On February 1, fearing an insurrection, he declared martial law and ordered 29 men whom he considered the leading troublemakers as well as all who had not taken an oath of allegiance to prepare to leave under escort to Fort George at Niagara. The 29 immediately accused Procter of violating the terms of the August 1812 surrender agreement. Woodward agreed to plead their cause. He offered Procter an alternative: the 29 would cooperate in maintaining order within Detroit if they were guaranteed the safety of their lives and property. Woodward also accused Procter of failing to observe the rules of international law and gave him a long list of incidents in which the British had failed to live up to them. He also blamed Procter for the atrocities that had been committed at Frenchtown. None of his arguments prevailed. The men designated by Procter were forced to leave.[42]

Realizing that he was accomplishing little for the citizens of Detroit in the face of Procter's protracted stubbornness, Woodward requested his passport so that he could travel through the lines and take up residence in the United States. He finally received it after a two-week delay. He would not return to Detroit until the war had ended.

After Woodward's departure, one man still remained to plague Procter—Father Gabriel Richard. His name had not been on the list of Procter's undesirables, a mystery in itself, for Father Richard was one of his most vociferous critics, especially for permitting the Frenchtown massacre and doing so little to aid the captives held by the Indians. Father Richard's criticism finally reached such a point that Procter demanded that he pledge allegiance to the British crown. Father Richard refused. He told Procter that he owed his allegiance only to the United States. Procter had him arrested and imprisoned in Sandwich for three weeks, probably under house arrest in the care of Father Marchand, pastor of the Church of the Assumption. On June 16 Procter went one step further and confronted Father Richard in the church rectory. He informed him that he would banish him from the territory unless he signed a bond stating that he would refrain from criticizing him in public. Wishing only to return to his congregation and be of future help to them, Father Richard reluctantly agreed. Some have speculated that Tecumseh, who held Father Richard in high esteem, forced Procter to make the offer.[43]

After he had entered the United States, Woodward wrote an account of the atrocities that took place at Frenchtown and Detroit in which he included the affidavits of French Canadians witnesses. The account appeared in the *Albany Argus* and was soon reprinted widely across the country, prompting strong condemnation of Procter's conduct. Woodward eventually went to Washington, where he spent the next 18 months working for Congress.[44]

Now free to act without the interference of either Woodward or Father Richard, Procter ordered the British Indian Department to move from Malden to Detroit. He intended to make the country along the river between Frenchtown and Detroit Indian country to serve as a buffer zone to repulse American attempts to reconquer Fort Detroit. To this end he invited Tecumseh and his people to settle on the Huron River near the river trail, and the Ottawa tribe to reside on the River Rouge.[45] The strategy proved to be fruitless as a guard against Harrison. After Perry's victory on Lake Erie, Harrison had no need to use the river trail to reach Detroit.

THE RECAPTURE OF DETROIT

The military events of 1813 leading up to the recapture of Detroit suggest what Hull also might have accomplished had he been afforded the same resources as Brigadier General William Henry Harrison and had the Americans been in control of the waterways of Lake Erie and the Detroit River. With these advantages Hull probably would have approached his Detroit campaign differently, and its outcome could have been completely different.

In March 1813, two months after Winchester's defeat at Frenchtown, Harrison constructed a new fort at the Falls of the Maumee. The site he selected, on the south side of the river near present-day Perrysburg, Ohio, could easily be supplied and defended. The choice was excellent, well elevated with a deep ravine behind and a small stream across its eastern edge. Its interior formed a rectangle 200 yards wide and 400 yards long, completely surrounded by picket fencing. Seven large two-story blockhouses, five raised batteries, and two storehouses filled out its complement. Ditches filled with a breastwork of sharpened stakes in key locations surrounded the exterior of the picket walls. Harrison named his armed camp Fort Meigs in honor of Ohio's governor, then settled down to see what the future would bring.[1]

At Malden, Procter viewed the construction of Fort Meigs with alarm. It forced him to plan an attack on Harrison before the latter became too strong. He also was running critically short of supplies, having to feed hundreds of Indians, his own troops, and the citizens of Detroit and Amherstburg. A victory over Harrison at Fort Meigs could provide him with the large store of supplies that Harrison had accumulated for his own

FORT MACKINAC

LAKE HURON

MICHIGAN TERRITORY

UPPER CANADA

BATTLE OF THAMES

FORT DETROIT

FORT MALDEN

LAKE ERIE

FRENCHTOWN

ERIE

BATTLE OF LAKE ERIE

FORT MEIGS

FORT STEPHENSON

URBANA   OHIO

Map of Northwest campaigns in the War of 1812.

troops. Unfortunately, the early winter weather had not been conducive to a winter campaign in Ohio. March and early April had been extremely wet, making it virtually impossible to haul artillery from Fort Malden to Fort Meigs for an assault on the latter's pickets.

On April 24 Procter finally was ready. His army, of 469 regular troops with their 26 officers and 27 sergeants, 462 Canadian militia, and 600 Indians under Chief Roundhead, boarded a fleet of six ships, two gunboats, and other transports and sailed across to the Ohio shore, disembarking near the entrance to the Maumee River. On April 27 Procter held an Indian council, to which Tecumseh brought 600 more warriors, bringing the total number of Indians to 1,200, about equal to that of all the American troops within Fort Meigs.[2]

The next day the British moved within easy range of the fort. Procter's artillery officers busily positioned their heavy guns: two 24-pounders, two 12-pounders, an eight-inch howitzer, and two five-and-one-half-pound mortars. These were augmented by the nine-pounder guns aboard the two British gunboats that had trailed the troops up the Maumee River from Lake Erie. By 10:00 a.m. May 1, the British artillery on the northern bank of the river approximately 300 yards across from Fort Meigs began bombardment of the fort.[3] Harrison countered with heavy fire from his own artillery: five 18-pounder guns, five 12-pounders, four six-pounders, and five howitzers.[4]

Over the next two days the British dropped 590 rounds onto Fort Meigs with little effect other than the loss of six men and the wounding of 11. They were stymied by Harrison's foresight in having built a 10-foot-high, 20-foot-thick earthen bank across the center of the fort's interior that extended from one picket wall to the other. Called the Grand Traverse, it formed a huge sponge into which British shells and bombs were buried without causing much harm. The Americans simply created cave-like shelters within its foundation for their protection.[5] On May 4, the third day after the British arrival, an exasperated Procter demanded the fort's surrender but was summarily rebuffed. Tecumseh added a note of derision to the surrender request, writing, "I have with me 800 braves. You have many in your hiding place. Come out with them and give me battle. You talked like a brave when we met at Vincennes, and I respected you, but now you hide behind logs and in the earth, like a groundhog. Give me your answer."[6] Harrison, of course, declined Tecumseh's invitation. His picket walls had yet to be breached and if a shell did pass through a portion it was quickly shored up.

Shortly before midnight on the day Procter demanded surrender, Harrison received a dispatch from Brigadier General Green Clay that he and a force of 1,200 Kentucky militiamen were coming down the Maumee River on flatboats and were about two hours distant. They were about to make camp for the night but should be at Fort Meigs early the next morning. Harrison's reply was an order for Clay to attempt to capture the main British battery on the north side of the river and spike its guns. Clay gave this detail to Lieutenant Colonel William Dudley and his regiment of 796 men. Clay emphasized to Dudley that as soon as he had captured and immobilized the guns, he was to join the rest of the Kentucky militiamen, who would have disembarked from their flatboats on the south bank. They would wait for Dudley to join them and they would then proceed to the fort together.

Dudley profited from a rare moment of laxity on the part of Tecumseh, who was off on a sortie against the fort and had neglected to have his Indians guard against an attack along the north shore of the river. Taken by surprise, the Indians and the British artillery troops camped at the battery were driven off the field by Dudley, whose Kentucky riflemen cried out, "Remember the Raisin!" as they swept through the British ranks.[7]

Flushed with success and before spiking the cannon, the left side of Dudley's force detached itself to pursue those Indians and British fleeing into the nearby woods, a course that took the troops away from the river. Instead of recalling them, Dudley committed the rest of his force to their support. From the ramparts of the fort, Harrison could see what was taking place and sent urgent signals for Dudley to regroup and cross the river to the south bank, but he was ignored.[8]

Procter, when he learned that his main battery had been overrun, realized that if he acted quickly he could trap Dudley's troops between his own reinforcements and the river and isolate them. He ordered three companies of the 41st regulars supported by several Canadian militia companies and Indians to recapture the battery, which they easily did, Dudley's troops now being scattered deep within the woods. Dudley, alerted by the firing behind him, quickly ordered a retreat. To divert Procter's troops away from Dudley, Harrison ordered Colonel John Miller with 350 men to attack another British artillery battery further downriver. Miller's attack was successful and he held the position to spike the British guns. However, his force now came under heavy attack by British troops four times its number. Having accomplished his mission, he wisely elected to retreat back to the fort, bringing with him 41 prisoners but unfortunately having lost 50 men of his own.[9]

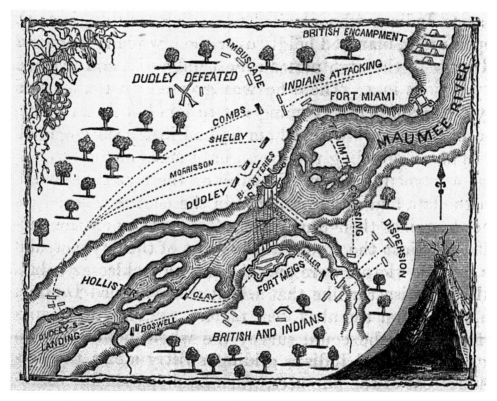

Overhead view of Fort Meigs attack formations. (From Benson J. Lossing, *The Pictorial Field-Book of the War of 1812* [New York: Harper & Brothers, 1868].)

Dudley's troops now became the pursued. They were in total disarray, and blocked from the river. When called upon to surrender by the British, those who were deep inside the woods did so in order to avoid capture by the Indians, who would tomahawk them to death. Those still outside the woods or on its fringes turned and attempted to fight their way to their boats. Only about 50 escaped to reach Clay on the other side of the river. The remainder were either killed or captured. Colonel Dudley was one of the fatalities.

Procter now was left with the task of removing 500 American prisoners of war to Fort Malden without interrupting his siege of Fort Meigs. He assigned 50 of his men to escort them back to his camp at the ruins of old Fort Miami. A large group of Indians trailed along, demanding that the prisoners give them their valuables, even their clothing, filling the air with their threats. The Americans expected to be free of them once they had reached the fort. It was not to be so. As they arrived at the entrance the

Indians formed a gauntlet through which the prisoners were forced to run to gain safety. They were buffeted, pushed, and tripped as they passed, only to discover that safety did not exist within the old fort's ruined walls, which had deteriorated to a height of only about four feet. The Indians simply pushed the British guards aside or scaled the pickets and dropped inside. Soon a general massacre was taking place, which the British could not or would not quell. At least 40 Americans had been killed when Tecumseh arrived on the scene with Matthew Elliott and threatened to take the life of any Indian who harmed an American prisoner.[10] Tecumseh allegedly became so irate with Procter's failure to defend the prisoners that he told him, "Begone, Proctor! You are not fit to command! Go put on petticoats!"[11]

The siege of Fort Meigs continued until May 7, when Procter once more called upon Harrison to surrender. Again Harrison refused. After arranging a truce to exchange prisoners Procter renewed the siege, but thanks to Harrison's stubbornness, the Indians began to lose heart and drift away. They were upset because Fort Meigs refused to fall, depriving them of the booty they were expecting. By May 9 only 10 were left of the 1,200 that had begun the attack. Nor was the Canadian militia too pleased with the time the siege was taking. The Essex and Kent militia captains informed Procter that it was absolutely necessary for them to return home soon so that they could plant their early wheat since the bad winter had ruined their normal winter grain crop. If they did not do so, they could expect a famine the coming winter.[12]

Procter finally concluded that it was useless for him to continue. Half of his Canadian militia already had left and only a handful of Indians remained. He found himself in an embarrassing position: his attacking force was outnumbered by the besieged.[13] On May 9 he placed his artillery and stores aboard his gunboats and departed for Amherstburg. He had accomplished nothing, and had suffered losses of 14 killed, 41 wounded, and 41 taken prisoner. American losses were far greater, at 130 killed, 189 wounded, and 630 taken prisoner, but the majority of the casualties resulted from Dudley's disobedience of orders. For the most part, Harrison's army was intact. He even considered an attack on the departing British but wisely changed his mind, realizing that the troops Procter still had with him were primarily regulars and would put up a stubborn resistance if Harrison attempted to harry them.

The failure to capture Fort Meigs did not sit well with Procter. It left him with a strong American outpost within reaching distance of Fort

Malden and blocked any attempt he might make to campaign west, but it could not be helped.

Two months later, on July 20, Procter, now a brigadier general in recognition of his Frenchtown victory, renewed his effort to remove Fort Meigs from his path. He crossed the Detroit River once again, but with a much smaller force than before: 450 regulars and militia, and 1,000 Indians. He also brought with him several six-pounder cannon, hardly sufficient firepower to subdue a fort as well protected as Fort Meigs, now better positioned to repel an attack than before. When Harrison went to the Lower Sandusky, the fort's command fell to Brigadier General Green Clay, who now held command of 2,000 troops who were better disciplined, better armed, and had sufficient provisions on hand to withstand a prolonged siege.

Procter would have preferred to attack Sandusky rather than Fort Meigs, but the Indians had balked at the notion. Sandusky was too distant; Fort Meigs was closer to home and as such was their preferred target. They made this well known to Procter during a council meeting held at Fort Malden in the middle of July in which Tecumseh, in cold, calculating language, called for a return to Fort Meigs. For the Indians the choice was obvious: to whip Harrison's troops would remove the threat of American settlers to their own families on the frontier.[14] The Indians' reluctance to travel eastward placed Procter in a bind since he could not afford to offend his Indian allies who, in fact, made up most of his striking force. Therefore, Fort Meigs it would be, although he considered his prospects for victory remote.[15]

News of the renewed attack on Fort Meigs invigorated the northwest Indian tribes. Soon between 2,000 and 3,000 warriors had gathered at Malden. Feeding so many Indians and his own men became a nightmare for Procter. To supplement what food they received from the British, the Indians ranged through the neighboring countryside, slaughtering farmers' livestock without compunction. Their disorderly conduct forced Procter to move on Fort Meigs as soon as possible so that they might better live off the land.[16]

Procter's force arrived at Fort Meigs on July 21. He immediately faced the inevitable question: how to draw the Americans out of the fort so he could engage them in the open. A bombardment lasting three days accomplished very little, and his small force of regulars was in no position to storm the fort. Finally Tecumseh suggested they set a trap. The Indians would stage a mock battle in the woods, giving the impression that they were attacking a detachment of American troops that had come to General Clay's aid. The Americans would sally out of the fort to the rescue and then could be attacked. Thus at 4:00 p.m. on July 26 the Indians raised a terrific din out of sight of the fort. British regulars lined the trail leading toward the mock battle, ready to pounce on those Americans who left Meigs. To their immense disappointment no troops came into sight. Clay was not fooled. He was not expecting a relief force, having received a dispatch from Harrison just that morning informing him that he was confident Clay could deal with the situation without his help.[17]

By July 28, with nothing significant having taken place and the Indians once again beginning to drift off, Procter terminated the siege.[18] What he did accomplish, however, was to prove to the Indians that his reluctance to make a second attack on Fort Meigs was well founded and that he, not they, would select their next target: Fort Stephenson on the Lower Sandusky (now Fremont, Ohio). Tecumseh agreed to Procter's decision, although most of the Indians, having no stomach for attacking another walled fort, departed for Amherstburg. Tecumseh and a few hundred of his followers went east with Procter.

The small post of Stephenson, in Procter's view, was ripe for capture. In the scale of things it was not very important, being used primarily as a storage depot for 200 barrels of flour. A double stockade 16 feet high topped by bayonets surrounded it, outside of which was a ditch nine feet wide and six feet deep. A blockhouse stood at both its northeast and southwest corners. Major George Croghan of the 17th Infantry, whose uncle was George Rogers Clark, was in command, with a garrison of about 160 men. Croghan had been a volunteer aide to Harrison, promoted to major for his valor during the first siege of Fort Meigs.

Harrison learned that Procter was heading in the direction of Fort Stephenson on the 29th of July. Believing that the fort could not withstand a siege, he ordered Croghan to burn it that night and remove his troops upriver to his headquarters at Seneca Town. The order did not reach Croghan until the next day. After a council with his officers, he sent word back to Harrison that he intended to stay. Harrison did not take the rebuff of his command too lightly, particularly since rumor had reached him that Tecumseh was headed toward Stephenson with 2,000 warriors, accompanied by Procter with a large body of troops. He feared for the fort's safety. He dispatched Colonel Wells to Stephenson to order Croghan to come to Seneca Town to explain why he had countermanded his order. Croghan apologized to Harrison for his curt reply to the original order, but explained that it would be safer for his troops to remain in the fort rather than be caught on the trail by the Indians. Harrison accepted his logic and returned him to his command at Stephenson, ordering Wells to return to Seneca Town. He did warn Croghan that should the fort come under fire from heavy artillery he was to retreat unless unable to do so.[19]

Procter appeared outside the fort the day after Croghan returned, August 1, eliminating any opportunity for the Americans to retreat. Procter immediately demanded that Croghan surrender, adding the usual postscript that an Indian massacre was probable if he did not do so. Croghan refused. Procter then brought up the two gunboats that had accompanied him downriver to join in a bombardment of the fort, to which he added the fire from his three six-pounder cannon.

After two days of bombardment with no great success Procter made plans to assault the fort's pickets by storm.[20] At 5:00 p.m. on August 2 three British columns, each with 120 men, advanced toward the pickets, led by Brevet Lieutenant Colonel William Shortt of the 41st Regiment. Only a few Indians accompanied them, most preferring to wait and see how things developed. If Shortt were successful, they would come to his support. Watching the British advance, Croghan held his fire until the troops had entered the ditch surrounding the fort's pickets. At that point his men discharged their muskets in their faces accompanied by the raking fire of Croghan's one piece of artillery, a six-pounder loaded with grapeshot. The British assault was suicidal. The attackers had no scaling ladders and could only chop away at the pickets with their axes. In doing so they were standing targets for the strong fire emanating from inside the fort. Gradually bravery gave way to reality, and the men took cover behind a ridge a distance from the fort where they were pinned down until dark. At 9:00 p.m. Procter had had enough and abandoned any further plans for attack, ordering his men to make for their boats.[21] Compared to one American killed and seven wounded in the action, the British casualties were disastrous: 26 killed, 41 wounded, and 29 captured.[22]

This would be the last offensive operation conducted by Procter in the Northwest, a situation made certain by events already beginning to take place on Lake Erie. As Procter took his force back to Fort Malden, Master Commandant Oliver Hazard Perry was maneuvering his newly constructed brigs *Lawrence* and *Niagara* over the sandbar that extended across the entrance to Presque Isle Bay. Both were more than a match for any British warship currently sailing on Lake Erie, which meant they were in a position to seriously disrupt Procter's supply line between Malden and Niagara.

Perry's presence at Presque Isle was the result of the administration's belated realization that control of Lake Erie was pivotal to reclaiming the Northwest from British hands, an argument that Hull had made several times before his Detroit campaign. Soon after Detroit's surrender the secretary of the navy appointed Captain Isaac Chauncey to head all naval operations on the Great Lakes. Chauncey had never been in a naval battle but as former commander of the New York Navy Yard he brought extensive ship-building experience with him, a skill sorely needed at this time at the Sackets Harbor dockyard. Although Chauncey gave most of his attention to maintaining a naval presence on Lake Ontario, he did initiate efforts to gain control of Lake Erie.[23]

For the Lake Erie operation Chauncey selected Lieutenant Jesse Elliott, a distant relative of Matthew Elliott, head of the British Indian Department. Elliott's orders were to select a site at which to build, repair, and service ships to act as a base from which to operate on Lake Erie. Elliott chose Black Rock, a few miles down the Niagara River, opposite the British Fort Erie.

Unknown to him or Chauncey, President Madison had appointed Daniel Dobbins as sailing master and authorized him to begin constructing a squadron at Presque Isle (Erie), Pennsylvania. Dobbins had extensive sailing experience on the Great Lakes as a merchant captain and considered Presque Isle an ideal place for a shipyard. When they learned of Dobbins's appointment, Chauncey and Elliott had no choice but to follow orders.[24] Dobbins had the shipyard operational by October 1812 and in December laid the keels for two 50-foot schooners. After a visit to Presque Isle Chauncey agreed that it was a better location than Black Rock, which could too easily be blockaded by British ships. He also had Dobbins begin cutting timber for two new brigs.[25]

Chauncey removed Lieutenant Elliott from his responsibilities on Lake Erie on November 26, naming him commander of the 24-gun USS *Madison,* newly launched at Sackets Harbor to operate on Lake Ontario. To replace him at the Lake Erie post, Chauncey asked the recently appointed secretary of the navy, William Rogers, to assign Master Commandant Oliver Hazard Perry to this duty. Perry had been languishing at Newport, Rhode Island, as commander of a fleet of gunboats. When he heard of the opening created by Elliott's transfer, he wrote Chauncey, promising to bring 50 of his men to serve on Lake Erie if he were selected. Chronically short of good seamen on the lakes, Chauncey readily accepted Perry's offer.[26]

Perry arrived at Presque Isle on March 27, 1813. Only 27 years of age, he had served as a midshipman aboard the ship of war USS *General Green,* which had been built by his father, under whom he sailed.[27] Perry received a lieutenancy in 1802 was and given command of several gunboats as well as the 12-gun schooner *Revenge.* His most recent assignment was that of constructing gunboats in Newport.

Shortly after being transferred to Chauncey's command, Perry volunteered to accompany Colonel Winfield Scott on a joint navy-army operation to capture Fort George on the Niagara River. Its success led to the British evacuating Fort Erie, further to the south, in May, thus breaking a blockade that had bottled up several American ships at Black Rock: the brig *Caldonia,* the schooners *Ohio, Amelia, and Somers,* and the sloop *Trippe.* Perry took the five to Presque Isle in a voyage that lasted almost two weeks. They arrived on June 18 after a harrowing sail through a dense fog in which they narrowly missed being detected by a British squadron in the area.[28]

On the British side of the naval equation, the removal of these ships to Presque Isle and news that Perry had completed four new gunboats, with two brigs well under way, deeply concerned Lieutenant Robert Barclay, commander of the British Lake Erie squadron. Barclay had arrived at Amherstburg in June and was appalled to discover that there was a severe shortage of provisions, manpower, and materials for his ships. Their lack would handicap his attempts to place his squadron on an equal footing with the navy that Perry was creating at Presque Isle. On June 29 he wrote Major General Procter that he was in need of stores of every type, especially iron, and was desperately short of seamen. The completion of a new brig, the *Detroit,* at Amherstburg had been going slowly because of material shortages and would not be ready for sea until mid-July. In reviewing the situation, Procter and Barclay came to the conclusion that the best way to rid themselves of Perry's ships would be to land a large force in the Presque Isle vicinity, then coordinate an attack on his fleet by troops on land while Barclay blockaded the entrance. Barclay wrote to Governor General Prevost of their plan and requested the necessary reinforcements to implement it. Prevost agreed to forward 200 men from the 41st Regiment in a letter dated June 20. Two weeks passed without the hint of any troops arriving at Amherstburg. Finally an apologetic dispatch arrived from Prevost: Major General Francis de Rottenberg, who had just replaced Sir Roger Sheafe as Procter's superior officer, had vetoed the request, claiming that the troops could be put to better use defending the Niagara frontier.[29]

At Presque Isle Perry was encountering difficulties as well. By the last week in July Perry's ships were ready for action, rigged and with their guns in place, but they lacked sufficient manpower. This problem was alleviated when Chauncey forwarded Lieutenant Elliott with 101 officers and men. Harrison also sent 130 soldiers from his camp to help.[30] The major problem now confronting Perry was that his two largest ships, the USS *Lawrence* and the USS *Niagara,* were too heavy to pass over the sandbar at the harbor entrance. Should either or both become stuck in the process, they would be sitting targets for British warships, which were waiting outside the harbor for just such an occurrence. Therefore, it was critical that any attempt to pass the sandbar be made at a time when Barclay and his Lake Erie squadron had temporarily lifted their blockade. Barclay himself knew the importance of his blockade. Should the *Lawrence* and the *Niagara* reach open water, his own ships would be in danger because of their size.

On July 29 Barclay's squadron abruptly disappeared from view, probably headed across the lake to Long Point, the British central depot for men and supplies. No doubt the British ships were running low on food, having been away from land for the past 10 days. At first Perry thought the departure was a ruse to entice him to attempt the bar crossing with all of his ships; then Barclay would return and strike while the largest were in their most vulnerable position. Perry decided to take the risk. Early Sunday morning, August 1, the *Scorpion* and several of the other schooners crossed over into open water and moored outside the entrance to be in position to fend off the British squadron should it suddenly appear. Each carried a single but highly effective long gun that, if necessary, would buy Perry sufficient time to float the two brigs over as well.[31]

The *Lawrence* and the *Niagara* each drew eight to nine feet. The depth of the water over the bar, however, was only four feet. Perry resorted to a system of camels (floating boxes) to overcome the difference. These would be filled with water, then submerged down low on either side of the two ships and attached to them, after which the water would be pumped out, lifting the vessels higher, sufficiently to permit them to float over the bar. It was extremely difficult work. The *Lawrence* was the first to reach open water. The *Niagara* was partially over when Barclay's squadron suddenly arrived on the scene. But Barclay, realizing what was taking place and assuming that Perry, even without the *Niagara,* was in a good position to fight with the *Lawrence* standing guard, turned his squadron away and headed for Amherstburg. Had Barclay chosen to attack at that moment there is a possibility he may have scuttled the American ships—he caught them while they still were being rearmed, their guns and stores having been removed to lighten them and ease their passing over the bar. This, however, he did not know.[32]

During the following week Perry's little fleet sailed around the lake hoping to catch Barclay's ships, but they remained moored at Amherstburg. Perry did make one stop at Sandusky Bay to confer with Harrison about a joint army-navy operation. They agreed it would be best to postpone any invasion of Canada until after the American and British fleets had engaged in battle, the outcome dictating how the invasion would take place. Perry was confident that Barclay would bring his ships out soon because he would experience a shortage of supplies, Perry having shut down their transport by water from Niagara.[33]

On August 13, having grown impatient with Barclay's lack of action, Perry tacked off the shore of Amherstburg to entice him to come out and meet his fleet in open water, but unfavorable winds sprang up, forcing him to retire to the open lake. On September 24 he returned once again to find the *Queen Charlotte,* the *Lady Prevost,* and other vessels anchored on a line between Bois Blanc Island and the mainland where the river was at its narrowest, about a third of a mile. In addition, a formidable battery had been erected on the tip of Bois Blanc to further discourage passage upriver. Perry also noted that the brig *Detroit* had been launched. Barclay had removed cannon, ammunition, and stores from Fort Malden to the *Detroit* in an attempt to make it battle-ready. Perry, not liking what he saw, decided that this was neither the time nor the place to initiate an attack and withdrew to Put-in-Bay.[34]

Nor was Barclay in any hurry to enter the lake with the *Detroit* because it lacked a large enough crew. After General Procter contributed 50 men from the 41st regiment and a detachment of 36 officers and seamen had arrived from Lower Canada, Barclay was ready to take his squadron out into the lake, out of necessity more than bravery. As Barclay later wrote to his superior, Commodore Yeo,

> The last letter I had the honor of writing to you dated 6th Instant, I informed you that unless certain intimation was Received of more Seamen being on their way to Amherstburg, I should be obliged to

sail with the Squadron deplorably manned as it was, to fight the Enemy to enable us to get supplies of Provision and Stores of every
description, so perfectly destitute of Provision was the Port that there
was not a day's flour in Store, and the crews of the Squadron under
my command were on half allowance of many things, and when that
was done there was no more, such were the motives which induced
Major General Procter. . . to conceive in the necessity of a Battle being risqued.[35]

Early on the morning of September 10 the two fleets came within sight of
each other. The British squadron consisted of six ships: the new corvette
Detroit, equipped with 17 long guns and two carronades; the corvette
Queen Charlotte, with 14 carronades and two long guns; the schooner
Lady Prevost, with 10 carronades and two long guns; the brig *General
Hunter,* with two carronades and eight long guns; the sloop *Little Belt,*
with three long guns; and the schooner *Chippeway,* with one long gun.
Perry's squadron was made up of nine ships: the brigs *Lawrence and Niagara,* each with 18 carronades and two long guns; the *Caldonia,* with one
carronade and two long guns; the schooner *Somers,* with one carronade
and one long gun; the sloop *Trippe,* with one long gun; and four gunboats:
the *Tigress,* with one long gun; the *Porcupine,* with one long gun; the
Scorpion, with one long gun and one carronade, and the *Ariel,* with four
small long guns.[36]

The type of guns with which the ships were equipped dictated the
initial sailing action of the two squadrons. Barclay's ships, for example,
had 33 long guns between them, compared to Perry's 15. This invited
Barclay to stand off at a distance from the American ships and engage in
long-range action. Perry's two largest ships, the *Lawrence* and the *Niagara,* were armed with 18 32-pounder carronades each; their shorter range
called for close action, causing Perry to instruct his ships' captains to fight
at close quarters. His orders called for the *Lawrence* to directly engage the
Detroit, the *Niagara* to attack the *Queen Charlotte,* and the rest to pair off
against British vessels their size.[37] At a meeting with his ship' officers he
showed them the special blue flag that the *Lawrence* would fly, on which
he had painted words taken from Captain James Lawrence: "Don't give
up the Ship."

As Barclay's squadron sailed into view Perry adjusted his line of battle
so that the *Scorpion* would lead, followed by the *Ariel,* then the *Lawrence,*
all three to focus upon Barclay's flagship, the *Detroit.* The *Caledonia,* next

in his line, would steer toward the *General Hunter,* while the *Niagara* was to go directly against the *Queen Charlotte.*

At 10:00 a.m., when the two squadrons were still about three miles apart, the wind shifted. Until then, it had favored the British ships, which held the weather gauge—that is, they were between the wind and Perry's vessels, allowing Barclay to dictate the sailing action of the ships in battle. The wind now veered, and Perry had the advantage; it would be very difficult for the British ships to break off the action and flee should Perry gain the upper hand.[38]

At 11:45 a.m., although still one and one-quarter miles distant, Barclay fired an exploratory shot at the *Lawrence* from one of his 24-pounder long guns. The *Lawrence* could not respond since the fire of it shorter-range carronades could not match that distance. Perry crowded more sail onto the *Lawrence* to bring the two ships closer together. By 12:20 p.m. Perry had maneuvered the *Lawrence* until it was sailing parallel to the *General Hunter* and the *Queen Charlotte* but at 250 yards' distance, which allowed him to bring the carronades into action against both in passing toward the *Detroit.* When the captain of the British *Queen Charlotte* realized that the *Niagara,* sailing behind the *Lawrence,* was too far out of position to be engaged because of her angle of travel, he added on more sail to leapfrog around the *General Hunter* and add his ship's firepower to that of the *Detroit* against the *Lawrence.* For two hours the three larger ships exchanged shot for shot. Gradually the deck of the *Lawrence* became a shambles. Eighty-three of the ship's crew of 103 were either killed or wounded. Perry, realizing that if he struck his colors he would be captured by Barclay, had four seamen lower one of his small boats and row him to the *Niagara.* That ship was still unscathed, having hardly participated in the action to this point. Perry transferred his flag to the *Niagara* and immediately attempted to sail around the *Detroit* to gain the weather gauge and resume action.[39]

Whether Perry realized it or not, Barclay's *Detroit* was hardly in better shape than Perry's *Lawrence.* Early on, broadsides from the American ship had shredded its sails and rigging and were ripping apart its belowdecks, killing the gun crews. At one point a flying splinter tore into Barclay's thigh, removing him from the action. Lieutenant George Inglish, who had taken command of the *Detroit* after Barclay was wounded, did his best to continue the fight, but his ship was too badly damaged. "I ordered the *Queen Charlotte* to Shoot ahead of us if possible, and attempted to back our Fore Topsail to get astern, but the ship laying completely unmanage-

Oliver Perry transfers his flag from the *Lawrence* to the *Niagara*. (Courtesy of the Burton Historical Collection, Detroit Public Library.)

able, every Brace cut away, the Mizen Topmast and Gaff down, all the other masts badly wounded, not a stay left forward, hull shattered very much, a number of guns disabled, and the Enemy's Squadron raking both ships, ahead and astern, none of our own in a situation to support us, I was under the painful necessity of answering the Enemy to say we had struck, the *Queen Charlotte* having previously done so."[40]

Both became floating targets for the guns of the *Niagara*. Barclay was indeed severely injured, his first officer had been killed, 52 of the *Detroit's* crew were casualties, and the ship's gun batteries were silenced. Things were not much better aboard the *Queen Charlotte*: its captain had been killed and his ship had suffered 42 casualties. Also injured was the captain of the British ship *Hunter*. By 3:00 p.m. the British ships had surrendered, first the *Detroit* and the *Queen Charlotte*, then the *Hunter* and the *Lady Prevost*, followed by the others.[41]

At 4:00 p.m. Perry returned to the wrecked *Lawrence*, from which he wrote a note on the back of an envelope and sent it off to Harrison's headquarters. It read, "Dear General: We have met the enemy and they are ours: Two ships, two brigs, one schooner, and one sloop."[42] Now that the waters of Lake Erie were secure for the Americans, Harrison could begin planning his invasion of Canada.

The defeat of Barclay meant only one thing to Procter. He could expect Harrison to assemble his forces as quickly as possible and bring them against Forts Detroit and Malden. On September 13, he wrote Sir George Prevost, "I evidently cannot maintain my present extensive position as the Enemy will now have undisputed command of these waters by which he be enabled to turn my Flank and cut us off probably in detail. I have made my arrangements to fall back on the Thames. The women and sick I send off tomorrow: the Stores . . . shall be removed with all convenient expedition . . . [but] the management of the Indians may be a delicate, difficult affair."[43]

Ironically, Procter's command had grown to 48 officers and 831 men plus the largest number of Indians ever assembled at Malden. Yet, because the British were no longer in command of the lake, he realized that Harrison could easily land his forces wherever he chose and block his support from Niagara. In an exchange of letters with Prevost, the governor-general advised Procter that should a retreat be unavoidable, it was to be conducted in an orderly fashion, the troops were not to be encumbered with unnecessary baggage, and the sick should be removed to safety. In short his retreat, should it come to that, was not to take on the characteristics of a flight. Prevost also approved Procter's plan to take a stand at the Thames River should he be forced to leave Malden.[44]

Procter already had decided that, despite his numbers, a retreat was unavoidable. Should he decide to stay and fight, even if he succeeded, his position would be just as untenable as Hull's had been at Detroit the previous year. Without control of the water, the large numbers of men under his command were more of a detriment than advantage because it meant a greater demand for supplies than circumstances allowed him to provide. By retreating eastward to the Thames River, however, using the river as a highway on which to transport his women and children, his artillery and his baggage, he should be able to reach Moravian Town, 70 miles away. This would bring the army and Indians within reaching distance of help from Niagara.

A retreat was unthinkable, however, without first winning the approval of the Indians. He called them to council on September 18, just over a week after Perry's defeat of the British squadron. He told them of the dire situation they were in and described the route of departure from Fort Malden, inviting the tribes to accompany him.

His announcement of a pending retreat took the Indians by surprise, as it also did Lieutenant Colonel Augustus Warburton, his second in command, in whom he had not confided his decision beforehand. The Indians were incensed. Many of them had left their ancestral homes to settle in the Detroit/Amherstburg area. For the past 14 months they had assisted the British in their struggle against the Americans. To retreat was unthinkable. Tecumseh urged that they stay and fight. He told Procter that the British now had 2,500 regulars at Fort Malden, his numerous Indians as well as the Canadian militia. They were in possession of a substantial fort with a strong battery. Why should they retreat? If necessary, the Indians under Tecumseh would fight alone.[45]

Realizing that the council had reached an impasse, Procter promised to provide the Indians with an answer in two days. On the morning of August 20 he called for Tecumseh, showed him a large map of the area eastward, and pointed to Chatham on the Thames River. There, he promised Tecumseh, they would make their stand. Tecumseh now understood the logic of the move and agreed to accompany the army as far as Moravian Town.

As Procter prepared to abandon Malden, Harrison's regulars and volunteers at South Bass Island, Put-in-Bay, prepared to board the ships that would carry them to Canada. Missing were Colonel Richard Johnson and his 500 mounted Kentucky riflemen, who were going by land around the western side of Lake Erie toward Detroit because their horses had proved too skittish on board ship.

Procter's troops marched out of Fort Malden on September 24 after destroying all the public property that they could not carry. That same day the British garrison at Fort Detroit put it to the torch along with all bulk supplies and any other buildings that could be helpful to American troops. Several more days were spent destroying all public works and stores in Amherstburg. By the 27th, after a brief stop at Sandwich, Procter's troops were on the road to the Thames.

Also that same day, at 3:00 p.m., Harrison's troops, 5,000 strong, disembarked onto Canadian soil three miles below Amherstburg where they made camp for the night. The next day they reached Amherstburg, which they found virtually deserted. An advance guard secured the two bridge crossings on the trail that led to Sandwich. It drove off a British rear guard attempting to burn the bridge over the Canard River, but could not save the other at Turkey Creek, which had to be rebuilt, causing a two-day delay in Harrison's progress.[46] The army reached Sandwich on September

30, six days after Procter had left. There it was met by Colonel Johnson, whose Kentucky mounted riflemen had just arrived at Detroit via the river trail.[47]

At Sandwich, Harrison detailed Duncan McArthur to ferry 700 men across the Detroit River and establish order in Detroit, whose citizens no longer had protection from the Indians, especially the warlike Potawatomi, Winnebago, Fox, Huron, and others who had chosen not to accompany Procter to the Thames. McArthur found that as soon as the British had left, the remaining Indians had immediately begun to occupy the town's vacant buildings and plunder or otherwise harass the people. McArthur crossed the river just as vessels from the American fleet arrived and peppered the Indians with grapeshot. Had McArthur not taken possession as quickly as he did, it is probable that a general massacre of Detroit citizens by the Indians would have occurred and many houses burned. As it was the Indians retreated only as far as the River Rouge, six to seven miles away. That evening Harrison issued a proclamation assuring the citizens of Detroit that U.S. civil law was back in place.[48]

By October 1 Procter's army had reached the Thames and begun to march upriver toward the Forks (Chatham, Ontario). Harrison advanced quickly in pursuit, setting out at sunrise, October 2, with about 3,000 men, having left 1,500 to protect Detroit and Sandwich. He reached the mouth of the Thames River 25 miles away that same night, a rather rapid march for an army to make in a single day. There four gunboats from Perry's squadron met him and accompanied the army along the river as the men set out the next day. When they reached Drake's farm, about 11 miles upriver (their progress had been slowed by the need to repair several of the bridges they encountered), they camped for the night. Here a shallow bar extending across the river impeded the progress of the gunboats. Only two were able to pass over and continue. Even they were left behind when Harrison reached Dolsen's farm, three miles above their previous night's camp, as the river's depth and width decreased, and its high, wooded banks provided excellent cover for British sharpshooters. Harrison detailed 150 men to guard the gunboats and the army continued onward.[49]

At one point Procter had expected to make his stand at Dolsen's farm, but the pressure of Harrison's pursuit forced him to continue five miles past the Forks (Chatham) to Bowle's farm. There the British set fire to several of their boats to speed up their advance, moving the ammunition and supplies they carried to a pair of gunboats and other small vessels before continuing upriver. The gunboats, unable to keep up with the rapid march of the British troops, were captured by Harrison. Especially disastrous to the British was the loss of their reserve ammunition.[50]

By 2:00 p.m., October 5, Harrison was within four miles of Moravian Town, forcing Procter to make a decision as to where to stand and fight that day. He opted for a location two miles from Moravian Town in a wooded, swampy area that might reduce the effectiveness of Johnson's mounted riflemen, yet still allow Procter to retire to Moravian Town to regroup his forces if the fight went against him.

That afternoon, the American troops finally came face-to-face with the British. Had an observer looked down on the impending battle scene from above, it would have appeared that Procter had deployed his forces quite well. The Thames River was on the British left on either side of a road winding along the bank through hardwood trees. On the troops' far right a large swamp ground extended parallel to the river. The battlefield between was divided partially in two by a smaller, narrow swamp. Procter

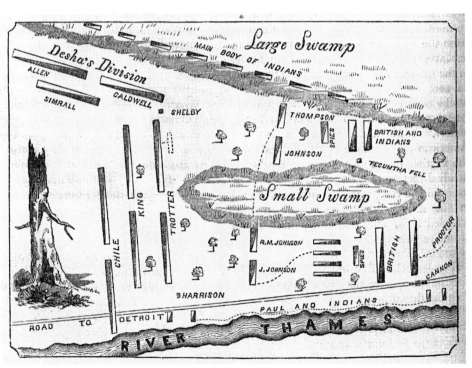

Overhead view of the battle of Thames. (From Benson J. Lossing, *The Pictorial Field-Book of the War of 1812* [New York: Harper & Brothers, 1868].)

placed his regulars in a loose formation among the trees between the small swamp and the river with a six-pounder cannon that was aimed down the trail. Tecumseh's Indians with some British waited opposite them on their right, with the small swamp separating the two forces. Spread across the large swamp extending along the far side of the battlefield some 1,000 men waited to attack Harrison's left flank once it entered the scene of action.

As he surveyed the positions of the British forces before him, Harrison made several adjustments to his own troop deployment, thanks to recommendations from his officers. His plan of battle was for Colonel Johnson and his mounted riflemen to charge directly toward the British regulars in the trees beside the river, with three brigades of infantry under General Henry following behind. Instead of supporting the charge of Johnson and Henry, the three brigades under General Desha would halt on the battlefield, turn to their left facing the mass of Indians in the large swamp, and ward off any attempt on their part to mount a flank attack.

As Colonel Johnson prepared to move forward against the British regulars, he discovered that the ground to be traversed was not wide enough for his two battalions of mounted riflemen to ride abreast. When the order to attack came, he instead diverted his battalion over a trail that led across the small swamp, to join Governor Shelby and his troops in attacking Tecumseh. His brother, Lieutenant Colonel James Johnson, and his mounted battalion continued forward. They charged the British regulars in the trees with such vigor that they swept right through them, turned, and struck again at their rear, capturing the six-pounder cannon before the British had time to fire a single shot. Seeing his regulars collapse in the face of Johnson's charge, Procter turned and quickly fled the field.

On the other side of the small swamp Richard Johnson and Governor Shelby found themselves fighting within thick underbrush. Johnson dismounted his men. A fierce firefight developed in which the colonel was wounded five times before the Indians finally gave way. At some point during the melee, Tecumseh went down. When the news of his death reached the mass of Indians in the large swamp, who were experiencing growing pressure from General Desha's troops, they gradually drifted away from the battle. As their numbers diminished, the remaining British troops on the field had no recourse but to surrender.[51]

The entire battle lasted less than one hour. No more than one half of Harrison's troops was directly involved. The mounted battalions of both Johnson brothers bore the brunt of the action. Reports of the number of casualties sustained by both sides vary, but most historians accept the numbers reported by Harrison to Washington: seven Americans killed and 22 wounded; 12 British killed and 22 wounded, with 601 taken prisoner. It proved to be a productive victory for Harrison, netting him eight pieces of artillery and wagons, and equipment worth more than $1 million.[52]

That night after the battle, Johnson's mounted men rode ahead and took possession of Moravian Town. The rest of the army camped on the battlefield in case the Indians decided to return and resume the fight. They did not. With the defeat of Procter, the northwest Indian tribes no longer were a factor in the war. Those who survived the Thames battle retreated eastward with the rest of the British army including Tenskwatawa, the Prophet, who had joined his brother, Tecumseh, months previously at Fort Malden. Not being a warrior, Tenskwatawa contributed nothing by his presence. After the British defeat, many of the warriors deserted and returned home.[53] After a day's rest the army started back to Detroit on October 7 instead of pursuing Procter. It was a decision made by expediency: the 60-day enlistment period of Governor Meig's volunteers would expire on October 14, and that of Colonel Johnson's mounted riflemen shortly thereafter.

While still at Detroit Harrison had planned a joint army-navy effort to recapture Fort Mackinac, but a violent storm rose up on Lake Erie, making it impossible for supplies to reach him by ship for this new action. After he and Perry discussed what options lay open to them, they concluded that by the time new supplies could arrive it would be too far into the winter season for sailing the lakes. The question became moot as Harrison received new orders transferring him to the Niagara region.

On October 29 President Madison appointed Lewis Cass the new civil governor of the Territory of Michigan; Cass accepted the nomination on December 2, thus bringing to a close William Hull's turbulent eight years as the territory's first governor. That Cass should have been selected as Hull's successor was fraught with irony, whether intended by Madison or not. Cass had been Hull's primary antagonist among the Ohio militia colonels and one of the ringleaders of the unrealized coup to remove him from command during the Detroit campaign.

Harrison gave Cass 400 regular troops and 1,300 Ohio militiamen to maintain the peace in Michigan, especially among the sullen Indian tribes in the area. Since Fort Detroit and the town's public buildings had been burned by the retreating British, Cass had to establish new living quarters for the troops. Equally important was the need to bring supplies in from Ohio, not only for the troops but for the men, women, and children living on both sides of the river who had been left destitute by the depredations of the Indians before Harrison's arrival. Cass's responsibility was further magnified because it included governance over the Canadian territory captured by Harrison on his sweep to the Thames River and Moravian Town.[54]

As Cass assumed control over the civil government, Washington announced that it would reopen Hull's court-martial proceedings. Considering that one and one-half years had passed since the surrender of Detroit, there seemed to be no reason for doing so—unless it was to distract the country from what was taking place on the battlefield. There may be some truth to this. Other than the capture of York (Toronto), the war had not been going well in the east. The inept General Dearborn had been replaced by General Wilkinson. Only in the Northwest, with Perry's victory on Lake Erie and Harrison's at the Thames River, had there been any cause for rejoicing. Both victories had vindicated Hull's pleas to the administration for naval support during the Detroit campaign, which might have led to his victory over the British rather than the surrender of the town and fort the previous year. Whether there still was a need to conduct a court-martial of Hull court-martial after so much time had passed remains an open question.

EPILOGUE

Hull's reputation as a Revolutionary War hero and governor suffered irreparable damage as result of his surrender and subsequent court-martial. In a twist of irony, those who helped bring about the surrender by their intentional as well as unintentional lack of cooperation with Hull during the Detroit campaign went on to achieve surprising political success. Only history can judge whether these careers were justified by merit or were the result of political patronage. Below are short biographies of the principal actors involved in the campaign either to invade Canada or recover Detroit.

Isaac Brock

Before the week was out after the surrender of Detroit, Brock was on his way back to York, arriving on August 27. He was at the Niagara front on October 13, when U.S. troops made a surprise attack on Queenston Heights. Brock immediately rushed to the scene from Fort George to take command as the Americans, who had scaled the Heights unseen in the half light of morning, suddenly stormed down the hill, driving the British before them. Brock rallied all the men he could in the village and counterattacked. He was shot in the chest and died almost immediately. He never knew that only three days before, he had been appointed Knight Commander of the Bath for his success at Detroit.[1]

Lewis Cass

On October 29, 1813, President Madison appointed Cass the governor of Michigan Territory to replace William Hull. Cass proved to be an excellent governor. He was especially adept at negotiating with Indian tribes over the land they controlled within the territory. He also became wealthy through his own land purchases. In 1831 President Andrew Jackson selected him as secretary of war, which placed him at the forefront of Indian policies at the national level. Five years later Jackson appointed him minister to France, one of his attributes being that he spoke French fluently. He resigned in 1842, returning to Detroit to become an influential figure in Democratic Party politics. His name was one of several entered in his party's convention for president in 1844 but the nomination went to Martin Van Buren. The following year the Michigan legislature elected Cass to the U.S. Senate, where he became an active spokesman for President Polk. In 1848 he was selected as his party's nominee for president at the Democratic National Convention but lost to Zachary Taylor in a close race. After being reelected to the Senate in 1849 and 1851, he once again was considered for the presidency during the Democratic Party's convention in 1852, only to lose to Franklin Pierce on the 49th ballot. Cass remained in the Senate as a leader of the Democratic Party until 1857 when President James Buchanan appointed him secretary of state. The two did not always agree on policy and Cass resigned in 1860. He spent the rest of his life in Detroit.[2]

Henry Dearborn

Dearborn's military record as commanding general in New York was disappointing, with a defeat at Queenston on the Niagara River followed by a march to the Canadian border that did not achieve anything. His career took a turn for the better in the spring of 1813 when he captured York (Toronto) in April and Fort George on the Niagara River in May. But by July Secretary of War Armstrong had lost faith in his leadership and removed him from active duty at the front lines, placing him in administrative command of New York City. In the spring of 1814 he served as president over the court-martial of William Hull. Dearborn was honorably discharged from the army on June 15, 1815. Seven years later President Madison selected him as the U.S. minister to Portugal, but after two years Dearborn asked to be released from duty. He retired in 1824 to spend the rest of his years in Roxbury, Massachusetts.[3]

William Eustis

Lacking the support of those around President Madison, Eustis resigned as secretary of war on December 3, 1812. On June 10, 1815, he left for Europe as envoy extraordinary and minister plenipotentiary to the Netherlands, a post he retained until May 1818, when he resigned because of poor health. In November 1820 he was selected to fill a vacant seat in the U.S. House of Representatives. Over the next three years he ran unsuccessfully for governor of Massachusetts while still in the House. In 1823 he finally won the governor's seat. He died suddenly while in office on February 6, 1825.[4]

James Findlay

After the war Findlay returned to his two loves—politics and business—in the Cincinnati area. He was a part owner of the *Liberty Hall and Cincinnati Gazette,* the Cincinnati Bell, Brass & Iron Foundry (along with Harrison), and the Merino Sheep Company, and chief trustee of the Cincinnati Manufacturing Company. He was a member of the House of Representatives from 1825 to 1833, when he was defeated for reelection. The following year, 1834, he campaigned for governor of Ohio against his old comrade in arms Robert Lucas, who was the incumbent, but was unsuccessful. Findlay is generally considered one of the most influential citizens of Cincinnati during its formative years.[5]

William Henry Harrison

After Harrison recaptured Detroit, with no more battles to be fought on the northwest frontier, he resigned his commission. Between 1816 and 1828 he served at various times in the U.S. Congress and in the Ohio Senate. In 1828 he served as ambassador to Columbia but was forced out of the country the following year, accused of fomenting a revolution. In 1840 the Whig Party chose him to run for president against Martin Van Buren, which prompted the famous campaign slogan "Tippecanoe and Tyler, Too" (Tyler being his running mate). Harrison defeated Van Buren by a wide margin, 234 electoral votes to 60, but died of pneumonia only one month after taking office.[6]

William Hull

Although Hull officially remained the governor of Michigan throughout his court-martial, the government refused to pay his salary. It was not until after his death that Congress awarded his heirs $1,628.32 for his services from April 10, 1812 to February 1, 1813, then later awarded another payment of $1,380.00. The two payments were not sufficient recompense, but Congress ignored the remainder and considered the matter closed. Ten years after his trial, in 1824, Hull finally gained access to the letters and documents that he had requested for his defense in his court-martial. These allowed him to publish a defense of his surrender of Detroit. It first appeared as a series of articles in the *Boston Statesman* and later was incorporated in book form under the title *Memoirs of the Campaign of the North Western Army of the United States, 1812,* published in 1824, a year before his death.[7]

Thomas Jessup

One of Hull's harshest critics during the court-martial, Jessup received rapid promotions, from lieutenant to captain in January 1813 and to major in March. At the battle of Chippewa on July 5 his bravery led to his being named brevet lieutenant colonel; he became a full brevet colonel after the battle of Lundy's Lane, during which he sustained four bullet wounds. After the war the army retained Jessup as lieutenant colonel in command of the Third Infantry Regiment. In 1818 the secretary of war made him quartermaster general of the army, with the rank of brigadier general. Jessup went on to serve in wars against the Creek Nation and the Seminole Indians, and in the Mexican-American War. At his death in 1860 he had served as quartermaster general of the army for 42 years, the longest tenure of any staff officer to the present day.[8]

Robert Lucas

Lucas's journal has for generations been considered a primary historical source of what took place during the Detroit campaign. Admittedly biased against Hull, it resonated well with a public that could not believe that Hull's surrender was warranted. Lucas served during the remainder of the War of 1812 as a recruiter for and staff officer in the Ohio militia. He was elected to the state senate for a number of terms: 1814–22, 1824–28, and 1829–30, then served in the lower house during 1831. In 1830 he ran unsuccessfully for governor against his wartime companion Duncan McArthur. Pitted against a different candidate in 1832, Darius Lyman, he was successful, then was reelected in 1834 in a campaign against another wartime friend, James Findlay. He held the governor's office during the territorial dispute known as the Toledo War, which decided the boundary between Ohio and Michigan. In 1838 President Van Buren appointed him governor of the new territory of Iowa. He served in this capacity until 1841, when the newly elected President Harrison replaced him, after which Lucas retired from politics.[9]

Duncan McArthur

Following his parole after the surrender of Detroit, McArthur resigned from the Ohio militia and was elected to the U.S. House of Representatives late in 1812. In March 1813 he was appointed a brigadier general in the U.S. Army under Harrison. He did not take part in the battle of the Thames, having been left in charge of the garrison at Fort Detroit. He testified against Hull in the latter's court-martial in 1814 and subsequently succeeded Harrison as head of the North Western Army when Harrison resigned on May 1. After the war ended McArthur served as a member of the Ohio House (1815–18), the Ohio Senate (1821–23), as a member of Congress (1823–25), then the Ohio House (1826–27), the Ohio Senate (1829–30), and narrowly defeated Robert Lucas as governor of Ohio in 1830. After serving only one term, he unsuccessfully ran for Congress in 1832, then retired from public office, having become a wealthy man through land speculation.[10]

James Miller

Miller's military career blossomed after his exchange as a prisoner of war. Assigned to the Sixth U.S. Infantry, he participated in the attack and capture of Fort George and in the ill-fated Montreal expedition led by General Wilkinson. Promoted to the rank of colonel, he fought in the battle of Lundy's Lane of July 25, 1814. His attempt to storm an entrenched

British battery at night with 300 men is considered one of the best-executed infantry attacks of the war. Congress awarded him a gold medal on November 3, 1814. His leadership during the Niagara campaign brought him a promotion to brevet brigadier general. He remained in the army after the war but resigned his commission on June 1, 1819 when appointed governor of the Territory of Arkansas. His health suffered from the Arkansas climate to the extent that he resigned his seat in 1823. He ended his public career as collector of the port of Salem, Massachusetts, a post he held for 24 years.[11]

Oliver Hazard Perry

Promoted to a full captain retroactive to the date of the battle of Lake Erie, Perry was then given command of the unfinished frigate *Java*. He finished the remainder of the War of 1812 superintending the ship's completion. The maiden voyage of the *Java* in 1816 was plagued by a gale that snapped its main topmast and disciplinary problems with several of the ship's Marine officers. In May 1819 President Monroe assigned Perry to a diplomatic voyage to the Venezuelan government, which he successfully concluded. In Venezuela he contracted yellow fever and died at Angostura on August 23, 1819. His men buried him at Port-of-Spain. In December 1823 his remains were transferred to Newport.[12]

Henry Procter

Before leaving Detroit, Brock appointed Procter both military commander of the region and civil governor of Detroit. On January 18, 1813, Procter delivered a stunning defeat to General Winchester at Frenchtown, for which he was appointed major general. Later that year he led an unsuccessful attack against Harrison at Fort Meigs and against Croghan at Fort Stephenson. After Perry's victory on Lake Erie, which prevented the transport of supplies by water from Niagara, he retreated from Forts Malden and Detroit. Harrison caught his army near Moravian Town on the Thames River and defeated it soundly. Procter escaped with part of his command, arriving at the British lines on Lake Ontario two weeks later. His defeat resulted in a court-martial early in 1815. He was found guilty; his original sentence of a suspension in rank and pay for six months was rescinded in favor of a public reprimand. However, it ended what looked like a promising career. He spent the rest of his life in partial retirement in Bath, England.[13]

Thomas Van Horne

After his exchange as prisoner of war, Van Horne was commissioned a lieutenant colonel in the regular army and spent the majority of the war as commander of Fort Erie. He was elected senator to the Ohio legislature in the years 1812, 1816, and 1817. President Monroe later appointed him registrar of the Land Office in northwestern Ohio, a position he held until 1837. At 45 he retired to become a farmer.[14]

James Winchester

After his capture by the British at Frenchtown, Winchester spent the remainder of 1813 as a prisoner of war. After his exchange he was ordered to join Andrew Jackson's army just prior to the battle of New Orleans, at which time Jackson placed him in command of the city of Mobile, Alabama, where he remained for the rest of the war. He resigned his commission in the regular army in March 1815 and retired to his home in Tennessee. In 1819 he served on the state commission regulating the Tennessee-Missouri boundary. He, John Overton, and Andrew Jackson founded the city of Memphis, Tennessee, on May 22, 1819.[15]

Appendixes

[1]

Madison's War Message to Congress, June 1, 1812

To the Senate and House of Representatives of the United States:

I communicate to Congress certain documents, being a continuation of those heretofore laid before them on the subject of our affairs with Great Britain.

Without going back beyond the renewal in 1803 of the war in Which Great Britain is engaged, and omitting unrepaired wrongs of inferior magnitude, the conduct of her Government presents a series of acts hostile to the United States as an independent and neutral nation.

British cruisers have been in the continued practice of violating the American flag on the great highway of nations, and of seizing and carrying off persons sailing under it, not in the exercise of a belligerent right founded on the law of nations against an enemy, but of a municipal prerogative over British subjects. British jurisdiction is thus extended to neutral vessels in a situation where no laws can operate but the law of nations and the laws of the country to which the vessels belong, and a self-redress is assumed which, if British subjects were wrongfully detained and alone concerned, is that substitution of force for a resort to the responsible sovereign which falls within the definition of war. . . .

The practice, hence, is so far from affecting British subjects alone that, under the pretext of searching for these, thousands of American citizens, under the safeguard of public law and of their national flag, have been torn from their country and from everything dear to them; have been dragged on board ships of war of a foreign nation and exposed, under the severities of their discipline, to be exiled to the most distant and deadly climes, to risk their lives in the battles of their oppressors, and to be the melancholy instruments of taking away those of their own brethren.

Against this crying enormity, which Great Britain would be so prompt to avenge if committed against herself, the United States have in vain exhausted remonstrances and expostulations, and that no proof might be wanting of their conciliatory dispositions, and no pretext left for a continuance of the practice, the British Government was formally assured of the readiness of the United States to enter into arrangements such as could not be rejected if the recovery of the British subjects were the real and sole object. The communication passed without effect.

British cruisers have been in the practice also of violating the rights and the peace of our coasts. They hover over and harass our entering and departing commerce. To the most insulting pretensions they have added the most lawless proceedings in our very harbors, and have wantonly spilt American blood within the sanctuary of our territorial jurisdiction. . . .

Under pretended blockades, without the presence of an adequate force and sometimes without the practicability of applying one, our commerce has been plundered in every sea, the great staples of our country have been cut off from their legitimate markets, and a destructive blow aimed at our agricultural and maritime interests. In aggravation of these predatory measures they have been considered as in force from the dates of their notification, a retrospective effect being thus added, as had been done in other important cases, to the unlawfulness of the course pursued. And to render the outrage the more signal these mock blockades have been reiterated and enforced in the face of official communications from the British Government declaring as the true definition of a legal blockade "that particular ports must be actually invested and previous warning given to vessels bound to them not to enter."

Not content with these occasional expeditions for laying waste our neutral trade, the cabinet of Britain resorted at length to the sweeping system of blockades, under the name of orders in council, which has been molded and managed as might best suit its political views, its commercial jealousies, or the avidity of British cruisers. . . .

Abandoning still more all respect for the neutral rights of the United States and for its own consistency, the British Government now demands as prerequisites to a repeal of its orders as they relate to the United States that a formality should be observed in the repeal of the French decrees nowise necessary to their termination nor exemplified by British usage, and that the French repeal, besides including that portion of the decrees which operates within a territorial jurisdiction, as well as that which operates on the high seas, against the commerce of the United States should not be a single and special repeal in relation to the United States, but should be extended to whatever other neutral nations unconnected with them may be affected by those decrees. . . .

It has become, indeed, sufficiently certain that the commerce of the United States is to be sacrificed, not as interfering with the belligerent rights of Great Britain; not as supplying the wants of her enemies, which she herself supplies; but as interfering with the monopoly which she covets for her own commerce and navigation. She carries on a war against the lawful commerce of a friend that she may the better carry on a commerce with an enemy—a commerce polluted by the forgeries and perjuries which are for the most part the only passports by which she can succeed. . . .

In reviewing the conduct of Great Britain toward the United States our attention is necessarily drawn to the warfare just renewed by the savages on one of our extensive frontiers—a warfare which is known to spare neither age nor sex and to be distinguished by features peculiarly shocking to humanity. It is difficult to account for the activity and combinations which have for some time been developing themselves among tribes in constant intercourse with British traders and garrisons without connecting their hostility with that influence and without recollecting the authenticated examples of such interpositions heretofore furnished by the officers and agents of that Government.

Such is the spectacle of injuries and indignities which have been heaped on our country, and such the crisis which its unexampled forbearance and conciliatory efforts have not been able to avert. . . .

Our moderation and conciliation have had no other effort than to encourage perseverance and to enlarge pretensions. We behold our seafaring citizens still the daily victims of lawless violence, committed on the great common highway of nations, even within the sight of the country which owes them protection. We behold our vessels, freighted with the products of our soil and industry, or returning with the honest proceeds of them, wrested from their lawful destinations, confiscated by prize courts no longer the organs of public law but the instruments of arbitrary edicts, and their unfortunate crews dispersed and lost, or forced or inveigled in British ports into British fleets, whilst arguments are employed in support of these aggressions which have no foundation but in a principle equally supporting a claim to regulate our external commerce in all cases whatsoever.

We behold, in fine, on the side of Great Britain a state of war against the United States, and on the side of the United States a state of peace toward Great Britain.

Whether the United States shall continue passive under these progressive usurpations and these accumulating wrongs, or, opposing force to force in defense of their national rights, shall commit a just cause into the hands of the Almighty Disposer of Events, avoiding all connections which might entangle it in the contests or views of other powers, and preserving a constant readiness to concur in an honorable reestablishment of peace and friendship, is a solemn question which the Constitution wisely confides to the legislative department of the Government. In recommending it to their early deliberations I am happy in the assurance that the decision will be worthy the enlightened and patriotic councils of a virtuous, a free, and a powerful nation.[1]

[2]

HULL'S PROCLAMATION TO CANADIANS
AFTER THE INVASION, JULY 13, 1812

INHABITANTS OF CANADA! After thirty years of Peace and prosperity, the United States have been driven to Arms, The injuries and aggressions, the insults and indignities of Great Britain have *once more* left them with no alternative but manly resistance or unconditional submission. The army under my Command has invaded your Country and the standard of the United States waves on the territory of Canada To the peaceful unoffending inhabitant. It brings neither danger nor difficulty. I come to *find* enemies not to *make* them. I come to *protect* not to *injure* you.

Separated by an immense ocean and an extensive Wilderness from Great Britain you have no participation in her counsels no interest in her conduct. You have felt her Tyranny, you have seen her injustice, but I do not ask *you* to avenge the one or redress the other. The United States are sufficiently powerful to afford you every security consistent with their rights & your expectations, I tender you the invaluable blessings of Civil, Political, & Religious Liberty, and their necessary result, individual, and general, prosperity: That liberty which gave decision to our counsels and energy to our conduct in our struggle for INDEPENDENCE and which conducted us safely and triumphantly thro' the stormy period of the Revolution.

The liberty that has raised us to an elevated rank among the Nations of the world has afforded us a greater measure of Peace & Security wealth and prosperity than ever fell to the Lot of any people.

In the name of my *Country* and by the authority of my Government I promise you protection to your *persons, property, and rights.* Remain at your homes, Pursue your peaceful and customary avocations. Raise not your hands against your brethern, many of your fathers fought for the freedom & *indepen . . . nce* we now enjoy. Being children therefore of the same family with us, and heirs to the same Heritage, the arrival of an army of Friends must be hailed by you with a cordial welcome, You will be emancipated from Tyranny and oppression and restored to the dignified station of freemen. Had I any doubt of eventual success I might ask your assistance but I do not. I have come prepared for every contingency. I have a force which will look down all opposition and that force is but a vanguard of a much greater. If contrary to your own interest & the expectation of my country, you should take part in the approaching contest, you will be considered and treated as enemies and the horrors, and calamities of war will Stalk before you.

If the barbarous and Savage policy of Great Britain be pursued, and the savages are let loose to murder our Citizens and butcher our women and children, this war, will be a war of extermination.

The first stroke with the Tomahawk the first attempt with the Scalping Knife will be the Signal for one indiscriminate scene of desolation. *No white man found fighting by the Side of an Indian will be taken prisoner.* Instant destruction will be his Lot. If the dictates of reason, duty, justice, and humanity, cannot prevent the employment of a force, which respects no rights & knows no wrong, it will be prevented by a severe and relentless system of retaliation.

I doubt not your courage and firmness; I will not doubt your attachment to Liberty. If you tender your services voluntarily they will be accepted readily

The United States offer you *Peace, Liberty,* and *Security* your choice lies between these, & *War, Slavery, and destruction,* Choose then, but choose wisely; and may he who knows the justice of our cause, and who holds in his hand the fate of Nations, guide you to a result the most compatible, with your rights and interests, your peace and prosperity.

WM. HULL[2]

[3]

Hull to Eustis Explaining His Withdrawal from Canada, August 4, 1812

Sir,

At the time when the army under my command took possession of the part of the Province of Upper Canada, everything appeared favourable and all the operations of the army have been successful. Circumstances have since occurred which seem materially to change our future prospect.

The unexpected surrender of Michilimakinac, and the tardy operations of the Army at Niagara are the circumstances to which I allude. I have every reason to expect in a very short time a large body of Savages from the North whose operations will be directed against this Army.

They are under the influence of the North and South-West Companies and the interest of the Companies depends on opening the Detroit River this Summer.

It is the channel by which they obtain their supplies, and there can be no doubt but every effort will be made against this Army to open that Communication. It is the opinion of the officers and the most respectable gentlemen from Mackinac that the British can engage any number of Indians they may have occasion for, and that including the engages of the North-west Companies, two or three thousand will be brought to this place in a very short time. Dispatches have been sent to Malden, and the messengers have returned with orders.

With respect to the delay at Niagara, the following consequences have followed.

A Major Chambers of the British Army with fifty-five regulars and four pieces of Brass Artillery, have been despatched from Niagara and by the last accounts had penetrated as far as Delaware, about one hundred and twenty miles—for this place. Every effort was making by this Detachment to obtain reinforcement from the Militia and Indians, considerable numbers had joined, and it was expected this force would consist of six or seven hundred. The object of this force is to operate against this Army. Two days ago all the Indians were sent from Malden with a small body of British troops to Brownstown and Maguago, and made prisoners of the Wyandotts of these places. There are strong reasons to believe that it was by their own consent, notwithstanding the professions they had made.

Under all these circumstances you will perceive that the situation of this Army is critical.

I am now preparing a work on this bank [Canada] which may be defended by about three hundred men. I have consulted with the principal officers and an attempt to storm the fort at Malden is thought inadvisable without artillery to make a breach.

The picketts are fourteen feet high and defended by bastions on which are mounted twenty-four pieces of cannon.

I am preparing floating batteries to drive the Queen Charlotte from the mouth of the river Canard, and land them below the river, and it is my intention to march down with the Army, and as soon as a breach can be made, attempt the place by storm. Circumstances, however, may render it necessary to recross the river with the main body of the Army to preserve the communication for the purpose of obtaining supplies from Ohio. I am constantly obliged to make strong detachments to convoy the provisions between the foot of the Rapids and Detroit. If nothing should be done at Niagara and the Force should come from the North and the East, as is almost certain, you must be sensible of the difficulties which will attend my situation.

I can promise nothing but the best and most faithful exertions to promote the honour of the Army and the interest of my country.

I AM,

VERY RESPECTFULLY,

YOUR MOST OBEDIENT SERVANT,

W. HULL[3]

[4]

HULL'S OFFICIAL REPORT TO THE SECRETARY OF WAR DESCRIBING THE EVENTS LEADING TO THE SURRENDER, AUGUST 26, 1812

Sir—

Inclosed are the articles of capitulation, by which the Fort of Detroit has been surrendered to Major-General Brock, commanding his Britannic Majesty's forces in Upper Canada, and by which the troops have become prisoners of war. My situation at present forbids me from detailing the particular causes which have led to this unfortunate event. I will, however, generally observe, that after the surrender of Michilimackinac, the Miamis and Delawares, north from beyond Lake Superior, west from beyond the Mississippi, south from the Ohio and Wabash, and east from every port in Upper Canada, and from all the intermediate country, joined in open hostility under the British standard, against the army I commanded, contrary to the most solemn assurances of a large portion of them to remain neutral; even the Ottawa Chiefs from Arbecrotch, who formed the delegation to Washington the last summer, in whose friendship I know you had great confidence, are among the hostile tribes, and several of them distinguished leaders. Among the vast number of chiefs who led the hostile bands, Tecumseh, Marpot, Logan, Walk-in-the-Water, Split-Log, &c. are considered the principals. This numerous assemblage of savages, under the entire influence and direction of the British commander, enabled him totally to obstruct the only communication which I had with my country. This communication had been opened from the settlements in the state of Ohio, two hundred miles through a wilderness, by the fatigues of the army, which I marched to the frontier on the river Detroit. The body of the Lake being commanded by the British armed ships, and the shores and rivers by gun-boats, the army was totally deprived of all communication by water. On this extensive road it depended for transportation of provisions, military stores, medicine, clothing, and every other supply, on pack-horses—all its operations were successful until its arrival at Detroit,—in a few days it passed into the enemy's country, and all opposition seemed to fall before it. One month it remained in possession of this country, and was fed from its resources. In different directions detachments penetrated sixty miles in the settled part of the province, and the inhabitants seemed satisfied with the change of situation, which appeared to be taking place—the militia from Amherstburg were daily deserting, and the whole country, then under control of the army, was asking for protection. The Indians generally, in the first instance, appeared to be neutralized, and determined to take no part in the contest. The fort of Amherstburg was eighteen miles below my encampment. Not a single cannon or mortar was on wheels suitable to carry before that place. I consulted my officers, whether it was expedient to make an attempt on it with the bayonet alone, without cannon to make a breach in the first instance. The council I called was of the opinion it was not—The greatest industry was exerted in making preparation, and it was not until the 7th of August, that two 24-pounders and three howitzers were prepared. It was then my intention to have proceeded on the enterprise. While the operations of the army were delayed by these preparations, the clouds of adversity had been for some time and seemed still thickly to be gathering around me. The surrender of Michilimackinac opened the northern hive of Indians, and they were swarming down in every direction. Reinforcements from Niagara had arrived at Amherstburg under the command of Colonel Procter. The desertion of the militia ceased. Besides the reinforcements that came by water, I received information of a very considerable force under the command of Major Chambers on the river Le Trench with four field-pieces, and collecting the militia on his route, evidently destined for Amherstburg; and in addition to this combination, and increase of force, contrary to all my expectations, the Wyandots, Chippewas, Ottawas, Pottawatamies, Munsees, Delawares, &c. with whom I had the most friendly intercourse, at once passed over to Amherstburg, and accepted the tomahawk and scalping knife. There being now a vast number of Indians at the British post, they were sent to the river Huron, Brownstown, and Maguago to intercept my communication. To open this communication, I detached Maj. Vanhorne of the Ohio volunteers with two hundred men to proceed as far as the river Raisin, under an expectation he would meet Capt. Brush with one hundred and fifty men, volunteers from the state of Ohio, and a quantity of provisions for the army. An ambuscade was formed at Brownstown, and Maj. Vanhorne's detachment [was] defeated, and returned to camp without effecting the object of the expedition.

In my letter of the 7th inst. you have the particulars of that transaction, with a return of the killed and wounded. Under this sudden and unexpected change of things, and having received an express from General Hall, commanding opposite the British shore on the Niagara river, by which it appeared that there was no prospect of any co-operation from that quarter, and the two senior officers of the artillery having stated to me an opinion that it would be extremely difficult, if not impossible, to pass the Turkey river and river Aux-Canard, with the 24-pounders, and that they could not be transported by water, as the *Queen-Charlotte* which carried eighteen 24-pounders, lay in the river Detroit above the mouth of the river Aux-Canard; and as it appeared indispensibly necessary to open the communication to the river Raisin and the Miami, I found myself compelled to suspend the operation against Amherstburg, and concentrate the main force of the army at Detroit. Fully intending, at that time, after the communication was open, to re-cross the river, and pursue the object at Amherstburg, and strongly desirous of continuing protection to a very large number of the inhabitants of Upper Canada who had voluntarily accepted it under my proclamation, I established a fortress on the banks of the river, a little below Detroit, calculated for a garrison of three hundred men. On the evening of the 7th, and the morning of the 8th inst. the army, excepting the garrison of 250 infantry, and a corps of artillerists, all under the command of Major Denny of the Ohio volunteers, re-crossed the river, and encamped at Detroit. In pursuance of the object of opening the communication, on which I considered the existence of the army depending, a detachment of six hundred men, under the command of lieut. Colonel Miller was immediately ordered. For a particular account of the proceedings of this detachment, and the memorable battle which was fought at Maguago, which reflects the highest honor on the American arms, I refer you to my letter of the 13th of August, a duplicate of which is enclosed, in this. Nothing however but honor was acquired by this victory; and it is a painful consideration, that the blood of seventy-five gallant men could only open the communication as far as the points of their bayonets extended. The necessary care of the sick and the wounded, and a very severe storm of rain, rendered their return to camp indispensably necessary for their own comfort. Captain Brush, with his small detachment, and the provisions, being still at the river Raisin, and in a situation to be destroyed by the savages, on the 13th inst. in the evening, I permitted Colonels M'Arthur and Cass to select from their regiment four hundred of their most effective men and proceed [by] an upper route through the woods, which I had sent an express to direct Capt. Brush to take, and had directed the militia of the river Raisin to accompany him as a reinforcement. The force of the enemy continually increasing, and the necessity of opening the communication, and acting on the defensive, became more apparent, I had, previous to detaching Colonels M'Arthur and Cass, on the 11th inst. evacuated and destroyed the fort on the opposite bank. On the 13th, in the evening, Gen. Brock arrived at Amherstburg about the hour Colonels M'Arthur and Cass marched, of which at that time I had received no information. On the 15th, I received a summons to surrender for Detroit, of which I herewith enclose you a copy, together with my answer. At this time I had received no information from Cols. M'Arthur and Cass. An express was immediately sent, strongly escorted, with orders for them to return.

On the 15th, as soon as General Brock received my letter, his batteries opened on the town and the fort, and continued until evening. In the evening all the British Ships of war came nearly as far up the river as Sandwich, three miles below Detroit. At daylight on the 16th (at which time I had received no information from Cols. M'Arthur and Cass, my express sent the evening before, and in the night, having been prevented from passing by numerous bodies of Indians), the cannonade recommenced, and in a short time I received information, that the British army and Indians, were landing below Spring wells under cover of their Ships of war. At this time the whole effective force at my disposal at Detroit did not exceed eight hundred men. Being new troops and unaccustomed to camp life; having performed a laborious march; having been in a number of battles and skirmishes, in which many had fallen, and more had received wounds, in addition to which a large number being sick, and unprovided with medicine, and the comforts necessary for their situation; are the general causes by which the strength of the army was thus reduced. The fort at this time was filled with women, children, and the old and decrepit people of the town and country; they were unsafe in the town, as it was entirely open and exposed to the enemy's batteries. Back of the fort, above or below it there was no safety for them on account of the Indians. In the first instance, the enemy's fire was directed principally against our batteries; and towards the close it was directed against the fort alone, and almost every shot and shell had their effect.

It now became necessary either to fight the enemy in the field; collect the whole force in the fort; or propose terms of capitulation. I could not have carried into the field more than six hundred men, and left an adequate force in the fort. There was landed at that time of the enemy a regular force of much more than that number, and twice that number of Indians. Considering this great inequality of force, I did not think it expedient to adopt the first measure. The second must have been attended with a great sacrifice of blood, and no possible advantage, because the contest could not have been sustained more than a day for the want of powder, and but a very few days for want of provisions. In addition to this, Cols. M'Arthur and Cass would have been in a most hazardous situation. I feared nothing but the last alternative. I have dared to adopt it—I well know the high responsibility of the measure, and I take the whole of it on myself. It was dictated by a sense of duty, and a full conviction of its expediency. The bands of savages which had then joined the British force, were numerous beyond any former example. Their numbers since have increased, and the history of the barbarians of the north of Europe does not furnish examples of more greedy violence than these savages have exhibited. A large portion of the brave and gallant officers and men I commanded would cheerfully have contested until the last cartridge had been expended, and the bayonets worn down to the sockets. I could not consent to the useless sacrifice of such brave men, when I knew it was impossible for me to sustain my situation. It was impossible in the nature of things that an army could have been furnished with the necessary supplies of provision, military stores, clothing, and comforts for the sick, on pack horses through a wilderness of two hundred miles, filled with hostile savages. It was impossible, sir, that this little army, worn down by fatigue, by sickness, by wounds and deaths, could have supported itself not only against the collected force of all the northern nations of Indians, but against the united strength of Upper Canada, whose population consists of more than twenty times the number contained in the territory of Michigan, aided by the principal part of the regular forces of the province, and the wealth and influence of the North-West, and other trading establishments among the Indians, which have in their employment, and under their entire control, more than two thousand white men.

Before I close this dispatch it is a duty I owe my respectable associates in command, Cols. M'Arthur, Findley, Cass, and Lieut. Col. Miller, to express my obligations to them for the prompt and judicious manner in which they have performed their respective duties. If aught has taken place during the campaign which is honorable to the army, these officers are entitled to a share of it. If the last act should be disapproved, no part of the censure belongs to them. I have likewise to express my obligation to General Taylor, who has performed the duty of quarter-master-General, for his great exertions in procuring every thing in his department which it was possible to furnish for the convenience of the army; likewise to brigade-major Jessup for the correct and punctual manner in which he discharged his duty; and to the army generally for their exertions, and the zeal they have manifested for the public interest. The death of Dr. Foster, soon after he arrived at Detroit, was a severe misfortune to the army; it was increased by the capture of the Chachaga packet, by which the medicine and hospital stores were lost. He was commencing the best arrangements in the department of which he was the principal, with the very small means which he possessed. I was likewise deprived of the necessary services of Capt. Partridge, by sickness, the only officer of the corps of engineers attached to the army. All the officers and men have gone to their respective homes, excepting the 4th United States' regiment, and a small part of the first, and Capt. Dyson's company of artillery. Capt. Dyson's company was left at Amherstburg, and the others are with me prisoners—they amount to about 340. I have only to solicit an investigation of my conduct, as early as my situation, and the state of things will admit; and to add the further request, that the government will not be unmindful of my associates in captivity, and of the families of those brave men who have fallen in the contest.[4]

[5]

CASS'S REPORT TO THE SECRETARY OF WAR DESCRIBING
THE EVENTS LEADING TO THE SURRENDER, SEPTEMBER 10, 1812

Sir—

Having been ordered on to this place [Washington] by Col. M'Arthur, for the purpose of communicating to the government particulars respecting the expedition lately commanded by Brig. General Hull, and its disastrous result, as might enable them correctly to appreciate the conduct of the officers and men; and to develop the causes which produced so foul a stain upon the national character, I have the honor to submit for your consideration, the following statement.

When the forces landed in Canada, they landed with an ardent zeal and stimulated with the hope of conquest. No enemy appeared within view of us, and had an immediate and vigorous attack been made upon Malden, it would doubtless have fallen an easy victory. I know General Hull afterwards declared he regretted this attack had not been made, and he had every reason to believe success would have crowned his efforts. The reason given for delaying our operations was to mount our heavy cannon, and to afford to the Canadian militia time and opportunity to quit an obnoxious service. In the course of two weeks the number of their militia, who were embodied, had decreased by desertion from six hundred to one hundred men; and, in the course of three weeks, the cannon were mounted, the ammunition fixed, and every preparation made for an immediate investment of the fort. At a council at which were present all the field officers, and which was held two days before our preparations were completed, it was unanimously agreed to make an immediate attempt, to accomplish the object of the expedition. If by waiting two days wee could have the service of our heavy artillery, it was agreed to wait; if not, it was determined to go without it, and attempt the place by storm. This opinion appeared to correspond with the views of the General, and the day was appointed for commencing our march. He declared to me, that he considered himself pledged to lead the army to Malden. The ammunition was placed in the waggons; the cannon embarked on board the floating batteries and every requisite article was prepared. The spirit and zeal, the ardor and animation displayed by the officers and men, on learning the near accomplishment of their wishes, was a sure and sacred pledge, that in the hour of trial they would not be found wanting in their duty to their country and themselves. But a change of measures, in opposition to the wishes and opinions of all the officers, was adopted by the General. The plan of attacking Malden was abandoned, and instead of acting offensively, we broke up our camp, evacuated Canada, and recrossed the river, in the night, without even the shadow of an enemy to injure us. We left to the tender mercy of the enemy the miserable Canadians who had joined us, and the *protection* we afforded them was but a passport to vengeance. This fatal and unaccountable step dispirited the troops, and destroyed the little confidence which a series of timid, irresolute and indecisive measures had left in the commanding officer.

About the 10th of August, the enemy received a reinforcement of four hundred men. On the twelfth the commanding officers of three of the regiments (the fourth was absent) were informed through a medium which admitted of no doubt, that the General had stated that a capitulation would be necessary. They on the same day addressed to Governor Meigs of Ohio, a letter, of which the following is an extract.

"*Believe all the bearer will tell you. Believe it, however it may astonish you, as much as if told by one of us. Even a c——n is talked of by the ——. The bearer will fill the vacancy.*"

The doubtful fate of this letter rendered it necessary to use circumspection in its details, and therefore these blanks were left. The word "capitulation" will fill the first, and "commanding general," the other. As no enemy was near us, and as the superiority of our force was manifest, we could see no necessity for capitulating, nor any propriety in alluding to it. We therefore determined in the last resort to incur the responsibility of divesting the General of his command. This plan was eventually prevented by two of the commanding officers of regiments being ordered upon detachments.

On the 13th the British took position opposite to Detroit, and began to throw up works. During that and the two following days, they pursued their object without interruption and established a battery for two 18 pounders and an 8 inch howitzer. About sun-set on the evening of the 14th a detachment of 350 men from the regiments commanded by Col. M'Arthur, and myself, was ordered to march to the river Raisin, to escort the provisions, which had some time remained there protected by a party under the command of capt. Brush.

On Saturday, the 15th about 1 o'clock, a flag of truce arrived from Sandwich, bearing a summons from General Brock for the surrender of the town and fort of Detroit, stating he could no longer restrain the fury of the savages. To this an immediate and spirited refusal was returned.

About four o'clock their batteries began to play upon the town. The fire was returned and continued without interruption and with little effect until dark. Their shells were thrown till eleven o'clock.

At day-light the firing on both sides recommenced; about the same time the enemy began to land troops at Spring wells, three miles below Detroit, protected by two of their armed vessels. Between 6 and 7 o'clock they had effected their landing, and immediately took up their line of march. They moved in close columns of platoons, twelve in front, upon the bank of the river.

The fourth regiment was stationed in the fort; the Ohio volunteers and a part of the Michigan militia, behind some pickets, in a situation in which the whole flank of the enemy would have been exposed. The residue of the Michigan militia were in the upper part of the town to resist the incursions of the savages. Two 24-pounders, loaded with grape, were posted upon a commanding eminence, ready to sweep the advancing column. In this situation the superiority of our position was apparent, and our troops, in the eager expectation of victory, awaited the approach of the enemy. Not a discontent broke upon the ear; not a look of cowardice met the eye. Every man expected a proud day for his country, and each was anxious that his individual exertion should contribute to the general result.

When the head of their column arrived within about five hundred yards of our line, orders were received from Gen. Hull for the whole to retreat to the fort, and for the 24-pounders not to open on the enemy. One universal burst of indignation was apparent upon the receipt of this order. Those, whose conviction was the deliberate result of a dispassionate examination of passing events, saw the folly and impropriety of crowding 1100 men into a little work, which 300 could fully man, and into which the shot and shells of the enemy were falling. The fort was in this manner filled; the men were directed to stack their arms, and scarcely was an opportunity afforded of moving. Shortly after a white flag was hung out upon the walls. A British officer rode up to inquire the cause. A communication passed between the commanding Generals, which ended in the capitulation submitted to you. In entering into this capitulation, the General took counsel from his own feelings only. Not an officer was consulted. Not one anticipated surrender, till he saw the white flag displayed. Even the women were indignant at so shameful a degradation of the American character, and all felt as they should have felt, but he who held in his hands the reins of authority.

Our morning report had that morning made our effective men present, fit for duty 1060, without including the detachment before alluded to, and without including 300 of the Michigan militia on duty.

About dark on Saturday morning the detachment sent to escort the provisions, received orders from Gen. Hull to return with as much expedition as possible. About 10 o'clock the next day they arrived in sight of Detroit. Had a firing been heard, or any resistance visible, they would have immediately advanced and attacked the rear of the enemy. The situation in which this detachment was placed, although the result of an accident, was the best for annoying the enemy and cutting off his retreat that could have been selected. With his raw troops enclosed between two fires and no hopes of succor, it is hazarding little to say, that very few would have escaped.

I have been informed by Col. Findley, who saw the return of their quarter-master-general the day after the surrender, that their whole force of every description, white, red, and black, was 1030. They had twenty nine platoons, twelve in a platoon, of men dressed in uniform. Many of these were evidently Canadian militia. The rest of their militia increased their white force to about seven hundred men. The number of the Indians could not be ascertained with any degree of precision; not many were visible. And in the event of an attack upon the town and fort, it was a species of force which could have afforded no material advantage to the enemy.

In endeavoring to appreciate the motives and to investigate the causes, which led to an event so unexpected and dishonorable, it is impossible to find any solution in the relative strength of the contending parties, or in the measure of resistance in our power. That we were far superior to the enemy; that upon any ordinary principles of calculation we would have defeated them, the wounded and indignant feelings of every man there will testify.

A few days before the surrender, I was informed by Gen. Hull, we had 400 rounds of 24 pound shot fixed, and about 100,000 cartridges made. We surrendered with the fort, 40 barrels of powder, and 2500 stand of arms.

The state of our provision has not been generally understood. On the day of the surrender we had fifteen days' provisions of every kind on hand. Of meat there was plenty in the country, and arrangements had been made for purchasing grain and grinding it to flour. It was calculated that we could readily procure three months' provisions, independent of 150 barrels of flour, and 1300 head of cattle, which had been forwarded from the state of Ohio, and which remained at the river Raisin, under Capt. Brush, within reach of the army.

But had we been totally destitute of provisions, our duty and our interest undoubtedly was to fight. The enemy invited us to meet him in the field.

By defeating him the whole country would have been open to us, and the object of our expedition gloriously and successfully obtained. If we had been defeated we had nothing to do but to retreat to the fort, and make the best defence which circumstances and our situation rendered practicable. But basely to surrender without firing a gun—tamely to submit, without raising a bayonet—disgracefully to pass in review before an enemy, as inferior in quality as in the number of his forces, were circumstances, which excited feelings of indignation more easily felt than described. To see the whole of our men flushed with the hope of victory eagerly awaiting the approaching contest, to see them afterwards dispirited, hopeless and desponding, at least 500 shedding tears, because they were not allowed to meet their country's foe and to fight their country's battles, excited sensations, which no American has ever before had cause to feel, and which, I trust in God, will never again be felt, while one man remains to defend the standard of the Union.

I am expressly authorised to state, that Colonel M'Arthur, Col. Findley, and Lieut. Col. Miller, viewed this transaction in the light which I do. They know and feel, that no circumstance in our situation, none in that of the enemy, can excuse a capitulation so dishonorable and unjustifiable. This too, is the universal sentiment among the troops; and I shall be surprised to learn that there is one man who thinks it was necessary to sheath his sword, or lay down his musket.

I was informed by Gen. Hull the morning after the capitulation, that the British forces consisted of 1800 regulars, and that he surrendered to prevent the effusion of human blood. That he magnified their regular force nearly five-fold, there can be no doubt. Whether the philanthropic reason assigned by him is a sufficient justification for surrendering a fortified town, an army and a territory, is for the government to determine. Confident I am, that had the courage and conduct of the General been equal to the spirit and zeal of the troops, the event would have been as brilliant and successful as it now is disastrous and dishonorable.[5]

NOTES

PREFACE

1. The quotes are from, respectively, James R. Jacobs and Glen Tucker, *The War of 1812: A Compact History* (New York: Hawthorne Books, 1969), 31; Garry Wills, *James Madison* (New York: Henry Holt, 2002), 102; Pierre Berton, *The Invasion of Canada* (Boston: Little, Brown, 1980), 1:178; A. J. Langguth, *Union 1812* (New York: Simon & Schuster, 2006), 193.

INTRODUCTION

1. James G. Forbes, *Report of the Trial of General William Hull: Commanding the Northwestern Army of the United States* (New York: Eastburn, Kirk, 1814), 119.
2. A. L. Burt, "Issues and the Evolution of Causes of the War of 1812," in *The War of 1812: Past Justifications and Present Interpretations*, ed. George Rogers Taylor (Boston: Heath, 1963), 88.
3. Robert S. Quimby, *The U.S. Army in the War of 1812: An Operational and Command Study* (Lansing: Michigan State University Press, 1997), 4.

CHAPTER 1

1. Brian Leigh Dunnigan, "Fortress Detroit, 1701–1826," in *The Sixty Years' War for the Great Lakes, 1754–1814,* ed. David Curtis Skaggs and Larry L. Nelson (Lansing: Michigan State University Press, 2001), 169–71.
2. Ibid., 173.
3. Philip Mason, *Detroit, Fort Lernoult, and the American Revolution* (Detroit:

Wayne State University Press, 1964), 9.

4. Ibid., 23.

5. Willis Frederick Dunbar, *Michigan: A History of the Wolverine State* (Grand Rapids, MI: Eerdman, 1965), 178; and F. Clever Bald, *Michigan in Four Centuries* (New York: Harper & Row, 1954), 106.

6. David Lee Poremba, *Detroit in Its World Setting* (Detroit: Wayne State University Press, 2001), 93, 99.

7. William L. Jenks, "Life of William Hull," *Michigan Historical Collections* 40 (1929): 25–51.

8. Alec R. Gilpin, *The Territory of Michigan: 1805–1837* (Lansing: Michigan State University Press, 1970), 9–10.

9. James Freeman Clarke, *History of the Campaign of 1812 and Surrender of the Post of Detroit* (New York: D. Appleton, 1847), 321.

10. George B. Catlin, *The Story of Detroit* (Detroit: Detroit News, 1920), 115–19; Dunbar, *Michigan,* 105; Bald, *Michigan in Four Centuries,* 107–8.

11. Dunbar, *Michigan,* 193–94.

12. Frank B. Woodford, *Mr. Jefferson's Disciple: A Life of Justice Woodward* (East Lansing: Michigan State College Press, 1953), 45.

13. Ibid., 198–99; Bald, *Michigan in Four Centuries,* 113.

14. Maria Campbell, *Revolutionary Services and Civil Life of General William Hull: Prepared from His Manuscripts* (New York: D. Appleton, 1848), 311.

15. Ibid., 320.

16. Reginald Horsman, *The Causes of the War of 1812* (New York: Octagon Books, 1975), 154.

17. Jenks, "William Hull," 38–39.

18. Dunbar, *Michigan,* 201.

19. Skaggs and Nelson, *The Sixty Years' War,* 180.

20. Almon E. Parkins, *The Historical Geography of Detroit* (New York: Kannikat, 1918), 132.

21. William Hull, *Memoirs of the Campaign of the North Western Army of the United States, 1812* (Boston: True & Greene, 1824), 19.

22. Ibid., 19–20.

23. Gilpin, *The Territory of Michigan,* 21.

24. R. David Edmunds, "Tecumseh, the Shawnee Prophet, and American History: A Reassessment," *Western Historical Quarterly* 14 (July 1983): 265–66; Alfred A. Cave, "The Shawnee Prophet, Tecumseh, and Tippecanoe: A Case Study of Historical Myth Making," *Journal of the Early Republic* 22 (Winter 2002): 641–43.

25. Edmunds, "Tecumseh, the Shawnee Prophet, and American History," 271.

26. Cave, "The Shawnee Prophet," 644.

27. Ibid., 273–74.

28. Alec R. Gilpin, *The War of 1812 in the Old Northwest* (East Lansing: Michi-

gan State University Press, 1958), 13.

29. John Sugden, *Tecumseh: A Life* (New York: Henry Holt, 1997), 232.

30. Ibid., 235–36.

31. Cave, "The Shawnee Prophet," 657–65.

32. Robert Leckie, *From Sea to Shining Sea* (New York: HarperCollins, 1993), 160–65.

33. Gilpin, *The Territory of Michigan*, 21

34. Forbes, *Report of the Trial*, appendix, 3

35. Sugden, *Tecumseh*, 258.

36. "Brig-General Hull to the Secretary of War, March 6, 1812," in *Documents related to the Invasion of Canada and the Surrender of Detroit*, ed. E. A. Cruikshank (Ottawa: Government Printing Bureau, 1962), 19–21.

37. Ibid., 22.

38. "John Armstrong to Secretary of War, January 2, 1812," in Cruikshank, *Documents*, 3.

39. Gilpin, *The War of 1812*, 28.

40. Forbes, *Report of the Trial*, appendix, 7.

CHAPTER 2

1. Horsman, *The Causes of the War of 1812*, 21.

2. Ibid., 30–31.

3. Ibid., 38–39.

4. Ibid., 69.

5. Burt, "Issues and the Evolution of Causes of the War of 1812," 70–71.

6. Kate Caffrey, *The Twilight's Last Gleaming* (New York: Stein & Day, 1977), 110–11.

7. Ibid., 112.

8. Sugden, *Tecumseh*, 156.

9. Ibid.

10. Noble E. Cunningham Jr., *The Life of Thomas Jefferson* (Baton Rouge: Louisiana State University Press, 1987), 297–99.

11. Garry Wills, *James Madison* (New York: Henry Holt, 2002), 83.

12. Caffrey, *Twilight's Last Gleaming*, 51.

13. Burt, "Issues and the Evolution of Causes of the War of 1812," 78.

14. "Embargo Act," in *Encyclopedia of the War of 1812*, ed. David S. Heilder and Jeanne T. Heilder (Santa Barbara: ABC-CLIO, 1997), 167.

15. Horsman, *The Causes of the War of 1812*, 138.

16. Ibid., 145–47.

17. Bradford Perkins, *Prologue to War: England and the United States, 1805–1812* (Berkeley: University of California Press, 1968), 250.

18. Ibid., 244–45.

19. Horsman, *The Cause of the War of 1812*, 187.
20. Ibid., 188.
21. Ibid., 196–97.
22. Ibid., 203–4.
23. Perkins, *Prologue to War*, 285.
24. Sandy Antal, *A Wampum Denied: Procter's War of 1812* (Ottawa: Carleton University Press, 1997) 20–21.
25. Ibid., 22–24.
26. Burt, "Issues and the Evolution of Causes of the War of 1812," 36.
27. Horsman, *The Cause of the War of 1812*, 239–40.
28. Burt, "Issues and the Evolution of Causes of the War of 1812," 90.
29. Caffrey, *Twilight's Last Gleaming*, 313.
30. Robert R. Rutland, *James Madison: The Founding Father* (New York: Macmillan, 1987), 223.
31. Leckie, *From Sea to Shining Sea*, 178–79.
32. Ibid., 178–79.
33. Rutland, *James Madison*, 226.
34. Robert Rutland, *The Presidency of James Madison* (Lawrence: University Press of Kansas, 1990), 105.
35. T. H. Williams, *The History of American Wars from 1745 to 1918* (Baton Rouge: Louisiana State University Press, 1981), 98.
36. Henry Adams, *The History of the United States of America during the Administration of Thomas Jefferson and James Madison,* ed. Earl H. Harbert (New York: Library of America, 1986), 2:440.
37. Leckie, *From Sea to Shining Sea*, 200; J. Mackay Hitsman, *The Incredible War of 1812: A Military History* (Toronto: University of Toronto Press, 1965), 42.
38. Horsman, *The Causes of the War of 1812*, 241.
39. Quimby, *The U.S. Army in the War of 1812*, 3.
40. Leckie, *From Sea to Shining Sea*, 183–84.
41. Quimby, *The U.S. Army in the War of 1812*, 3, 9.
42. Irving Brant, *James Madison: Commander in Chief* (New York: Bobbs-Merrill, 1961), 44.
43. Richard Lee Morton, "Enlisted Men in the United States Army: 1812–1815," *William and Mary Quarterly* (October 1986): 645.
44. Quimby, *The U.S. Army in the War of 1812*, 5.
45. Ibid., 7.
46. Ibid., 9–10.
47. Rutland, *The Presidency of James Madison*, 106.
48. Hitsman, *The Incredible War of 1812*, 29.
49. Gilpin, *The War of 1812*, 64.

CHAPTER 3

1. Robert McAfee, *History of the Late War in the Western Country* (Lexington, KY: Worsley & Smith, 1816), 50.
2. "Duncan McArthur," ohiohistorycentral.org, April 3, 2008, 1.
3. "James Findlay," ohiohistorycentral.org, October 17, 2008, 1.
4. William Carl Klunder, *Lewis Cass and the Politics of Moderation* (Kent, OH: Kent University Press, 1996), 8.
5. Frank B. Woodford, *The Last Jeffersonian* (New Brunswick, NJ: Rutgers University Press, 1950), 10–18.
6. Klunder, *Lewis Cass,* 9.
7. Gilpin, *The War of 1812,* 33–34.
8. Hull, *Memoirs,* 34.
9. Ibid., 34.
10. Gilpin, *The War of 1812,* 36.
11. Ibid., 36–37.
12. Klunder, *Lewis Cass,* 10.
13. Parkins, *Historical Geography of Detroit,* 254.
14. Gilpin, *The War of 1812,* 36.
15. Ibid., 38.
16. McAfee, *History of the Late War,* 53.
17. Gilpin, *The War of 1812,* 40–41.
18. McAfee, *History of the Late War,* 54.
19. John C. Parish, ed., *The Robert Lucas Journal of the War of 1812* (Iowa City: State Historical Society of Iowa, 1906), vi.
20. Ibid., 55.
21. Eustis to Hull, in Michigan Pioneer and Historical Society, *Historical Collections,* vol. 25 (Robert Smith: Lansing, 1896), 307.
22. Hull to Eustis, in Cruikshank, *Documents,* 38.
23. Gilpin, *The War of 1812,* 52–53.
24. Ibid., 52.
25. Eustis to Hull, in Cruikshank, *Documents,* 35.
26. Benson J. Lossing, *The Pictorial Field-Book of the War of 1812* (New York: Harper & Brothers, 1868), 258.
27. Gilpin, *The War of 1812,* 53.
28. Testimony of Lieutenant Aaron Forbush, in Forbes, *Report of the Trial,* 145.
29. Gilpin, *The War of 1812,* 54.
30. Parish, *Lucas Journal,* 18–19.
31. Hull, *Memoirs,* 39.
32. Gilpin, *The War of 1812,* 59.
33. Milo M. Quaife, *War on the Detroit: The Chronicle of Thomas Vercheres de Boucherville* (Chicago: Lakeside, 1940), 220.

34. St. George to Hull, in Cruikshank, *Documents,* 41.

35. Secretary of War to Hull, June 24, 1812, in Cruikshank, *Documents,* 37.

36. Quimby, *The U.S. Army in the War of 1812,* 57.

37. Ibid., 57–58.

CHAPTER 4

1. Gilpin, *The War of 1812,* 65.

2. Ibid.

3. Dixon to Bruyeres, in Cruikshank, *Documents,* 47.

4. Ibid., 46, 47.

5. Gilpin, *The War of 1812,* 67.

6. Antal, *A Wampum Denied,* 44.

7. Hull to Secretary of War, in Cruikshank, *Documents,* 50.

8. Milo M. Quaife, ed., *The Capitulation; or, A History of the Expedition Conducted by William Hull, Brigadier-General of the North Western Army by an Ohio Volunteer* (Chillicothe, OH: James Barnes, 1812), 225, 226.

9. Gilpin, *The War of 1812,* 75; Parish, *Lucas Journal,* 27.

10. Quaife, *The Capitulation,* 226.

11. Proclamation of General Hull, in Cruikshank, *Documents,* 58–60.

12. Clarke, *History of the Campaign,* 338.

13. Hull, *Memoirs,* 53.

14. Quaife, *The Capitulation,* 234.

15. Gilpin, *The War of 1812,* 78.

16. Ibid., 77, 78; McAfee, *History of the Late War,* 63; Gilpin, *The War of 1812,* 234–36. Virtually every account of McArthur's march to the Thames differs from the others.

17. Antal, *A Wampum Denied,* 47.

18. Cass to Hull, in Cruikshank, *Documents,* 71.

19. Parish, *Lucas Journal,* 33, 34.

20. St. George to Hull, in Cruikshank, *Documents,* 70.

21. Gilpin, *The War of 1812,* 81.

22. Parish, *Lucas Journal,* 34, 35.

23. Ibid., 36–39.

24. Ibid., 40.

25. Hull to Secretary of War, in Cruikshank, *Documents,* 80.

26. Proclamation of Major-General Brock, in Cruikshank, *Documents,* 81–83.

27. Parish, *Lucas Journal,* 41, 42.

28. Quaife, *The Capitulation,* 255.

29. Ibid., 256–61; Gilpin, *The War of 1812,* 87.

30. Antal, *A Wampum Denied,* 67–69.

31. Procter to Brock, in Cruikshank, *Documents,* 80.

32. Hull to Scott, in Cruikshank, *Documents,* 103.

33. Roberts to Baynes, in Cruikshank, *Documents,* 65.

34. Hanks to Hull, in Cruikshank, *Documents,* 67.

35. Articles of Capitulation, in Cruikshank, *Documents,* 63, 64.

36. Askin to Claus, in Cruikshank, *Documents,* 67.

37. Harrison to Secretary of War, in Cruikshank, *Documents,* 132–33.

38. Antal, *A Wampum Denied,* 72.

39. Ferdinand Brock Tupper, *The Life and Correspondence of Major-General Sir Isaac Brock, K.B.* (London: Simpkin, Marshall, 1847), 231.

40. Dearborn to Secretary of War, in Cruikshank, *Documents,* 127.

41. Dearborn to Hull, in Cruikshank, *Documents,* 129.

42. Prevost to Bathurst, in Cruikshank, *Documents,* 179.

CHAPTER 5

1. Forbes, *Report of the Trial,* 148.

2. Gilpin, *The War of 1812,* 94–95.

3. Parish, *Lucas Journal,* 45.

4. Jeffrey Kimball, "The Fog and Friction of Frontier War: The Role of Logistics in American Offensive Failure during the War of 1812," *Old Northwest* 5 (Winter 1979): 334–35.

5. Cass file, Burton Historical Collection, Detroit Public Library, folder 1810–13.

6. Forbes, *Report of the Trial,* 56.

7. Ibid., 77–78.

8. Ibid., 72.

9. Ibid., 56.

10. Quaife, *War on the Detroit,* 88–89.

11. Forbes, *Report of the Trial,* 57.

12. Parish, *Lucas Journal,* 47–48.

13. Ibid., 48–51.

14. Quaife, *War on the Detroit,* 89–92; Sugden, *Tecumseh,* 76, 77; Antal, *A Wampum Denied,* 292.

15. Parish, *Lucas Journal,* 51; McAfee, *History of the Late War,* 75; Quaife, *War on the Detroit,* 89.

16. Forbes, *Report of the Trial,* 47–49.

17. Ibid., 49.

18. Ibid., 50.

19. Ibid., 52.

20. Ibid.

21. McAfee, *History of the Late War,* 77.

22. Gilpin, *The War of 1812,* 99.

23. Forbes, *Report of the Trial,* 55.
24. Clarence M. Burton, ed., *The City of Detroit, Michigan, 1701–1922* (Detroit: S. J. Clarke, 1922), 1006.
25. Gilpin, *The War of 1812,* 100–101; Quaife, *War on the Detroit,* 96–97; Sugden, *Tecumseh,* 296–97; Antal, *A Wampum Denied,* 80–82.
26. Quaife, *War on the Detroit,* 98.
27. Gilpin, *The War of 1812,* 101.
28. Proctor to Brock, in Cruikshank, *Documents,* 135–36.
29. Hull to Eustis, in Cruikshank, *Documents,* 139–40.
30. Forbes, *Report of the Trial,* 107.
31. Gilpin, *The War of 1812,* 101–2.
32. Forbes, *Report of the Trial,* 108.
33. McAfee, *History of the Late War,* 84.
34. Harrison to Secretary of War, August 10, 1812, in Cruikshank, *Documents,* 131–33.
35. Gilpin, *The War of 1812,* 105.
36. General Orders of August 14, 1812, in Cruikshank, *Documents,* 141–42.
37. Antal, *A Wampum Denied,* 83.
38. Parish, *Lucas Journal,* 59–60.
39. McAfee, *History of the Late War,* 82.
40. Ibid., 83–84.
41. Tupper, *Correspondence of Brock,* 242–46.
42. Gilpin, *The War of 1812,* 110–11.
43. Burton, *The City of Detroit,* 1009.

CHAPTER 6

1. Heald to Secretary of War, in Cruikshank, *Documents,* 225–27; McAfee, *History of the Late War,* 98–101; Quimby, *The U.S. Army in the War of 1812,* 49–50. There are numerous accounts of the surrender of Fort Dearborn, none of which agrees with another. The account presented here is Heald's own official report to the secretary of war, which presumably would be the most accurate.
2. Quimby, *The U.S. Army in the War of 1812,* 43.
3. Brock to Hull, in Cruikshank, *Documents,* 144.
4. Hull to Brock, August 15, 1812, in Cruikshank, *Documents,* 144.
5. Brian Leigh Dunnigan, *Frontier Metropolis* (Detroit: Wayne State University Press, 2001), 137.
6. Forbes, *Report of the Trial,* 32.
7. Burton, *The City of Detroit,* 1012.
8. Forbes, *Report of the Trial,* 36, 37.
9. Gilpin, *The War of 1812,* 115.

10. Reginald Horsman, *Matthew Elliott, British Indian Agent* (Detroit: Wayne State University Press, 1964) 195, 196.

11. Prize Pay List—Surrender of Fort Detroit, in Cruikshank, *Documents,* 147, 148.

12. Forbes, *Report of the Trial,* 42, 43.

13. Brock to Prevost, in Cruikshank, *Documents,* 158.

14. Forbes, *Report of the Trial,* 24.

15. Ibid., 60, 61.

16. Hull to Secretary of War, in Cruikshank, *Documents,* 118; Gilpin, *The War of 1812,* 121.

17. Pierre Berton, *The Invasion of Canada* (Boston: Little, Brown, 1980), 1:116.

18. Forbes, *Report of the Trial,* 86.

19. Gilpin, *The War of 1812,* 122.

20. Clarke, *History of the Campaign,* 455, 456.

21. Cruikshank, *Documents,* 241.

22. Burton, *The City of Detroit,* 1013.

23. Ibid., 1014.

24. Forbes, *Report of the Trial,* 91.

25. Ibid., 94.

26. Cruikshank, *Documents,* 146, 147.

27. Ibid., 147.

28. Burton, *The City of Detroit,* 1018.

29. Ibid., 155, 156.

30. Gilpin, *The War of 1812,* 121; Quimby, *The U.S. Army in the War of 1812,* 47; Steven J. Rauch, "The Eyes of the Country Were upon Them: A Comparative Study of the Campaigns of the Northwestern Army Conducted by William Hull and William Henry Harrison: 1812–1813" (master's thesis, Eastern Michigan University, 1992), 128; Forbes, *Report of the Trial,* 93–96, appendix, 74.

31. Clarke, *History of the Campaign,* 384; John G. Van Deusen, "Court Martial of Gen. William Hull," *Michigan History Magazine* 12 (1928): 681.

32. Gilpin, *The War of 1812,* 120, 121.

33. Woodford, *The Last Jeffersonian,* 70, 71.

34. Elliott to Procter and Chambers to Procter, in Cruikshank, *Documents,* 172, 175.

35. Clarke, *History of the Campaign,* 456, 457.

36. Brant, *James Madison,* 76.

37. Klunder, *Lewis Cass,* 14.

38. Cruikshank, *Documents,* 222.

39. Brant, *James Madison,* 75.

40. Cruikshank, *Documents,* 221. (The entire text of Cass's letter is in appendix 2.)

41. Merrill D. Peterson, ed., *James Madison: A Biography in His Own Words* (New York: Newsweek, 1974), 329, 330.
42. Rutland, *The Presidency of James Madison*, 111.

CHAPTER 7

1. Michigan Pioneer and Historical Society, *Historical Collections*, 25:424.
2. Burton, *The City of Detroit*, 1027.
3. Ibid., 1027–28.
4. Michigan Pioneer and Historical Society, *Historical Collections*, vol. 15 (Lansing: Wynkoop Hallenback Crawford, 1909) 388–89.
5. Burton, *The City of Detroit*, 1028.
6. Hull, *Memoirs*, 142–43.
7. Forbes, *Report of the Trial*, 14.
8. Hull, *Memoirs*, 101; Gilpin, *The War of 1812*, 159; Michigan Pioneer and Historical Society, *Historical Collections*, vol. 22 (Lansing: Robert Smith, 1903), 519.
9. Hull, *Memoirs*, 80–81.
10. Forbes, *Report of the Trial*, 117.
11. Hull, *Memoirs*, 148–49.
12. Ibid., 156–57.
13. Forbes, *Report of the Trial*, 47.
14. Cruikshank, *Documents*, 35.
15. Forbes, *Report of the Trial*, 138–39.
16. Ibid., 25.
17. Ibid., 26.
18. Ibid., 55–56.
19. Ibid., 110.
20. Ibid., 111.
21. Ibid., 131.
22. Ibid., 140.
23. Ibid., 39–43.
24. Ibid., 62.
25. Ibid., 89.
26. Ibid., 130.
27. Ibid., 128, 130.
28. Ibid., 83.
29. Ibid., 151.
30. Ibid., 98.
31. Ibid., 99.
32. Ibid., 104.
33. Ibid., 40.

34. Ibid.
35. Ibid., 123.
36. Ibid., 124.
37. Ibid., 45.
38. Ibid., 92.
39. Ibid., 85.
40. Ibid., 71.
41. Ibid., 131.
42. Ibid., 133.
43. Ibid., 149.
44. Ibid., 110.
45. Ibid., 96.
46. Ibid., 68.
47. Ibid., 113.
48. Ibid., 84.
49. Ibid., 132–33.
50. Ibid., 140.
51. Gilpin, *The War of 1812*, 97.
52. Forbes, *Report of the Trial*, 82.
53. Ibid., 117.
54. Ibid., 84.
55. Klunder, *Lewis Cass*, 13.
56. Forbes, *Report of the Trial*, 20.
57. Ibid., 141.
58. Ibid., 74–75.
59. Ibid., 76–77.
60. Ibid., 86.
61. Ibid., 31.
62. Ibid., 118–19.
63. Letter 6 to Senator Thomas Worthington, January 31, 1813, Cass file, Burton Historical Collection, Detroit Public Library.
64. Forbes, *Report of the Trial*, 154.
65. Ibid., 119.
66. Burton, *The City of Detroit*, 1032–33.
67. Forbes, *Report of the Trial*, 145.
68. Burton, *The City of Detroit*, 1035.

CHAPTER 8

1. Kimball, "The Fog and Friction of Frontier War."
2. Gilpin, *The War of 1812*, 158.
3. Philip de Ste. Croix, ed., *Patrick O'Brian's Navy* (London: Salamander

Books, 2003), 114.

4. Lossing, *Pictorial Field-Book,* 271.

5. Michigan Pioneer and Historical Society, *Historical Collections,* 15:436–39.

6. Cruikshank, *Documents,* 188–89.

7. Rauch, "The Eyes of the Country Were upon Them," 67.

8. Ibid., 85–87.

9. Ibid., 72.

10. Ibid., 100–102.

11. George B. Catlin, "Michigan's Early Military Roads," *Michigan History Magazine* 13 (Spring 1929): 199.

12. Gilpin, *The War of 1812,* 72.

13. Ibid., 112.

14. Ibid., 145.

15. Ibid., 137.

16. Parish, *Lucas Journal,* 80.

17. John R. Elting, *Amateurs, to Arms! A Military History of the War of 1812* (New York: Workman, 1991), 34.

18. Quimby, *The U.S. Army in the War of 1812,* 47–48.

Chapter 9

1. Gilpin, *The War of 1812,* 124.

2. Ibid., 159.

3. Antal, *A Wampum Denied,* 117.

4. Burton, *The City of Detroit,* 1037–38.

5. Woodford, *Mr. Jefferson's Disciple,* 110–11.

6. Ibid., 112.

7. Antal, *A Wampum Denied,* 121.

8. Ibid., 119.

9. Silas Farmer, *History of Detroit and Wayne Country and Early Michigan* (Detroit: Silas Farmer, 1890), 281.

10. Ibid., 281, 282.

11. Frank B. Woodford and Alfred Hyma, *Gabriel Richard: Frontier Ambassador* (Detroit: Wayne State University Press, 1958), 75.

12. "Memorial of the Citizens, January 6, 1813," Woodward Papers, Burton Historical Collection, Detroit Public Library.

13. Woodford, *Mr. Jefferson's Disciple,* 114.

14. Quimby, *The U.S. Army in the War of 1812,* 104.

15. Kimball, "The Fog and Friction of Frontier War," 333–34.

16. Elting, *Amateurs,* 58.

17. Quimby, *The U.S. Army in the War of 1812,* 126.

18. Ibid.

19. Ibid., 127.
20. Elting, *Amateurs,* 59.
21. Ralph Naveaux, *Invaded on All Sides* (Marceline, OH: Walworth, 2008), 101.
22. Antal, *A Wampum Denied,* 8.
23. Ibid., 60.
24. Quimby, *The U.S. Army in the War of 1812,* 132, 133; Antal, *A Wampum Denied,* 161–63.
25. Antal, *A Wampum Denied,* 166.
26. Naveaux, *Invaded on All Sides,* 133.
27. Ibid., 140.
28. Wells to Cushing, Michigan Historical Commission, *Michigan Historical Collections,* vol. 40 (Lansing: Michigan Historical Commission, 1929), 505.
29. Quimby, *The U.S. Army in the War of 1812,* 134–36; Antal, *A Wampum Denied,* 169–70.
30. Naveaux, *Invaded on All Sides,* 193.
31. Ibid., 137.
32. Proctor to Sheafe, in Michigan Pioneer and Historical Society, *Historical Collections,* 15:229.
33. Antal, *A Wampum Denied,* 174; Naveaux, *Invaded on All Sides,* 211.
34. Dudley, in Michigan Pioneer and Historical Society, *Historical Collections,* 22:441.
35. Farmer, *History of Detroit,* 280.
36. Burton, *The City of Detroit,* 1042.
37. Farmer, *History of Detroit,* 280.
38. General Friend Palmer, *Early Days in Detroit* (Detroit: Hunt & June, 1906), 135.
39. Michigan Pioneer and Historical Society, *Historical Collections,* 15:228.
40. Ibid., 234.
41. Ibid., 235, 236.
42. Woodford, *Mr. Jefferson's Disciple,* 117, 118.
43. Woodford and Hyma, *Richard,* 76.
44. Ibid.
45. Procter to McDonald, May 13, 1813, in Michigan Pioneer and Historical Society, *Historical Collections,* 15:297.

CHAPTER 10

1. Gilpin, *The War of 1812,* 175.
2. Ibid., 183; Jon Latimer, *1812: War with America* (Cambridge, MA: Harvard University Press, 2007), 134, 135.

3. "Chambers to Freer, in Michigan Pioneer and Historical Society, *Historical Collections,* 15:290.

4. Latimer, *1812,* 135.

5. Gilpin, *The War of 1812,* 180.

6. James A. Thom, *Panthers in the Sky* (New York: Ballantine Books, 1989), 607.

7. Latimer, *1812,* 136.

8. Gilpin, *The War of 1812,* 186.

9. Ibid., 188, 189.

10. Alexander C. Casselman, ed., *Richardson's War of 1812* (Toronto: Historical Publishing, 1902), 50, 51; Sugden, *Tecumseh,* 335.

11. Thom, *Panthers in the Sky,* 619.

12. "Chambers to Freer," in Michigan Pioneer and Historical Society, *Historical Collections,* 15:291.

13. Antal, *A Wampum Denied,* 230.

14. Sugden, *Tecumseh,* 344–45.

15. Gilpin, *The War of 1812,* 202; Latimer, *1812,* 178; Sugden, *Tecumseh,* 344–46.

16. Sugden, *Tecumseh,* 346.

17. Ibid., 348.

18. Gilpin, *The War of 1812,* 205.

19. Quimby, *The U.S. Army in the War of 1812,* 208.

20. Latimer, *1812,* 178.

21. Quimby, *The U.S. Army in the War of 1812,* 208, 209; Gilpin, *The War of 1812,* 206, 207.

22. Wilson Wood, ed., *Select British Documents of the War of 1812* (Toronto: Champion Society, 1920), 2:50, 51.

23. David Curtis Skaggs and Gerard T. Altoff, *A Signal Victory: The Lake Erie Campaign* (Annapolis, MD: Naval Institute Press, 1997), 37, 38.

24. Ibid., 41.

25. Quimby, *The U.S. Army in the War of 1812,* 260.

26. Skaggs and Altoff, *A Signal Victory,* 45.

27. Barry Gough, *Fighting Sail on Lake Huron and Georgian Bay* (Annapolis, MD: Naval Institute Press, 2002), 40.

28. Ibid., 33.

29. Robert Malcomson and Thomas Malcomson, *HMS Detroit: The Battle for Lake Erie* (Annapolis, MD: Naval Institute Press, 1990), 67–69.

30. Skaggs and Altoff, *A Signal Victory,* 81.

31. Malcomson and Malcomson, *HMS Detroit,* 76.

32. Ibid.

33. Quimby, *The U.S. Army in the War of 1812,* 265, 266.

34. Malcomson and Malcomson, *HMS Detroit,* 83.

35. Barclay to Yeo, in Michigan Pioneer and Historical Society, *Historical Collections,* 25:525.
36. Robert Malcomson, *Warships of the Great Lakes, 1754–1834* (Annapolis, MD: Naval Institute Press, 2001), 85.
37. Gough, *Fighting Sail,* 41–42; Malcomson, *Warships of the Great Lakes,* 85.
38. Malcomson and Malcomson, *HMS Detroit,* 95.
39. Ibid., 101–2.
40. Inglis to Barclay, in Michigan Pioneer and Historical Society, *Historical Collections,* 25:524.
41. Gough, *Fighting Sail,* 43.
42. Quimby, *The U.S. Army in the War of 1812,* 269.
43. Proctor to Prevost, in Michigan Pioneer and Historical Society, *Historical Collections,* 25:523.
44. Qimby, *The U.S. Army in the War of 1812,* 272.
45. Sugden, *Tecumseh,* 358–59.
46. Ibid., 275.
47. Antal, *A Wampum Denied,* 316–17.
48. McAfee, *History of the Late War,* 374.
49. Ibid., 381–88. McAfee gives an excellent account of the army's march up the Thames River.
50. Michigan Pioneer and Historical Society, *Historical Collections,* 15:428, 429.
51. Quimby, *The U.S. Army in the War of 1812,* 282–85; McAfee, *History of the Late War,* 389–93; Gilpin, *The War of 1812,* 224–25.
52. Logan Esarey, ed., *Messages and Letters of William Henry Harrison* (Indianapolis: Indiana Historical Commission, 1922), 2:565.
53. Cave, "The Shawnee Prophet," 668–69.
54. Qumby, *The U.S. Army in the War of 1812,* 292.

EPILOGUE

1. Latimer, *1812,* 79.
2. John A. Garraty and Mark C. Carnes, eds., *American National Biography* (New York: Oxford University Press, 1999), 14:546, 547; Samuel Eliot Morison, *The Oxford History of the American People* (New York: Oxford University Press, 1972), 2:168, 332–33, 342, 370.
3. Garraty and Carnes, *American National Biography,* 6:174–76.
4. Ibid., 7:590–91.
5. Ibid., 7:917–18.
6. Ibid., 10:223–26.
7. Michigan Historical Commission, *Michigan Historical Collections,* 48–51.
8. Heilder and Heilder, *Encyclopedia of the War of 1812,* 267.

9. Garraty and Carnes, *American National Biography,* 14:86.

10. Ibid., 331; Garraty and Carnes, *American National Biography,* 14:814–15.

11. Garraty and Carnes, *American National Biography,* 15:499–500.

12. Ibid., 17:369–71.

13. Heilder and Heilder, *Encyclopedia of the War of 1812,* 431–33.

14. *The History of Warren County, Ohio* (Chicago: W. H. Beers, 1882), 392.

15. "James Winchester," Wikipedia, November 22, 2009.

APPENDIXES

1. Caffrey, *Twilight's Last Gleaming,* 310–13.

2. Cruikshank, *Documents,* 58–60.

3. Burton, *The City of Detroit,* 1000–1001.

4. Cruikshank, *Documents,* 184–90.

5. Ibid., 218–23.

INDEX

GREAT LAKES BOOKS

*A complete listing of the books in this series
can be found online at wsupress.wayne.edu*

Editor
Charles K. Hyde
Wayne State University

Advisory Editors

Jeffrey Abt
Wayne State University

Fredric C. Bohm
Michigan State University

Michael J. Chiarappa
Western Michigan University

Sandra Sageser Clark
Michigan Historical Center

Brian Leigh Dunnigan
Clements Library

De Witt Dykes
Oakland University

Joe Grimm
Bloomfield Hills, Michigan

Richard H. Harms
Calvin College

Laurie Harris
Pleasant Ridge, Michigan

Thomas Klug
Marygrove College

Susan Higman Larsen
Detroit Institute of Arts

Philip P. Mason
*Prescott, Arizona and Eagle Harbor,
Michigan*

Dennis Moore
Consulate General of Canada

Erik C. Nordberg
Michigan Technological University

Deborah Smith Pollard
University of Michigan–Dearborn

David Roberts
Toronto, Ontario

Michael O. Smith
Wayne State University

Joseph M. Turrini
Wayne State University

Arthur M. Woodford
Harsens Island, Michigan